LIBRARY

LIBRARY S

D0396817

T. E. T.
Teacher
Effectiveness
Training

By the same author

Group Centered Leadership: A Way of Releasing the
    Creative Power of Groups
P.E.T.: Parent Effectiveness Training

371.102
G 658

c. 2

T.E.T.
Teacher
Effectiveness
Training

by Dr. Thomas Gordon
with Noel Burch

WITHDRAWN

DAVID McKAY COMPANY, INC.
New York

LIBRARY ST. MARY'S COLLEGE

127920

T.E.T.: TEACHER EFFECTIVENESS TRAINING

COPYRIGHT © 1974 BY THOMAS GORDON

All rights reserved, including the right to reproduce
this book, or parts thereof, in any form, except for
the inclusion of brief quotations in a review.

Quotation on page 297-298
from "On Teaching" in THE PROPHET,
by Kahlil Gibran, with permission
of the publisher, Alfred A. Knopf, Inc.
Copyright 1923 by Kahlil Gibran;
renewal copyright 1951 by
Administrators C.T.A. of Kahlil Gibran
Estate and Mary G. Gibran.

This book was previously published
by Peter H. Wyden/Publisher.

LIBRARY OF CONGRESS CATALOG CARD NUMBER: 74-17798

ISBN: 0-679-30347-2

MANUFACTURED IN THE UNITED STATES OF AMERICA

First paperback edition, April 1977
Second Printing, September 1977

How Teachers Can Get the Most Out of This Book

1. Teachers can use the methods of Teacher Effectiveness Training more successfully in the school when backed up by a compatible learning environment in the home. We therefore suggest that you encourage the parents of your students to familiarize themselves with T.E.T. (The Special Section focuses on the role of the parent as a teacher and how the home can be made a better learning environment.)

2. Teachers can apply the T.E.T. approach in their classrooms more completely if their principal and colleagues understand and support the T.E.T. philosophy. It is important therefore to acquaint your administrator and other faculty members with T.E.T. (Chapter XI suggests specific ways you can share your T.E.T. experiences within your school or school district.)

3. T.E.T. is a complete and integrated system. Its specific skills and principles work best once *all* of them have been understood.

4. Level with your students about T.E.T.—what it is, why and how you and they will use it together in the classroom. This will reduce their resistance to your new methods and make them partners with you in making their learning more enjoyable.

5. T.E.T. provides you with specific skills for making your job easier and more enjoyable, but you will need to practice those skills until they become second nature to you. It will be up to you to create opportunities, both inside and outside the classroom, where you can get the practice you will need.

To all the young people
whose pain sent me
searching for new pathways
to parent and teacher
effectiveness.

How Parents Can Get the Most Out of This Book

1. Because parents are the first and usually most influential teachers of their children, every chapter in this book will help you increase your effectiveness as a teacher in the home. Think of yourself as a teacher as well as a parent, and think of your home as a kind of classroom—a learning environment. The skills and methods in T.E.T. will help you make your home a much better learning environment.

2. When your youngsters are old enough for school, you must turn over part of your teaching function to professional teachers. We therefore suggest that you do all you can to influence your youngsters' teachers to familarize themselves with T.E.T. (See Special Section for ways to increase your impact on teachers' relationships with your children.)

3. As a parent you will be the one to hear all of your children's complaints about teachers and school. Don't take the side of the teachers and the school, but also don't automatically assume that your children's reactions are always justified. Learn how to be an effective non-judgmental listener. (See Chapters III and IV to become more effective in helping your children resolve their own school problems.)

4. T.E.T. is a complete and integrated system. Its specific skills and principles work best once *all* of them have been understood. If you understand this approach to effective teaching, not only will you be a better teacher for your children, but you will know when the other teachers of your children are being effective or ineffective. This *should* be your responsibility. After all, they are your children.

Behind this Book:
The Idea and the People

WERE IT NOT for some very special children and young people whose lives became intimately involved with mine, I am certain I would not have written a book about teaching. They were the youngsters brought to my offices by their parents, who hoped that I might "fix them up," "bring them around," or make them "better adjusted." Although I seldom felt I produced any such unrealistic results, thanks to my previous training as a professional counselor or psychotherapist, my attitudes and skills did enable me to get accepted by most of these youngsters into a unique kind of relationship with them—one in which there was trust, open and honest communication, warmth, and mutual caring.

From these relationships, certainly as enriching to me as to them, I learned (or perhaps re-learned) how parents, inadvertently yet inexorably hurt children and youth—damage their self-esteem, chip away their self-confidence, stifle their creativity, break their spirit, lose their love. Listening hour after hour to these youngsters, I also began to understand more clearly just how adults produce such crippling effects on the very ones in their lives they least want to hurt. They seem to do it by the way they talk to them, by the way they handle everyday conflicts with them, by the way they try to discipline them, and by the way they force their values on them by the use of power and authority.

Yet seldom were the intentions of these parents anything but good ones, and I rarely discerned in these parents much of what professional psychologists usually label as "pathological" or "sick." Quite simply, they were very uninformed.

I don't mean *uneducated,* because many of the fathers were successful attorneys, physicians, engineers, ministers, and businessmen; and most of the mothers were college graduates, some professionals themselves. Yet their formal education had not provided them even the most elementary knowledge about the principles and skills of effective human relations, honest interpersonal communications, or constructive conflict resolution.

Could they be taught such principles and skills? Because I thought so, I proceeded to design a training program that might do it. Now, twelve years later, that course, called Parent Effectiveness Training, or simply P.E.T., is providing training for thousands of parents each week in every state and several foreign countries. In 1970 the textbook for the course was published and within four years had been purchased by over a half million readers. Clearly, parents do need help in raising children, and many seize the opportunity to become better informed and better trained as parents.

It was inevitable that some parents, after completing the P.E.T. course and after seeing marked improvements in their relationships with their children in the home, would then want to influence the administrators of their children's schools to make the course available to teachers ("the other parents of their children"). I am grateful to those parents, because their concern (and courage) influenced a number of school districts to begin offering Effectiveness Training to their teachers.

Thus, Teacher Effectiveness Training was born—a special course for teachers, focusing on the teacher-student relationship. Its expansion may soon equal that of the P.E.T. course throughout the country. This book presents the principles and skills we have been teaching successfully in the T.E.T. course for more than eight years.

I would have hesitated starting the book without the assurance of having a colleague in Effectiveness Training Associates with extensive experience in education—as a teacher, counselor, coach, and principal. Noel Burch, then director of educational programs for our organization, knew from firsthand experience how a school can become more humanized by using the skills and applying the philosophy of the T.E.T. course. As a consultant and collaborator, Noel Burch participated with me in working out the general organization of the book, as well as developing its style and much of its content. In addition, he brought to the project rich insights which resulted from his having been so immersed in trying to make schools better places for students and teachers alike.

Dr. Thomas Gordon
Founder and President,
Effectiveness Training Associates

Contents

I. Teacher-Learner Relationships: The Missing Link   1

What's Crucial About the Teacher-Student Relationship
Tested Skills, Not Vague Abstractions
Skills That Help Students Grow
An Alternative to the "Hoop-Jump-Biscuit" Game
One Philosophy for All Ages and Types of Students
What To Do About the Ubiquitous Discipline Problem
How To Resolve the Authoritarian-Permissive
      Controversy

II. A Model for Effective Teacher-Student
Relationships   19

Myths, Expectations, and Playing Roles
What Is a Good Teacher-Student Relationship?
A Way of Viewing the Teacher-Student Relationship
Unaccepting Teachers and Accepting Teachers:
      A Crucial Difference
The Unfixed Line in the Ever-Changing Rectangle
How To Understand Changes in the Self (Teacher)
How To Understand Different Feelings Toward
      Different Students
How To Understand the Influence of the Environment
      or Situation
Is Pretended Acceptance Ever All Right?
Who Owns the Problem?
Why "Problem Ownership" Is So Important
Why the No-Problem Area Is Important

III. What Teachers Can Do When Students Have
Problems   43

Why Teachers Fail in Helping with Student-Owned
      Problems
The Language of Unacceptance: The Twelve
      Roadblocks to Communication

Why Twelve Roadblocks Are So Ineffective
Three Common Misunderstandings
Why the Language of Acceptance Is So Powerful
More Constructive Ways of Helping Students Who
        Have Problems
Passive Listening (Silence)
Acknowledgment Responses That Work
What Door Openers Can Do
The Need For Active Listening
What Communication Is Really All About
How To Learn Active Listening
What's Required For Effective Active Listening
"Why Counsel Students? I'm a Teacher!"

**Two Types of Verbal Communication and Their
    Effects on Students: A Catalogue**   80
Communication Roadblocks
    Ordering, Commanding, Directing
    Warning, Threatening
    Moralizing, Preaching, Giving "Shoulds and Oughts"
    Advising, Offering Solutions or Suggestions
    Teaching, Lecturing, Giving Logical Arguments
    Judging, Criticizing, Disagreeing, Blaming
    Praising, Agreeing, Giving Positive Evaluations
    Name-Calling, Stereotyping, Ridiculing
    Interpreting, Analyzing, Diagnosing
    Reassuring, Sympathizing, Consoling, Supporting
    Questioning, Probing, Interrogating, Cross-
        Examining
    Withdrawing, Distracting, Being Sarcastic, Humoring,
        Diverting
Communication Facilitators
    Passive Listening (Silence)
    Acknowledgment Responses
    Door Openers, Invitations to Talk
    Active Listening (Feedback)

IV. The Many Uses of Active Listening   90
How To Foster Effective Content-Centered Classroom
        Discussions
How To Use Active Listening To Handle Resistance

How To Use Active Listening To Help
Dependent Students
How To Make the Most of Student-Centered
Discussion Groups
How Active Listening Helps Parent-Teacher
Conferences
What Three-Way Conferences Can Accomplish
Summing Up

V. What Teachers Can Do When Students Give Them Problems   125

What To Do About Teacher-Owned Problems
What Typical Ineffective Confrontations Do
Why Solution Messages Fail
Why Put-Down Messages Fail
Why Indirect Messages Fail
You-Messages versus I-Messages
What's Wrong with You-Messages
Why I-Messages Are More Effective
How To Put an I-Message Together
How To Shift Gears After Sending an I-Message
How Teachers Make Themselves Angry
Sending I-Messages Can Be Risky
What Effective I-Messages Can Accomplish

VI. How to Modify the Classroom Environment To Prevent Problems   156

The Inadequacies of the Typical Classroom
How To Think Creatively About Change
How To Think Systematically About the Classroom
Environment
How To Enrich the Environment
How To Impoverish the Environment
How To Restrict the Environment
How To Enlarge the Environment
How To Rearrange the Environment
How To Simplify the Environment
How To Systematize the Environment
How To Plan Ahead

How To Upgrade the Quality of Time in the Classroom
    Why Diffused Time Causes Problems
    Why Individual Time Is Vital—and How To Get It
    Why Optimum Time Is Vital—and How To Create It
The Great Potential of the Teaching-Learning Area

VII. **Conflict In the Classroom**   **179**
What Conflict Really Is
What Really Produces Conflict?
How Teachers Typically Resolve Conflicts
The Two Win-Lose Approaches: Method I and
    Method II
    What Is Known About Method I
    What Is Known About Method II
    When Vacillation Is the Name of the Game
    How Methods I and II Rely on Power
Authority in the Classroom
    Authority Type 1
    Authority Type 2
Serious Limitations of Power in the Classroom
    Teachers Inevitably Run Out of Power
    Power Is Destructive to Students
The Coping Mechanisms Students Use
    Rebelling, Resisting, Defying
    Retaliating
    Lying, Sneaking, Hiding Feelings
    Blaming Others, Tattling
    Cheating, Copying, Plagiarizing
    Bossing, Bullying, Pushing Others Around
    Needing To Win, Hating To Lose
    Organizing, Forming Alliances
    Submitting, Complying, Buckling Under
    Apple-Polishing
    Conforming, Taking No Risks, Trying Nothing New
    Withdrawing, Dropping Out, Fantasizing, Regressing
Why Not Use Method II?
How Power Affects the Winner
How Power and Authority Are Rationalized
    The Myth of "The Wisdom of Age and Experience"
    "Students Really Want Limits on Their Behavior"
    The Myth of "Responsibility to Transmit the Culture"

"Isn't Power Necessary with Certain Kids?"
The Myth of "Firm, but Fair"

VIII. The No-Lose Method of Resolving Conflicts   217
Method III: The No-Lose Method of Resolving Conflicts
How Method III Works in the Classroom
Prerequisites for Method III
Method III: The Six-Step Problem-Solving Process
  Step 1: Defining the Problem (Conflict)
  Step 2: Generating Possible Solutions
  Step 3: Evaluating the Solutions
  Step 4: Making the Decision
  Step 5: Determining How To Implement the Decision
  Step 6: Assessing the Success of the Solution
Working with Method III in the Classroom
A Tape-Recorded Method III Meeting
The Benefits and Rewards of Method III in Schools
  No Resentment
  Motivation Increases To Implement the Solution
  "Two Heads Are Better Than One"
  No "Selling" Is Needed in Method III
  No Power or Authority Is Required
  Kids Like Teachers, and Teachers Like Kids
  Method III Helps Uncover Real Problems
  Students Become More Responsible, More Mature

IX. Putting the No-Lose Method to Work: Other Uses of Method III In Schools   250
How To Resolve Teaching-Learning Conflicts with
     Method III
How To Resolve Conflicts Between Students with
     Method III
How To Use Method III To Set Classroom Rules and
     Policies
How Rule-Setting Class Meetings Work
  Overcoming the Threat
  Preparations
  Conducting the Meeting
  The Teacher's Role
  The Benefits of the Rule-Setting Meeting
  What About the Time Involved?

How to Deal With Typical Problems Teachers
     Encounter Using Method III
Competing "Solutions" versus Competing "Needs"
When Students Don't Stick to the Agreement
What About Problems Outside the Teacher's Area
     of Freedom?
"What If We Can't Agree on a Solution?"
When Youngsters Build Punishment into a Solution
How To Enforce Rules Outside the Teacher's Area
     of Freedom
Are There Times When Method I Is Necessary?

X. When Values Collide in School   283

How To Identify a Value Collision
Why I-Messages Seldom Work in Resolving Value
     Collisions
Why Method III Seldom Works in Resolving Value
     Collisions
Why Method I Is Ineffective in Resolving Value
     Collisions
Why Method II Is Ineffective in Resolving Value
     Collisions
How To Deal with Value Collisions
  Become an Effective Consultant
  Model What You Value
  Modify Yourself To Become More Accepting
  Find the "Serenity To Accept"

XI. Making the School a Better Place for Teaching 307

Characteristics of Schools That Cause Problems for
     Teachers
  Teachers Are Subordinates
  Teachers Do Not Participate in Decision Making
  Rigidity and Resistance to Change
  Imposition of Uniform Values
  Putting the Blame on Others
What Teachers Can Do To Increase Their Effectiveness
     in the Organization
  Accept the Importance of Your Role
  Always Look Through Your "Window"
"Can I Use the Confronting Skills with My Boss?"
  Strength in Numbers

How To Become More Effective in Group Meetings
   Before the Meeting
   During the Meeting
   After the Meeting
How To Be an Effective Consultant
Become an Advocate for Your Students

**Special Section   How To Handle Learning Problems in the
   Home: The Parent-Teacher-Student Relationship**   **323**
   The Parent as Teacher To the Child
   Who Owns Your Child's Learning?
   How To Make Your Home a Learning Environment
   Yes, Parents Must Be Hired as Teachers
   "You Can Lead a Horse to Water, but. . . ."
   How Parents Can Teach Their Values
   When Your Children Have Problems at School
   What To Do About Homework Hassles
   "Look, Mom, I Only Got Two C's!"
   How Parents Can Be more Influential with Teachers
   How To Use the Parent-Teacher-Principal Team
   How To Evaluate Your Child's School
   Building Better Relationships

Acknowledgments   **356**

Suggested Reading   **357**

Index   **361**

I. TEACHER-LEARNER RELATIONSHIPS:
The Missing Link

TEACHING is a universal pursuit—everybody does it. Parents teach their children, employers teach their employees, coaches teach their players, wives teach their husbands (and vice versa), and of course professional teachers teach their students. This is a book about how teaching can become remarkably more effective than it usually is; how it can bring more knowledge and maturity to learners and simultaneously cut down on conflicts and create more teaching time for teachers.

Although Teacher Effectiveness Training (T.E.T.) is a complete program for professionals, the methods and skills we offer here will increase the effectiveness of anyone else who instructs, particularly parents. Indeed, a special section beginning on page 323 deals specifically with teaching problems encountered in the home and with the difficulties and opportunities that develop from the delicate (and so often troubled) teacher-parent-student triangle.

Adults spend an amazing amount of time teaching young people. Some of that time is richly rewarding because helping youngsters (of whatever age) learn new skills or acquire new insights is a joyous experience. It makes one feel good, as a parent, a teacher, or youth leader, to contribute to the growth of a youngster, to realize one has given something of oneself to enrich the life of another human being. It is exhilarating to watch a young person take from a teaching relationship something new that will expand his* understanding of his world or add to his repertoire of skills.

But as everybody knows, teaching young people can also be terribly frustrating and fraught with disappointments. All too often, parents, teachers, and youth workers discover to their dismay that their enthusiastic desire to teach something worthwhile to young people somehow fails to engender an enthusiastic desire in their students to learn it. Instead, they encounter stubborn resistance, low motivation, short attention spans, inexplicable disinterest, and often open hostility.

Whenever that happens, nothing seems to work for the would-be teacher—not even such messages as: "It's for your own good," "You'll be glad you learned it when you grow up," or "You have such great potential if you would only put your mind to it." When young people, seemingly without reason, refuse to learn what adults are so unselfishly and altruistically willing to teach them, teaching is anything but exhilarating. In fact, it can be a miserable experience leading to feelings of inadequacy, hopelessness, sheer exasperation— and, too frequently, deep resentment toward the unwilling and ungrateful learner.

What makes the difference between teaching that works and teaching that fails, teaching that brings rewards and teaching that causes pain? Certainly, many different factors influence the outcome of one's efforts to teach another. But it is the thesis of this book that one factor contributes the most—namely, the degree of effectiveness of the teacher in establishing a particular kind of relationship with students.

---

* We advocate equal rights for all young people, regardless of sex, age, intellectual endowment, etc. The word "his" is used throughout this book only because of the limitations of the language.

It is the quality of the teacher-learner relationship that is crucial. More crucial, in fact, than what the teacher is teaching, how the teacher does it, or whom the teacher is trying to teach. How to achieve this effective quality is what this book is all about.

WHAT'S CRUCIAL ABOUT THE
TEACHER–STUDENT RELATIONSHIP

It is essential to zero in on the fact that teaching and learning are really two different functions—two separate and distinct processes. Not the least of the many differences between teaching and learning is that the process of teaching is carried out by one person while the process of learning goes on inside another. Obvious? Of course. But worth thinking about. Because if teaching-learning processes are to work effectively, a unique kind of relationship must exist between these two separate organisms—some kind of a "connection," link, or bridge between the teacher and the learner.

Much of this book therefore deals with the *communication skills* required by teachers to become effective in making those connections, creating those links, and building those bridges. These essential communication skills actually are not very complex—certainly not hard for any teacher to understand—although they require practice like any other skill, such skills as sewing, wood-working, skiing, singing, or playing a musical instrument. Nor do these critical communication skills place unusual demands on teachers to absorb vast amounts of knowledge about the "philosophy of education," "instructional methodologies," or "principles of child development."

On the contrary, the skills we shall describe and illustrate primarily involve talking—something most of us do very easily. Since talk can be destructive to human relationships as well as enhancing, talk can separate the teacher from students or move them closer together. Again, obvious. But again, worth further thought. For the effect that talk produces depends on the *quality* of the talk and on the teacher's selection of the *most appropriate kind of talk* for different kinds of situations.

Our instruction for teacher effectiveness, then, builds on top of elementary operations that teachers already perform every day. It is an additional set of skills, an extra sensitivity, an extra accomplishment.

Take praise, as an example. Every parent and every teacher knows how to praise youngsters. The teacher effectiveness training we offer builds from that point on. We will demonstrate how one kind of praising message will most likely cause students to feel terribly misunderstood and slyly manipulated, while a slightly different message has a high probability of making students see you as a person who is human and genuine, as well as a person who really cares.

Research—literally volumes of it—has shown how critical *listening* is in facilitating learning. Here again, every parent and teacher, with a few unfortunate exceptions, is biologically equipped to listen and well practiced in the act of listening to what youngsters communicate. They do it every day. Yet what they think they hear is not necessarily what the learner is trying to communicate. Our kind of teacher effectiveness training will teach you a simple method by which you can check on the accuracy of your listening to make sure that what you hear is what the student really meant. At the same time, it will prove to the student that you have not only heard him but have understood.

Parenthetically, we will also point out when it is very inappropriate to listen to kids. At certain times, when you are teaching them something in the classroom or at home and you find their behavior disruptive or unacceptable, the hackneyed advice, "Be a good listener," should be ignored. We will show you why at such times you must send your own strong message instead, confronting the youngsters with how they are interfering with *your rights*—and we will demonstrate how you can send such a message with little risk of their feeling squelched, put down, or even defensive.

It seems necessary now to make an important disclaimer: *This book is not about what teachers or parents should be teaching children and youth.* That issue must be left to others far more experienced in designing curricula, formulating educational objectives, and making value judgments about what is important for young people to learn—at home and in school. In fact, opinions on such matters will vary from home to home, from school to school, and from one type of community to another.

Our training rests basically on the assumption that the quality of the teacher-learner relationship is crucial if teachers are to be effective in teaching *anything*—any kind of subject matter, any "content," any skills, any values or beliefs. Latin, Greek history, math, English composition, literature, mechanical drawing, or chemistry—all can be made interesting and exciting to young people by a teacher who has learned how to create a relationship with students in which the needs of the teacher are respected by the students and the needs of the students are respected by the teacher.

Face it: even basketball, home economics, tennis, finger painting, gymnastics, sculpture, or sex education can be taught so that students are bored, turned off, and stubbornly resistant to learning—if the teacher fosters relationships that make students feel put down, distrusted, misunderstood, pushed around, humiliated, or critically evaluated.

In most schools a very high percentage of time that could be teaching-learning time is taken up with student problems that teachers are rarely trained to help solve, or teacher problems created by reactive or rebellious students whom teachers cannot control. The skills and methods for teacher effectiveness we offer in this book will give teachers *more time to teach*, whatever the subject matter. They will also open up *more time in which real learning occurs*. In each chapter we will introduce a new set of skills; each will have the effect of enlarging what we call "teaching-learning time" —periods when teachers are permitted by their students to teach ("do their thing") and students are motivated by their teacher to learn.

TESTED SKILLS, NOT VAGUE ABSTRACTIONS

The skills and methods offered in this book have been taught to tens of thousands of teachers in every state in a thirty-hour training program known as "Teacher Effectiveness Training," or simply "T.E.T."

Designed in 1966, T.E.T. has been widely accepted for inservice training of teachers in public and private schools— teachers who teach in preschools, elementary schools, intermediate schools, or high schools. The T.E.T. course evolved quite naturally from the first effectiveness training course, called "Dr. Thomas Gordon's Parent Effectiveness Training," which came to be called "P.E.T." and is now taught by more than 5000 instructors throughout the United States and several foreign countries. Teachers and administrators began to hear from parents about what they had learned in P.E.T., and asked that the course be given to their districts' teachers, so they could apply the same communication skills and conflict-resolution methods to students in the classroom. Within a year a special course was designed for schoolteachers, tailored to fit the special and unique human relations problems teachers face in classes with thirty to forty captive students all at once.

This book transfers to the printed page the same principles, skills, and methods that we developed, refined, and tested in our in-service work with teachers in the T.E.T. course. Many of the illustrations and case histories throughout the book have been drawn from these teachers.

Based on this experience, the teacher effectiveness we describe step by step in this book is naturally oriented toward developing very specific skills—that is, we will focus on practical things that teachers can say and do every day in the classroom, not on abstract educational concepts.

Experience with teachers in the T.E.T. classes has made us somewhat critical of the formal education of most teachers; it seems to familiarize them with terms, ideas, and concepts without providing them with practical ways to put these abstractions to work in the classroom. We are talking about such concepts as "respect for the needs of students," "affective education," "classroom climate," "freedom to learn," "humanistic education," "the teacher as a resource person," "two-way communication," and the like.

In the T.E.T. course such ideas and concepts are given what scientists call "operational definitions"—they are defined in terms of specific operations, things teachers actually can do, specific messages they can communicate.

Take for example a concept most teachers have heard over and over again in their training—"respect for the needs of the student." Few teachers we enroll in T.E.T. have any idea what specific operations they can perform that would show respect for the needs of students. It becomes eminently clear, however, how they can make that concept real when they learn in T.E.T. about Method III, the no-lose method of resolving conflicts between teachers and students. Method III is a six-step process: Teacher and students problem-solve until they come up with a solution that permits the teacher's needs to be met (respected) and the students' needs to be met (respected), too.

Method III offers teachers a specific tool they can use every day for insuring that their students' needs are respected without teachers paying the price of having their own needs frustrated. In T.E.T., respect for students' needs becomes something more than an abstraction for teachers—they actually learn how to bring it off.

The same is true with the concept of "democracy in the classroom." T.E.T. shows teachers the skills and procedures required to create a living democracy through the classroom rule-setting meeting in which all members of the class, including the teacher, participate in determining the rules everyone will be expected to follow. T.E.T. also offers teachers workable alternatives to the traditional use of power and authority (which is, of course, the direct antithesis of democratic relationships).

Many teachers have described the T.E.T. course as an experience in learning how to bring about what previously had been only idealistic abstractions which they were taught to value highly.

SKILLS THAT HELP STUDENTS GROW

Student "growth and development" are goals to which all schools and all teachers wholeheartedly subscribe. Yet the teaching methods used by most teachers and sanctioned by most school administrators all but insure that students will remain helplessly dependent, immature, infantile. Instead of fostering the growth of *responsibility*, teachers and administrators dictate and control students of all ages as if they were not to be trusted and could never be responsible. Instead of encouraging independence, schools actually reinforce students' dependence on their teachers—for determining what they should learn, how they should learn it, when they should learn it, and, of course, how well they learn it.

Not that teachers really want students who are irresponsible and dependent—most of them don't. It's more that they have not been taught the skills and methods by which a person, in his relationships with others, can foster self-direction, self-responsibility, self-determination, self-control, and self-evaluation. Such qualities are not developed accidentally; they must be nurtured and deliberately fostered by parents and teachers.

In T.E.T. we show what can be done to make growth and development happen, rather than remain an empty ideal. In

Chapters III and IV, for example, teachers can learn how to use a new counseling skill called "active listening" that will greatly increase their effectiveness in helping students with problems that interfere with learning. But this help is supplied in a way that enables *the student to find his own solution,* as opposed to being given solutions or suggestions—the typical way most teachers respond to student problems. When students are allowed to keep the responsibility for solving their problems, the outcome is an increment of growth toward self-responsibility and self-confidence.

In the following meeting between a student and her teacher, note how the teacher skillfully kept responsibility with the youngster by using active listening—a way of responding so that the listener feeds back or "reflects back" messages of the sender. The class had been studying the Revolutionary War, and the student had been given an assignment to write a theme on any aspect of it.

STUDENT: I came in to see you to get your ideas about what I should write about in my theme.

TEACHER: You're uncertain about what topic to choose, is that right?

STUDENT: I sure am. I've stewed about this now for days, but I still haven't come up with anything. I knew you'd have an idea.

TEACHER: You've really struggled with this, but no progress yet.

STUDENT: What have other students written on that made a really good theme?

TEACHER: You want a topic that would make an exceptionally good theme, right?

STUDENT: Yeah. I just have to get an "A" on the theme so that I can make an "A" in the course.

TEACHER: It sounds like you're feeling some strong pressures to get an "A" in the course.

STUDENT: I'll say! My parents would really be upset if I didn't. They always want me to do as well as my older sister. She's really a brain.

TEACHER: You feel they expect you to be just as good as your sister in school.

STUDENT: Yeah. But I'm not like her. I have other interests. I wish my parents would accept me for what I am—I'm different from Linda. All she ever does is study.

TEACHER: You feel you're a different kind of person than your sister and you wish your parents recognized that.

STUDENT: You know, I've never told them how I feel. I think I will now. Maybe they'll stop pushing me so hard to be a straight-A student.

TEACHER: You're thinking maybe you should tell them how you feel.

STUDENT: I can't lose. And maybe it'd help.

TEACHER: Everything to gain, nothing to lose.

STUDENT: Right. If they stopped pushing me, I wouldn't have to worry so much about my grades. I might even learn more.

TEACHER: You might get even more out of school.

STUDENT: Yeah. Then I could write a theme on a topic I'm interested in and learn something. Thanks for helping me with my problem.

TEACHER: Any time.

By refraining from giving this troubled student a solution to her problem (suggesting a topic or giving advice), this teacher employed one of the T.E.T. skills rather effectively, and the result was that the student got down to the deeper problem (parental pressure) and eventually came up with her own strategy for trying to solve it. In this brief interaction, the teacher contributed far more significantly to the growth of this student than if she had not used the active-listening skill.

In Chapter V we will show teachers how they can learn to send "I-messages" when students are behaving in ways that interfere with the teaching function. These I-messages *put responsibility directly on the student* for modifying his behavior—they give him a chance to initiate a change in his behavior out of consideration for the teacher's needs. As a result, the student is more apt to respond with behavior that is self-chosen and self-determined—and he grows yet another inch in self-responsibility and maturity.

These are but two examples of skills teachers and other adults can acquire so they can contribute to the growth and development of youngsters toward responsible and independent adulthood. It is time adults stopped *wishing* that our youth would act more responsibly, and instead learned how to encourage and foster greater responsibility in the young people they teach. We already know what skills and methods will do this; it is only a matter of giving parents, teachers, and administrators an opportunity to learn these alternatives to power and authority. As long as the lives of children are directed and controlled by punishment and threats of punishment or by rewards and promises of rewards, they will be locked into babyhood with little chance to learn to take responsibility for their own behavior—they simply won't grow up.

AN ALTERNATIVE TO THE "HOOP-JUMP-BISCUIT" GAME

As students see it, schools require them to play a game, which John Holt, in his provocative book *Freedom and Beyond*, calls the "hoop-jump-biscuit" game. Teachers hold up a hoop and say "Jump." Students jump, and if they make it, they get a doggy biscuit. Then the teachers raise the hoop higher and say "Jump." Again, another biscuit if they make it. Raise the hoop still higher, and another biscuit if they make it, and so on.

This is not only the way most schools try to get students to perform, but it is commonly accepted in our society as "the way it's s'pozed to be." Schools simply reflect the traditional ways of thinking in the society. Using rewards to motivate students to learn what some teacher or principal or school board or state has decided would be best for them to learn is deeply ingrained, both in teachers and in the other adults in our society. After all, it is the same game they had to play when they were in school, and the game their parents had to play, and their parents' parents. What other way is there? Why change?

In recent years, in fact, teachers in many school districts throughout the country have been exposed to training programs which promise to give them even greater proficiency in setting up and operating conditions so that students will be even more motivated to perform certain educational tasks or modify behavior deemed unacceptable or unproductive by their teachers. Social scientists have developed a rather advanced and complicated science of "behavioral engineering" or "behavioral modification" which can in fact make teachers even more proficient at doing what they have been doing for hundreds of years—trying to get kids to do learning tasks or to behave in the classroom by promising and handing out various kinds of rewards.

Although the rules of the "hoop-jump-biscuit game" are rather straightforward, students' responses to the game are quite variable and sometimes unexpected. A student may suddenly decide it's too difficult to do all that jumping; so he refuses to jump, even though he knows the biscuit will be forthcoming if he should make it. Another student complains that he is jumping as high as he is capable of jumping and makes only a feeble gesture at jumping. Another student gets angry and accuses the teacher of unfairly raising the hoop too high. Still another student leaves the game discouraged because his friends have learned to jump higher and now ridicule him for being a dummy or a below-average jumper.

For those parents, teachers, and administrators who may have become disillusioned with this approach in education, or whose school problems have not been solved by the hoop-jump-biscuit technology, our concept of teacher effectiveness may be a promising alternative. For it is an approach that offers students more freedom, but not license; more responsibility; more self-direction; more voice in their lives at school; and more democratic relationships with their teachers and their peers.

ONE PHILOSOPHY FOR ALL AGES
AND TYPES OF STUDENTS

Most books about teaching imply that different skills, strategies, and methods are required for each of the various ages of youngsters—as if a different pedagogy were required by teachers for each age bracket. Teaching preschoolers, it is said, is very different from teaching high-school students or sixth-graders, and so on. While it is true that the various developmental stages of children must be taken into consideration in determining materials and educational experiences, the basic human relationship between teacher and student remains the same.

The skills and methods we present in this book and in the T.E.T. course are equally useful and applicable for effective teaching of students of all ages, up to and including college students. Teachers need not learn one set of skills for preschoolers, another for elementary students, another for students in junior high school, etc. Our philosophy is that students of whatever age are human beings, and with their teachers they will develop human relationships, good or bad, depending on how they are treated by their teachers.

Similarly, we feel far too much emphasis has been placed on other differences among students—their color, their ethnic origins, their IQs, their abilities, and the social and economic status of their families. This universal practice of classifying, testing, evaluating, labeling, and stereotyping students seems not only unnecessary but harmful. It has brought into schools a way of thinking about students not unlike the way many physicians view their patients—e.g., my allergy patient, my heart problem, my ulcer patient, my hyperactive-colon case. Too often schools see their students not as persons but as faceless cases: underachievers, gifted, educationally handicapped, culturally deprived, economically handicapped, high or low IQ, hyperkinetic, emotionally disturbed, high or low potential, retarded, and so on. The harmful effects of such diagnosing and subsequent grouping of students is just beginning to be exposed by research studies. These clearly demonstrate that such groupings not only lower students' self-concepts but also bias teachers' expectations and hence lower the quality of instruction.

We believe there are far more similarities than differences among students. All are human beings, first of all. All have human characteristics, human feelings, human responses. Teacher effectiveness can therefore be based on a general theory of human relationships—assuming, as we do, that teachers are also human. All kids get turned on when they are really learning, and get bored when they are not. All youngsters feel discouraged when they are put down if they have done poorly or have failed. All kids develop self-defeating coping mechanisms to deal with teachers' use of power. All kids have a tendency to want to be dependent, yet struggle desperately for autonomy; all kids get angry and retaliative; all kids develop self-esteem when they achieve and lose it when they are told they don't achieve enough; all kids value their needs and protect their civil rights.

Our skills and methods are designed for this homogeneity of students. This is why teachers find T.E.T. as useful for a child labeled "retarded" as for one labeled "gifted," for a black youngster from a low-income family as for a white one from a wealthy family. The active-listening skill offered in Chapters III and IV, for example, will work wonders with all kinds of kids because all kinds of kids need to be heard, understood, accepted. The I-message technique for confronting students who are interfering with the teacher (or other students) will greatly reduce the defensiveness of all kinds of students, because all students defend themselves when attacked and put down. And particularly useful with students from different cultural backgrounds, with their unique value systems, are the methods outlined in Chapter X for effectively handling the inevitable value collisions between teachers and students.

WHAT TO DO ABOUT THE UBIQUITOUS DISCIPLINE PROBLEM

No question about it, students do behave unacceptably and create problems for their teachers and other students. For most teachers this causes their most difficult problems. They simply cannot ignore the issue of discipline in the school and in the classroom.

This book does not ignore the discipline problem either. But we approach discipline in a way that will be novel to most teachers. It has been a revelation to us to discover in our T.E.T. courses that only a handful of teachers have been given adequate preparation in their training for what they must face when they get into a classroom full of rambunctious, energetic youngsters.

When teachers finally do get into their classrooms, they naturally want to *teach*, not discipline. Most new teachers hope they never will have to discipline, because they are certain that as teachers they are going to be so competent and stimulating that the need for discipline will seldom arise. Most experienced teachers have learned that while they must discipline, they actually find it odious, as well as inadequate. They, too, want, to teach, not discipline. As teachers, they want the supreme satisfaction of seeing their learners learn.

What goes wrong? Why do so many teachers spend so much of their teaching time trying to maintain discipline in the classroom? Our answer is that teachers, by and large, rely too heavily on disciplining by means of threats of punishment, actual punishment, or verbal shaming and blaming, and these methods simply do not work well. Repressive, power-based methods usually provoke resistance, rebellion, retaliation. Even when they do bring about a change in a student's behavior, the old behavior often recurs the minute the teacher leaves the room or goes to the chalkboard.

In the T.E.T. classes, teachers are taught substitutes for power and authority—methods that actually give them *more* influence, not less. They learn how to conduct the rule-setting meeting in which they involve all the students in setting the class rules and regulations. One result of such meetings is that students are much more motivated to follow the rules because they see them as *their* rules, not just the teacher's. Another benefit from these rule-setting meetings is that teachers spend less time having to act as enforcers of rules.

When teachers become skilled in using nonpower methods to achieve discipline and order, they find themselves using a whole new language in talking about discipline. The traditional language of power is replaced by the language of nonpower. Teachers report a gradual reduction in their use of such terms as "control," "direct," "punish," "threaten," "setting limits," "policing," "enforcing," "laying down the law," "being tough," "reprimanding," "scolding," "ordering," "demanding," and so on. Even the term "discipline" tends to drop out of their vocabulary.

In place of such terms, teachers begin using a new vocabulary—e.g., problem solving, conflict resolution, influencing, confronting, collaboration, cooperation, joint decision making, working out contracts with students, obtaining mutual agreements, negotiating, meeting needs, working things through.

When teachers forego using power and authority, they cease using the language required to administer the old, ineffective type of discipline. They begin to use the words and terms of their other relationships, where nonpower methods are absolutely necessary to make those relationships mutually satisfying—e.g., the husband-wife, friend-friend, colleague-colleague relationships. What teachers would ever speak of "disciplining" their spouses or friends? In their marriages or friendships, rarely would teachers even think, let alone speak, in such terms as giving orders, commanding, reprimanding, punishing, setting limits, making rules. The reason is obvious: Teachers know that power and authority inevitably destroy those relationships. In Chapter VII we will try to show that power and authority will just as surely destroy teachers' relationships with students.

HOW TO RESOLVE THE
AUTHORITARIAN–PERMISSIVE CONTROVERSY

As most parents and teachers know, a controversy has been raging for years in school districts in every part of the country over whether schools should be strict or lenient, "free" or regimented, traditional or progressive, student-centered or teacher-centered, conservative or liberal, authoritarian or permissive. This pervasive controversy never seems to get resolved; it constantly emerges as a fundamental issue that polarizes parents, teachers, administrators, and the media. Schoolboard members run for office on platforms that proclaim either their "conservative" or their "liberal" stance toward schools. Candidates for state superintendent are often stereotyped as "right-wing" or "liberal." Parents fight in P.T.A. meetings over whether the schools are too permissive or too strict. Administrators admit being harassed by parents who feel they are too progressive as well as by parents who are as certain they are too conservative. Bond issues are won or lost over the issue of whether the school system is too far "right" or too far "left" of the majority values of the community—particularly when it comes to "authority versus freedom" in dealing with youngsters.

Our teacher effectiveness cuts through this controversy. It

exposes both of the two polar positions as destructive philosophies, not only in dealing with young people in schools but in all human relationships. In Chapter VII we will clearly show how both postures, under whatever label, are "win-lose" approaches and power-based philosophies. Those who advocate strictness, strong authority, regimentation, and so on want adults to direct and control youngsters by using the power and authority that adults possess. Those who advocate permissiveness and freedom for kids in the schools unwittingly are opting for conditions in which students are permitted to use their power and make life miserable for their teachers and administrators. Whichever one of these schools of thought prevails, somebody is bound to lose.

This book, like the T.E.T. course, presents an alternative to the two win-lose philosophies. Teachers will learn how to establish and maintain rules and order in the classroom *without using their power*. Teachers will also learn about the inevitable price they have to pay for being either permissive or strict—student-centered or teacher-centered. It is our hope that this no-lose method, which replaces conflicts in the classroom with cooperation and mutual respect, will finally help to end this unproductive controversy that has needlessly kept parents and school people at each other's throats for over a half century.

II. A MODEL FOR EFFECTIVE
TEACHER-STUDENT RELATIONSHIPS

IF TEACHING can and should be one of the most rewarding, gratifying, and exciting of professions yet unfortunately, for many teachers, it is not, what can be done about it?

Recently, a teacher said:

When I started teaching I saw myself as the leader of a happy band of students, eager to learn, to explore, to discover. It didn't turn out that way. I don't look forward to teaching, I dread each new class, each new day. So do the students. I feel like a slave driver cracking the whip over the heads of a bunch of lazy, good-for-nothing slobs whose only interest is to get out of work. They lie, cheat, put each other down, and seem to be interested only in how little they can do and still pass the course. Worst of all, I'm now told that *I* am going to be judged by how well *they* do on standardized tests!

A shockingly large number of teachers echo this instructor's frustration. Apparently the majority of teachers begin their professional lives with the idea that they will experience feelings of joy and accomplishment, but instead find school life filled with strife, a world where they feel pitted against their students in what often seems to be a struggle for survival.

When teachers experience this letdown, they try to figure out what happened. They know something went wrong and they feel there must be some explanation for why teaching isn't the satisfying job they anticipated it would be. What could it be?

Sometimes they blame their professors and college counselors for not letting them know what the "real world out there" is like. Some say, "Kids are really different than they were when I was in school," or, "The school I work in sure isn't as good as the one I went to." Often their administrators catch the blame because of large class sizes, poor working conditions, or low pay. Administrators are also the target for criticism when there is a problem of low morale, lack of school spirit, or poor student attitudes.

Worst of all, some teachers conclude that the fault lies within themselves, that they were not "cut out to be teachers." Many leave the profession each year, discouraged, frustrated, and suffering deep feelings of personal failure.

While all these explanations have some validity, they are really off target. For example, professors of education with all their knowledge and expertise cannot transfer their experience to teachers. Each person must experience life in a school for himself in his own unique way, and *that* experience is not transferable. Some professors do warn their students that teaching is a tough and demanding job, but until the student tries it for himself he cannot know in just exactly what ways the job is tough and demanding.

As for blaming the difference in students, it is unlikely that any great changes have taken place in young people in the four or five years between a teacher's leaving high school as a student and returning as a faculty member. The change people experience on returning as teachers is not a change in human nature, it is a change in roles. One of the characteristics of the institution we call "school"* is the separation of the roles of "teacher" and "student."

We believe that school administrators are more the victims than the cause of the problem. This is not to defend incompetent administrators. Rather, it recognizes that the problem of teacher disillusionment and disenchantment is so widespread that almost all administrators would have to be incompetent to account for it.

Working conditions and pay do not seem to hold the answer either. We find that teachers may feel just as frustrated and unrewarded in schools with "ideal" working conditions and small class sizes. And, obviously, being paid more money for an unsatisfying job isn't going to make it any more satisfying. For the most part this is why teachers' unions have seldom succeeded in alleviating the problems. They have concentrated on improving working conditions, fringe benefits, and salaries (not that these don't warrant improvement), but have left teachers still frustrated, still disenchanted, still feeling ineffective and helpless.

Experience with thousands of teachers tells us that, far from being failures, *most of them know a great deal about teaching. They just don't get many opportunities to do it.*

If the causes of their "winters of discontent" are not what teachers think they are, what are they?

MYTHS, EXPECTATIONS, AND PLAYING ROLES

To begin to understand the problem we need to take a look at the definition of the ideal teacher which most teachers seem to adopt. This definition, we believe, is based on commonly accepted myths about teachers and teaching.

Check yourself out. Do you "buy into" these ideas about the nature of Good Teachers?

---

* For an excellent definition of the institution of school, see Postman and Weingartner, *The School Book*. Delacorte Press, New York. 1973. pp. 16–27.

MYTH NUMBER 1. Good Teachers are calm, unflappable, always even-tempered. They never lose their "cool," never show strong emotions.

MYTH NUMBER 2. Good Teachers have no biases or prejudices. Blacks, whites, Chicanos, dumb kids, smart kids, girls, boys, all look alike to a Good Teacher. Good Teachers are neither racists nor sexists.

MYTH NUMBER 3. Good Teachers can and do hide their real feelings from students.

MYTH NUMBER 4. Good Teachers have the same degree of acceptance for all students. They never have "favorites."

MYTH NUMBER 5. Good Teachers provide a learning environment that is exciting, stimulating, and free, yet quiet and orderly at all times.

MYTH NUMBER 6. Good Teachers, above all, are consistent. They never vary, show partiality, forget, feel high or low, or make mistakes.

MYTH NUMBER 7. Good Teachers know the answers. They have greater wisdom than students.

MYTH NUMBER 8. Good Teachers support each other, present a "united front" to the students regardless of personal feelings, values, or convictions.

In short, Good Teachers must be better, more understanding, more knowledgeable, more perfect than average people. To those who accept these myths, teaching means they must rise above human frailty, exhibit uniform qualities of fairness, organization, consistency, caring, empathy. They must be, in a word, virtuous.

The essential fallacy here is basic: These myths ask teachers to deny their humanity. This is something they cannot do except through elaborate role playing and self-deception. Still, an astoundingly large number of teachers support, somewhere in their heads, an idealized model of the "Good Teacher" that includes some if not all of these myths (and sometimes many more). They measure themselves against this model—and come up short. In this book we would like to replace the definition of the "Good Teacher" with a model that not only is more human, attainable, and real, but will permit teachers to drop their roles and be what they are: people.

A teacher with twenty-five years of experience recalled the feelings of frustration that he experienced as he struggled with the problem of dropping the role of the Good Teacher:

For most of my teaching career I saddled myself with the role of Superteacher. My intentions were seemingly reasonable. I wanted to be the best teacher I could be. From time to time, out of frustration or weariness, I would drop my role and be just me, a person. When this happened the relationships between me and the students changed, became closer, more intimate, more real. This frightened me since I had been taught to keep "distance" between me and my students, warned that "familiarity breeds contempt" and that I would "lose control" of the situation if the students really got to know me.

Yet, as afraid as I was when I dropped my role, I recognized that these were the times when I could really teach and the students really learn.

Sometimes during these periods of realness students did or said things I didn't like. At these times I reverted to my teacher-role to maintain control, restore order, or express my displeasure.

I spent years vacillating between the real me, when I could teach, and the role of teacher, when I could maintain order.

This teacher brings up another point. He talks about the problem of wanting to have closer, more intimate relationships with his students, but fearing to do so because he felt that the students wouldn't respect him anymore, that he would lose control. His solution to this dilemma was to develop two roles, a sort of Jekyll and Hyde personality, one to teach, the other to control. This seems to happen often. Teachers throughout the country tell us that they feel trapped in a situation much like this teacher's, where the role used to teach seems incompatible with the one used to maintain order. Universally, they hate "doing themselves in" this way, but don't know what to do about it.

We will present a model and set of skills that will get you out of this trap, allow you to behave as a real person, the authentic person you are, no matter what the situation. You can learn the skills necessary to maintain good classroom discipline *and* still be able to teach, without role playing, pretending, or being untrue either to yourself or to the students.

Students are freed to learn only when *the teacher-student relationship is good.* They need not spend their time working up strategies of defense or trying to outwit the task-giver and disciplinarian. If teachers establish good relationships, they need not shift from role to role, be tough drill sergeants, pretend to be virtuous and inhuman. Unless their relationships are good, teachers will find that even outstanding teaching techniques are useless.

WHAT IS A GOOD TEACHER-STUDENT RELATIONSHIP?

The relationship between a teacher and a student is good when it has (1) *Openness or Transparency,* so each is able to risk directness and honesty with the other; (2) *Caring,* when each knows that he is valued by the other; (3) *Interdependence* (as opposed to dependency) of one on the other; (4) *Separateness,* to allow each to grow and to develop his uniqueness, creativity, and individuality; (5) *Mutual Needs Meeting,* so that neither's needs are met at the expense of the other's needs.

Many teachers respond to this list of characteristics by saying, "Well, that sounds very nice, but can I have that kind of relationship in *my* classroom?" The answer is a qualified yes. While humans never achieve perfection in anything they do, every teacher can improve relationships with young people so that they become *more* open, *more* caring, *more* interdependent, *more* separate, and *more* satisfying. It is through such improvements that the social institution we call "school," with all of its limiting characteristics, can be made into a humane and vital organization where "education" *can* take place.

For teachers to improve, they need to learn and practice a number of skills. These skills, new to most teachers, are explained in this book, which has been written for teachers who want their classes to be true educational experiences, not "holding tanks" to keep young people out of the job market, off the streets, or out of their parents' hair while they "do their thing" in the home and marketplace.

A WAY OF VIEWING THE TEACHER-STUDENT RELATIONSHIP

Teachers are seldom helped by merely being told that they will be more effective if they would only improve their relationships with the young people they teach. This is far too abstract. They want to know *how* to do it.

Fine. But most teachers we have worked with in the Teacher Effectiveness Training course demonstrate a surprising lack of understanding of the teacher-student relationship —and often of human relationships in general. It seems that in their formal education teachers acquire either an oversimplified view of what goes on between people or they come out with a complex theoretical mulligan stew consisting of parts of Freud, Rogers, Adler, or Erickson, to which has been added small chunks of everyone else they have read, all sprinkled generously with B. F. Skinner.

Few teachers enter the classroom with a workable view of interpersonal relationships—a model they can use to guide their own behavior. No wonder that they have difficulty creating and maintaining effective human relationships with students!

For the T.E.T. course, we designed a model that teachers can easily understand and utilize almost daily to help them find behavior appropriate to problems that inevitably arise in the classroom. We show this model as a series of rectangular diagrams.

First, look at Figure 1, a simple rectangle, and then think of the area within the rectangle as representing all the behaviors of a student with whom you have a relationship—everything a student may do or say in your presence. You might think of thousands of little dots filling the rectangle, each representing one kind of behavior.

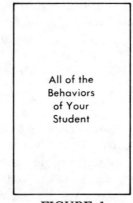

All of the
Behaviors
of Your
Student

FIGURE 1

Everything the student might do or say is contained within the rectangle—nothing is excluded. Another way of thinking about the rectangle is to imagine that it is a window through which you view the student. Everything he can possibly do or say is visible to you, but only through this window.

We now divide the rectangle into two parts, an area representing acceptable behaviors and an area of unacceptable behaviors. Figure 2 shows the divided rectangle with some typical behaviors of the student that might be *acceptable* to you in the top area and behaviors that might be *unacceptable* to you in the lower area.

As everyone knows, all teachers have feelings about what students say or do which range from very accepting (positive) to very unaccepting (negative), with all degrees in between. Although it would be helpful to students if teachers could be unconditionally accepting of them, they can't, except for short periods. It usually takes no convincing to get

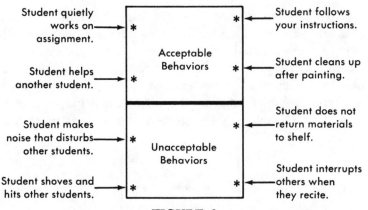

FIGURE 2

teachers in our T.E.T course to accept that no matter how hard they may try to be accepting, students behave in ways that are displeasing (and sometimes downright painful) to them.

For purposes of illustration, the line separating acceptable from unacceptable behaviors is drawn in the center of the rectangle. This would seem to indicate that exactly half of the student's behaviors are acceptable and the other half unacceptable. If this happens in reality, it is accidental. One reason why the line of demarcation between acceptable and unacceptable behaviors is seldom right in the middle of the rectangle is that people's acceptance of other people varies. The same is true for teachers. Some teachers find many student behaviors unacceptable. Others find a large percentage acceptable. The difference between these two types of teachers is important.

UNACCEPTING TEACHERS AND ACCEPTING TEACHERS: A CRUCIAL DIFFERENCE

In your own school experiences you undoubtedly have encountered at least one teacher who let you know that many of your behaviors were unacceptable to him or her. These teachers tend to criticize. They set "high standards" for their students (and usually also for other people), seldom really enjoy unconventional behavior or unusual situations in the classroom, and have an inflexible sense of "right and wrong." Students refer to them as "uptight," bossy, or overly strict, and tend to avoid them if at all possible. The window through which such teachers view students looks very much like Figure 3.

FIGURE 3

Figure 4 shows a more accepting teacher's window. This teacher finds far more behaviors of students in the area of Acceptable Behaviors and tends to be far less judgmental, more flexible. Such a teacher has greater tolerance, and less need to impose his or her versions of "right" and "wrong" on others. Usually such persons are quite accepting in all their human relationships.

People tend to seek the company of people who are very accepting and avoid those who are very critical and judgmental. Constant evaluation produces discomfort and anxiety. A high-school student in California says:

I hate one of my classes. I feel like a bug under a microscope in there. I'm so afraid that I'll do something wrong that I get all uptight and make mistakes on the simplest things. Then I get yelled at. I don't think there's any way to make that teacher happy. You can't please her.

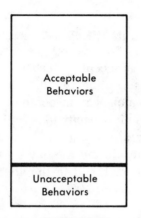

FIGURE 4

Teachers who are very critical or judgmental usually believe that it helps students to zero in on unacceptable behavior or faults and weaknesses. They believe that students are not sufficiently motivated to please or are downright incapable of self-correction. They therefore feel that if change is desired in a student it must be prompted from outside.

The exact opposite is usually true. Criticism, negative evaluation, and other ways of pointing out weaknesses tend to inhibit rather than promote change. Can you remember how you felt and reacted to teachers who were very critical of your behavior or your work? Didn't you respond like the just-quoted student who "froze up"? Did you feel that this critical attitude liberated you, or did it make you fight or be especially cautious?

Many students react to such teachers by playing it safe, taking as few risks as possible. Others rebel and retaliate by continuing the behavior that they know bugs the teacher—just to find out how far they can go before provoking a response. Evaluative and critical responses obviously stop the learning process. Without intent, unaccepting teachers actually interfere with the teaching-learning activity in the classroom and thereby reduce the amount of time when the teacher can teach and the student can learn.

THE UNFIXED LINE IN THE EVER-CHANGING RECTANGLE

Even the most accepting teacher will find that he or she is sometimes unaccepting, that the very behavior that was okay at one time is not okay at another. Everyone changes from time to time in his capacity to accept others. It happens for any number of reasons. Figure 5 shows the same teacher at two different times during the day: in the morning when she is fresh and cheerful, and in the afternoon when she is tired and grumpy.

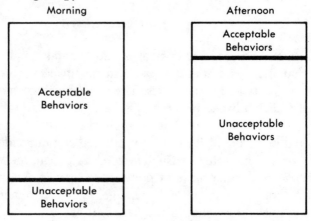

FIGURE 5

To indicate such changes in the rectangle, we refer to the dividing line going up and down. For purposes of discussion and explanation it is convenient to refer to a "high line" or "low line"—meaning a relatively unaccepting condition and a relatively accepting condition. One cause of a high line is the character or personality of the specific teacher, but we also need to remember that even the most unaccepting teacher's line will go down in some situations and up in others. Similarly, a relatively accepting teacher will on occasion be looking through his or her rectangular window and seeing mostly unacceptable behaviors.

Three factors drive the line up and down: (a) changes in self (teacher), (b) changes in the other person (student), and (c) changes in the situation or the environment. We need to look at each in some depth.

HOW TO UNDERSTAND CHANGES IN THE SELF (TEACHER)

As we have noted, people sometimes change in their ability to accept others because of what is happening *inside* them, things altogether *unrelated to the other person* or what that other person is doing. The left-hand rectangle in Figure 5 showed a teacher's view of a student early in the morning when the teacher was fresh and eager for the day's activities. The right-hand rectangle showed the same teacher's view of the student thirty minutes before the close of school that day, when the teacher was tired, hungry, or possibly worried about having to attend a long meeting before leaving for the day. As a result that rectangle shows many more of the student's behaviors as unacceptable. These *internal* changes can be either physical or psychological. A teacher in a crowded metropolitan area said:

By the time I drive to school through the morning rush-hour traffic, worrying about being late or even having an accident, I'm worthless for the first few minutes of the day. I need about a half hour to come down from the traffic jitters.

This teacher's line is high principally because of what she experiences before she even gets to school.

A kindergarten teacher, troubled about problems with her own son, admitted:

My son is cutting school and has gotten in a couple of scrapes with the law. Sometimes I'm so worried that I find myself barking at the children in my class. Usually, after a while I'm able to forget about my troubles and teach, but sometimes they come flooding back and I start yelling at the children again. Poor kids! They usually haven't done anything wrong at all.

The point, of course, is that teachers are never machines, unfailingly and unfeelingly functioning without troubles or emotions. And because they are human, teachers act and react differently from moment to moment, from hour to hour, from day to day. Inevitably, to be human is to be inconsistent—variable, changing, and unpredictable.

HOW TO UNDERSTAND DIFFERENT FEELINGS
TOWARD DIFFERENT STUDENTS

Figure 6 illustrates a teacher's window view of the behavior of two different students.

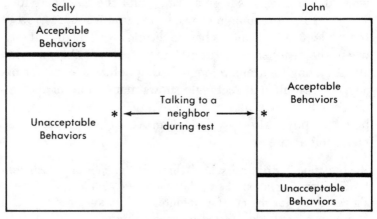

FIGURE 6

The asterisk indicates a particular behavior. In this illustration the behavior might be talking to a neighbor during a test. In the case of Sally, this behavior is unacceptable to the teacher. But in the case of John, the same behavior is in the area of acceptable behavior. The teacher may view the same behavior in entirely different ways for two different students simply because Sally was just told not to talk (and now she has done it), while John was not so instructed.

There may be many other reasons for this difference in the teacher's attitude. For example, teachers do develop personal likes and dislikes. While "individual differences" is a term misused in education, it does exist in real life. There *are* important differences in people—students as well as teachers. Everyone responds differently to different people for a variety of reasons.

When you were a teen-ager, why did you choose to date one person rather than another? Why do you extend an acquaintance into a friendship with one person and drop another? Obviously, no one feels equally accepting of all people. In the above case of Sally and John, the teacher may have greater empathy for boys than for girls, or may find John to be honest and trustworthy while Sally is sneaky. Sally might be a very bright and challenging student, always pushing the limits, while John is plodding and nonthreatening.

Whatever the cause, the crucial point is: *There will always be individual differences.* Teachers *will* be more accepting of some students than others.

HOW TO UNDERSTAND THE INFLUENCE OF THE ENVIRONMENT OR SITUATION

The third influence on your acceptance of a learner is the environment or situation in which a behavior occurs. To quote an old saw: "There is a time and a place for everything." When a behavior occurs in the wrong place or at the wrong time it tends to be unacceptable no matter how acceptable it might be under different circumstances. Yelling and pushing are usually acceptable to most teachers when they occur on the playground at recess; in the classroom they are usually unacceptable.

Reconsider now the myths we listed earlier about the Good Teacher. Can you see that many of them, in the light of our concept of acceptance and unacceptance, require a denial of the realities of your humanness? If you believe that a good teacher should always be unbiased, calm, unflappable, accepting, and consistent, you are inviting frequent feelings of failure—in short, you will never feel you are an effective teacher.

IS PRETENDED ACCEPTANCE EVER ALL RIGHT?

Sometimes teachers feel pressured (either from within themselves or from someone else) to pretend to accept student behavior that they really don't like. (Or the reverse: to pretend to be unaccepting of something that they actually think is perfectly okay.) Figure 7 illustrates the area of False Acceptance, in which we place behaviors of the student that are really unacceptable, yet the teacher acts as if he or she were accepting.

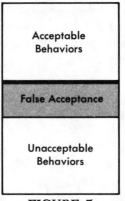

Acceptable
Behaviors

False Acceptance

Unacceptable
Behaviors

FIGURE 7

Because teachers accept many "shoulds" and "oughts" as guides for governing their own behavior, they sometimes get trapped into pretending. They rationalize: "Kids will be kids." "Don't frustrate the needs of children, because it might permanently damage their personalities." "Children should be given complete freedom in the classroom." "Children should never be reprimanded in front of others." These and other such standards that teachers pick up in their training create a false permissiveness. They smile and nod and act warm and accepting, but inside they are tied up in knots. Also, many teachers are uncomfortable with negative feelings (unacceptance) and hence try to force themselves to feel as they think they *should* feel.

The reverse is also true: Teachers can, and do, force themselves to pretend to *disapprove* of behaviors by students when they don't really feel disapproving. Some teachers even put pressure on colleagues to feel the same way they do about certain behaviors, so the teachers can present a "united front" toward the students.

Whatever the cause, if you pretend to feel accepting when you are really uptight about the behavior, or pretend to be unaccepting because you "should" be unaccepting, the message will come through to students—at best as confusion, at worst as phoniness.

Students are remarkably sensitive to the nonverbal messages teachers send. They learn to read the muscle tenseness, tightness around the mouth, facial expressions, and body movements. If these "body messages" are in conflict with the verbal messages, the students may become confused. Or they believe the nonverbal message and see the contrasting verbal message as phony. A high-school student talked about this problem with a counselor:

Some teachers are really strange. There's one or two here who like to make you think they're really cool. They talk real hip, you know, but anybody can see that they're uptight. Who do they think they're fooling?

It's almost impossible to pull off the task of being untrue to one's real feelings. Remember, students see teachers day after day, in good times and bad. The real feelings will ultimately come through.

When asked, "What's wrong with adults?" young people everywhere list two features of adult behavior as their chief criticisms:

(1) Adults don't listen to us, and
(2) Adults are phony.

A former teacher and coach, now a counselor in a large high school, recalls his experience and feelings when he was a student in high school:

When I was in school most of the teachers seemed to be unreal. Do you know what I mean? They sort of appeared at the beginning of the day, did their thing, and disappeared with the last bell. We used to sit around and speculate on who they really were. Did they have families? Eat? Love? It always came as a shock if one of the kids happened to live near a teacher and could give us firsthand evidence that he or she did what everyone else did. Part of the problem in those days was that teachers were expected to be like Caesar's wife, above suspicion. They couldn't smoke or have babies or, heaven forbid, swear.

Things have changed. The only thing that keeps teachers from being "real people" now is their own hang-ups. This may sound like heresy to my colleagues, but I don't think we would need "counselors" in our high schools if the teachers would quit hiding behind their desks, charts, books, and tests and start relating with the kids. The kids really want that, but they write off most of the teachers because they play "distance games."

Double standards are another cause of teacher phoniness. Few schools are without two sets of rules, expectations, and standards of acceptable behaviors: one set for adults, the other for young people. In many schools the teachers' right to smoke in their lounge makes some teachers feel phony when they are required to enforce the no-smoking rule for students. To the extent that the double standard grants freedoms, privileges, and rights to teachers that are denied to students, the school is posing an extremely difficult and delicate problem in ethics. Chapter X will explore this problem of values (and related ones) in more depth.

Without reading further you can now focus on one major cause of classroom confusion: phony messages. Remember, student behavior is either above your line in the Acceptable area of the rectangle or it is below your line in the Unacceptable area. You have only to get in touch with how you are feeling to know where in the rectangle to place the behavior—above or below the line. Then you can send a single message that clearly and directly tells the students where you are.

How? Here is how one elementary school teacher in the second session of a T.E.T. class expressed her feelings about her need always to appear pleasant, calm, and accepting with her fourth-grade students, and how she first tried "being real."

One afternoon last week it was hot. I was tired and had a headache. I realized that my face was hurting from keeping a smile on it and that the noise the kids were making was really "below my line." I decided to stop smiling and tell them how I was feeling. I said, "I'm tired, my head hurts, and I'm sick of smiling and pretending that all the noise you are making doesn't bother me. It does. I don't think I can stand it anymore." I was amazed! The children quieted down right away. One of them even brought me a glass of water! I guess I shouldn't have been so surprised. They didn't know how I felt until I told them. After all, I'd been smiling and acting as if I were feeling good until then. One of the boys met me on my way into the classroom the next morning. He wanted to know if I felt better.

Although your mind can recall the past and even create a fantasy future, your body lives in the here-and-now. Its messages reflect what is happening in the present. Unless highly controlled, it will communicate the here-and-now feelings. So in the classroom do make an effort to match your verbal with your nonverbal messages. If you find yourself feeling unaccepting of some student behavior, try saying "I don't like what you're doing now." At least you are being honest with the student, giving him the opportunity to interact with the *real* you, not some image of what you think you ought to be.

As the fourth-grade teacher discovered when she confessed

her headache, students will often be considerate of teachers' needs. But first it takes an act of humanness on the part of teachers to reveal honestly what they are feeling.

WHO OWNS THE PROBLEM?

The rectangle we use to differentiate between acceptable and unacceptable behaviors of students can also be used to help teachers better recognize and cope with the problems that inevitably arise in all teacher-student relationships.

Consider first the lower part of the rectangle, the area of unacceptable behaviors—behaviors that interfere with the teacher's meeting his or her needs, or cause the teacher to feel frustrated, upset, irritated, angry, and so on. Obviously, such behaviors cause the teacher a *problem*. For teaching and learning to be resumed, the teacher needs to resolve each such problem when it occurs.

When the behavior of a student is "below the line" (in the area of Unacceptable behaviors), the teacher is experiencing a problem. It is *his* problem—he has it; it belongs to him; he *owns* it. This concept of ownership is crucial in maintaining effective teacher-student relationships. In Figure 8 the asterisk representing the behavior of a student carving initials on the desktop is in the area of Unacceptable behaviors because it causes the teacher a problem. The teacher *owns* this problem.

Now, here is an entirely different kind of problem. A student reveals to her teacher that she is angry and disappointed because her mother will not let her go out of town with a group of her friends. This student is experiencing a problem in her own life—quite separate from the teacher's life. In no way does the student's anger and disappointment *tangibly and concretely* affect the teacher. In fact, unless the student volunteers something about it, the teacher probably would not even know about it. It *does* affect the student—

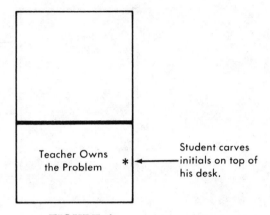

FIGURE 8

she has a problem. It belongs to her. She owns it. Consequently, we place this student's behavior in the top part of the rectangle: Problems owned by the student.

What about behaviors of the student that neither cause the teacher a problem nor create a problem for the student? When such behavior occurs there is no problem in the relationship. The center portion of Figure 9 represents No-Problem situations. An example of a behavior that would belong in the No-Problem area is a student quietly working on his math in a corner of the classroom. He is meeting his needs. In no way is his behavior interfering with the teacher meeting her needs. Nobody has a problem.

WHY "PROBLEM OWNERSHIP" IS SO IMPORTANT

One of the chief stumbling blocks on the path toward good relationships is the failure to understand the concept of "ownership of problems." It is absolutely *imperative* that teachers be able to distinguish between those problems students have in their lives that cause *them* a problem but not the teacher, and those that have a tangible and concrete effect on the teacher by interfering with the teacher's needs.

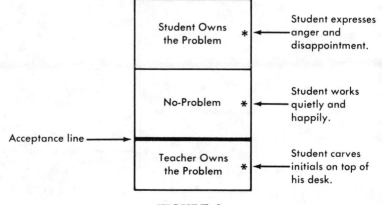

FIGURE 9

As we will demonstrate in later chapters, teachers should behave in quite different ways when students own problems than when the teachers own them. That is why *ownership definition* is crucially significant.

The difference between student-owned and teacher-owned problems is essentially one of tangible and concrete (or *real*) effect. Teachers can separate their own problems from those of their students by asking themselves: "Does this behavior have any *real*, tangible, or concrete effect on me? Am I feeling unaccepting because I am being interfered with, damaged, hurt, impaired in some way? Or am I feeling unaccepting merely because I'd like the student to act differently, not have a problem, feel the way I think he should?

If the answer is "yes" to the latter, the problem belongs to the student. If it is "yes" to the former, the teacher certainly has a real stake in the problem. Chapter III explores student-owned problems in depth and shows how teachers can best help students with these problems. For the time being, it is only necessary that you identify the two kinds of problems and place them in the appropriate area of the rectangle.

WHY THE NO-PROBLEM AREA IS IMPORTANT

While students are never entirely free of life problems (some related to school, others unrelated), they *are* able to resolve enough of them, and temporarily suspend others, to be able to think about and perform learning tasks. This ability is vital because *it is only in the No-Problem area of the relationship that teaching and learning can be effective.*

If a student is experiencing difficulties and problems in his life (he is afraid his classmates think he is stupid), he will find it difficult to concentrate on academics. If the student's behavior is "below the line" and is causing a problem for the teacher (the student is about to ruin a valuable map), the teacher will find it difficult to concentrate on teaching.

We have designated the No-Problem area as the *Teaching-Learning area.* Remember: The overall goal of Teacher Effectiveness Training is to help teachers increase the size of the Teaching-Learning area so that a greater proportion of their time is spent productively engaged in teaching and far less time is spent dealing with behaviors in the two problem areas. Figure 10 illustrates how an effective teacher's "window" view of students might look after mastering the skills taught in T.E.T.

FIGURE 10

Notice that even in this optimum situation problems remain at both ends. No matter how skillful a teacher becomes, students will continue to have their own problems that are unresolved, perhaps unresolvable. And students will always behave in ways that will interfere with teachers' needs and desires, so some problems will remain in the Teacher-Owned-Problem area. But an effective teacher's relationships with students will reserve a very large portion of the rectangle for the No-Problem or Teaching-Learning area.

How does Figure 10 compare with your own classroom time allotment? Are you able to spend a large percentage of your time teaching? Or are you one of those teachers who can only occasionally give glowing reports of rare "teachable moments"?

In the remaining chapters we will explain and demonstrate the specific skills that will enable you to have teachable *hours* and teachable *days*, not just teachable *moments*.

Teacher Effectiveness Training offers a model for effective relationships in classrooms so that the time of both teachers and students is spent more profitably and with a greater sense of satisfaction and achievement for both.

III. WHAT TEACHERS CAN DO
WHEN STUDENTS HAVE PROBLEMS

RALPH, a senior in high school, is frequently absent from class. Melissa, a twelve-year-old, stares out the window instead of reading. Kenneth, a kindergartener, cries when he hears loud voices. Jane, a fourth-grader, never plays games at recess time, preferring to sit under a tree watching the other children play. Jose restlessly wanders around the room, occasionally pushing or poking another student. Even the mildest reproach causes Loretta to fly into a rage. Don is loud, argumentative and given to calling his classmates names. Beautiful Diane suddenly starts coming to school in dirty clothes, no makeup, her usually squeaky-clean hair unwashed and uncombed. Betsy unexpectedly resigns as Student Council president.

These and countless other behaviors are cues, clues, and tips—messages students send that indicate something is wrong, that they are having problems.

What are teachers to do when they receive such messages? Ignore them and hope the problems will go away? Tell the students their problems do not belong in the classroom? Send the students to the school counselor (if there is one)? Squelch the behavior with threats of punishment? Ask for a transfer to a school that hopefully will have young people with fewer problems?

Many teachers don't really know what to do when their students come up with feelings or problems. Some feel very reluctant to move in as a helping person or counselor. Or they are confused about whether counseling falls within their job definition as "teacher." Or they believe that handling student problems is alien to the purposes of the school, which they define as working with students' minds. Many teachers feel about student problems the same way managers and supervisors feel about employees' problems—they ought to be left at home where they belong.

That kind of wishful thinking belies the fact that student problems *cannot* be left at home. Inevitably they get brought into the school and, once there, seriously interfere with the learning process and at times make learning virtually impossible. When students experience strong feelings or emotional distress because their security is threatened, when they have unmet physiological needs or when they think they are isolated, unworthy, or unliked, their ability to do schoolwork will be hampered. At these times attempts by the teacher to teach are more or less bound to be frustrating, perhaps even futile.

One experienced teacher recalls what happened when she transferred to a school whose students had lots of problems:

When I was assigned to what they called a "disadvantaged school" my years of experience had all been in suburban upper-middle-class neighborhoods. As I worked for the first time with children from the inner city, I realized why I had never felt I was a really good teacher, even though the children in my classes had always achieved well. These ghetto children made me understand quickly that their fears, frustrations, and angers had to be taken care of first. Then, and only then, could they work on the "stuff" I had to dish out. I was forced to set aside my preplanned curriculum and help them begin to feel good about themselves. They taught me that school isn't cramming a lot of stuff into the heads of the students. It's helping them get ready to grab ideas and concepts when they can and how they can.

This teacher discovered for herself an important idea: Students need help from their teachers in ways other than "booklearning."

Most teachers we have worked with in T.E.T. classes would help students with life problems, but very few have had useful training other than their own life experiences. Very few teachers have had the opportunity to interact with (and learn from) professional people trained in counseling. Their own life models were untrained and usually ineffective as "helping agents." In our Teacher Effectiveness Training classes instructors ask teachers if they can recall times in their lives as students when they were so troubled that they didn't care about schoolwork. Most can. When asked to recall whether any of their teachers were actually helpful to them at these times, most of them say that their teachers, even when they tried, were seldom helpful.

Can you remember such times? Were your teachers helpful to you?

So even though teachers really want to help, it is apparent that students seldom feel that they get help, and teachers seldom feel that they have really been helpful. The intent is good, the results poor.

The frustration of not being able to help troubled students is expressed by a junior-high teacher:

I see kids having all kinds of problems. Everything from puppy love to drugs. The counselors at our school are swamped. I'd like to help but I feel so inadequate. I don't know what to do, so I don't do anything except hope that everything works out all right.

Another teacher talks about this same frustration, but in a different way:

Kids today don't appreciate what they've got. They're always complaining and griping, but will they listen to me when I try to warn them that they're heading for a fall? Oh, no, they turn me off and then complain some more when they get in trouble.

These teachers state the two most common complaints—their feeling of inadequacy in being a helping person, and their feeling of rejection by students when attempts are made to be helpful.

WHY TEACHERS FAIL IN HELPING WITH STUDENT–OWNED PROBLEMS

Most teachers are more than adequately sensitive in picking up the cues and clues students send in their messages when they are experiencing problems. They certainly hear plenty of such messages. However, *recognizing* when problems occur is not enough. Teachers fail to be helpful because they do not know how to *respond effectively*. It is what they say to a student with a problem that makes them so often ineffective as a helping person.

In this chapter we will first focus on how teachers typically talk to students with problems, and suggest some new ways of talking—ways of responding that are successfully used by professional counselors who work with young people.

To demonstrate how teachers typically respond when young people have problems, we bring back our familiar rectangular window. In our T.E.T. classes, instructors present teachers with sample problems of students and then ask, "Who owns the problem?" If a student has been frequently daydreaming, for example, who owns the problem? Invariably some teachers say, "The teacher owns that problem," but most recognize that it is the student who owns the problem. For those who claim it is the teacher's problem, we must remind them that the daydreaming behavior of one child does not tangibly and concretely interfere with his or her teaching activities, so it is not the teacher's problem. This is often hard for teachers to accept, because they somehow want to assume ownership of all the behaviors of students in their classrooms.

Even those teachers in our T.E.T. classes who do identify daydreaming behavior as a cue or clue that the student has a problem, and who correctly place that behavior in the top part of the rectangle, invariably respond incorrectly to the daydreamer.

Most teachers send messages that communicate to the student that his daydreaming is unacceptable—that is, the teacher wants him to change, wants him to act as if he did not have a problem, wants him to be different, wants him to *stop having whatever problem he has*. The language of the teacher is what we call in T.E.T. the "language of Unacceptance."

While it is often appropriate to use the language of Unacceptance when the student's behavior is giving the teacher a problem, it is neither appropriate nor helpful to use such language when the *student owns a problem*.

In the next pages we will first list and describe the different categories of unaccepting language and then point out in some detail why they are not helpful to students; why they usually block further communication with students; why they do not facilitate problem solving; and why they so frequently bring about a deterioration of the teacher-student relationship. Then we will present four categories of accepting language, which for most teachers are new ways of responding.

THE LANGUAGE OF UNACCEPTANCE: THE TWELVE ROADBLOCKS TO COMMUNICATION

The thousands of possible unacceptance messages that a teacher can send can be classified into twelve categories. These twelve kinds of messages tend to block further communications; they slow down, inhibit, or completely stop the two-way process of communication that is so necessary in helping students solve the problems that interfere with learning.

Suppose a student is having a difficult time getting an assignment completed. In one way or another he communicates that he has a problem; it is really bothering him. Following are five typical teacher responses that communicate unacceptance. We have lumped these five types of responses together because in one way or another they all offer a solution or solutions to the student's problem.

1. *Ordering, commanding, directing.* Example: "You stop complaining and get your work done."

2. *Warning, threatening.* Example: "You'd better get on the ball if you expect to get a good grade in this class."

3. *Moralizing, preaching, giving "shoulds" and "oughts."* Example: "You know it's your job to study when you come to school. You should leave your personal problems at home where they belong."

4. *Advising, offering solutions or suggestions.* Example: "The thing for you to do is to to work out a better time schedule. Then you'll be able to get all your work done."

5. *Teaching, lecturing, giving logical arguments.* Example: "Let's look at the facts. You better remember there are only thirty-four more days of school to complete that assignment."

Now examine the next three categories. They all communicate judgment, evaluation, or put-downs. Many teachers firmly believe that it is helpful to a student to point out his faults, inadequacies, and foolish behaviors. Three kinds of messages are employed for this purpose:

6. *Judging, criticizing, disagreeing, blaming.* Example: "You're just plain lazy or you're a big procrastinator."

7. *Name-calling, stereotyping, labeling.* Example: "You're acting like a fourth-grader, not like someone almost ready for high school."

8. *Interpreting, analyzing, diagnosing.* Example: "You're just trying to get out of doing that assignment."

Two other kinds of messages are attempts by teachers to make a student feel better, to make a problem go away, or to deny that he even has a real problem:

9. *Praising, agreeing, giving positive evaluations.* Example: "You're really a very competent young man. I'm sure you'll figure how to get it done somehow."

10. *Reassuring, sympathizing, consoling, supporting.* Example: "You're not the only one who ever felt like this. I've felt that way about tough assignments, too. Besides, it won't seem hard when you get into it."

The most frequently used roadblock of all is probably category 11, even though teachers realize that questions often produce defensiveness. Also, questions are most often used when the teacher feels she needs more facts because she *intends to solve the student's problem by coming up with her best solution,* rather than help the student to solve the problem himself.

11. *Questioning, probing, interrogating, cross-examining.* Examples: "Do you think the assignment was too hard?" "How much time did you spend on it?" "Why did you wait so long to ask for help?" "How many hours have you put in on it?"

Category 12 consists of messages that teachers use to change the subject, divert the student, or avoid having to deal with the student at all.

12. *Withdrawing, distracting, being sarcastic, humoring, diverting.* Examples: "Come on, let's talk about something more pleasant." "Now isn't the time." "Let's get back to our lesson." "Seems like someone got up on the wrong side of the bed this morning."

Of the many thousands of teachers with whom we have worked in our T.E.T. course, a surprisingly large percentage (from 90% to 95% in most classes) respond with one of these twelve roadblocks when they hear typical messages from students who have a problem.

Parents in our Parent Effectiveness Training (P.E.T.) classes also rely heavily on the twelve roadblocks with their own children, and the explanation for these talking habits of teachers and parents is no mystery: Very few have been trained in alternative ways of responding and, as young people, they too were talked to in the same ways by their own parents and teachers.

Why the Twelve Roadblocks Are So Ineffective

To understand the effects of the twelve roadblocks, teachers must first be shown that their verbal responses to students usually carry more than one meaning or message. Suppose a junior-high student has expressed a feeling of being dumped or rejected by her girl friend. To say, "I think this would not have happened if you'd treated her better, so why don't you go and apologize for whatever you did?" conveys much more to the youngster than the words or content of your response. The student undoubtedly hears any or all of these hidden messages:

"You are to blame."

"You did something wrong."

"You are not seeing things correctly."

"You are not a very good friend."

"You can't be trusted to find your own solution to this problem."

"You are not as wise as I."

Or suppose a teen-ager says disgustedly, "I can't stand school or anything about school." If you respond, "Oh, everybody has felt that way about school at one time or another—you'll get over it when you're older," the student is entitled to infer these hidden messages:

"You don't think my feelings are very valid and real."

"You don't accept me or my judgment about school."

"You must think I'm nuts or something."

"You obviously think it's not the school that needs changing, just me."

"You don't even take me very seriously."

"You think I'm very immature to have this evaluation of the school."

When teachers say something *to* a youngster, they say something *about* him. Every message adds another building block to the relationship you are constructing with that student. Each message reveals what you think of him and defines what he will ultimately think of himself. *Your messages today become his self-concept tomorrow.* This is why talk can be either *constructive or destructive* to a student's self-esteem and to the relationship you have with him.

One way we help teachers understand how the twelve roadblocks can be destructive is to ask them in class to remember their own reactions when they shared their feelings with a friend who responded with roadblocks. Invariably, they report that most of the time the roadblocks had a destructive effect on them or on their relationship with the person they told their troubles to. Here are some of the effects our teachers commonly report:

They make me stop talking, shut me off.

They make me defensive and resistive.

They make me argue, counterattack.

They make me feel inadequate, inferior.

They make me feel resentful or angry.

They make me feel guilty or bad.

They make me feel I'm being pressured to change—that I'm not accepted as I am.

They make me feel the other person doesn't trust me to solve my problem.

They make me feel I'm being treated paternalistically, as if I were a child.

They make me feel I'm not being understood.

They make me feel my feelings aren't justified.

They make me feel I've been interrupted.

They make me feel frustrated.

They make me feel I'm on the witness stand being cross-examined.

They make me feel the listener is just not interested.

The teachers in our classes immediately recognize that if the roadblocks have these effects on *them* in their relationships with others, they will have the same effects on their *students.*

And they are right. These twelve kinds of verbal responses

are the very ones that professional therapists and counselors have learned to avoid when they work with children. These ways of responding are potentially nontherapeutic or destructive. Professionals learn to rely on other ways of responding to children's messages—ways that carry far less risk of causing the young person to stop talking, making him feel guilty or inadequate, reducing his self-esteem, producing defensiveness, triggering resentment, making him feel unaccepted, and so on.

(At the end of this chapter you will find an even more detailed catalogue of the Twelve Roadblocks and the various destructive or nonhelpful effects each can have on the students in your classroom.)

Teachers in our T.E.T. classes have found it very useful to check or underline those effects which they as youngsters most often experienced from the messages of their teachers and/or parents. You may want to try this yourself when you read this section at the end of the chapter.

Three Common Misunderstandings

While most teachers in T.E.T. classes find the concept of the language of Unacceptance (the Twelve Roadblocks) a very useful device for analyzing and modifying their own habits of communication with students, in almost every class the discussion focuses on three fundamental questions:

1. What is wrong with giving facts, lecturing, and providing information? ("Isn't this the principal function of a teacher?")

2. Why are praise and positive evaluation classified as a roadblock? ("We've been taught to use praise to reinforce and encourage good behavior.")

3. Why is questioning considered ineffective? ("Asking questions is one of the most valuable tools we use in teaching—you know, the 'Socratic method' or the 'Inquiry method.'")

Usually when teachers bring up these questions they are momentarily forgetting that we use the Twelve Roadblocks to illustrate ineffective responses to messages that indicate a student is *experiencing a problem* in his life—at school or out of school. The Twelve Roadblocks, we propose, are usually nonhelpful or nonfacilitative when the behavior of the student has been located in the top part of the rectangular window—the area of *the student-owned problem*.

When the behavior of the student is in the *No-Problem area*—the Teaching-Learning area—the roadblocks are much less inappropriate, simply because there is no problem in the teacher-student relationship.

Take "Giving Facts and Information" as an example. When a student is in a learning frame of mind (has no problem) and the teacher is in a teaching frame of mind (has no problem), facts and information may most certainly be offered by the teacher and accepted by the student. Not so when the student is preoccupied or distressed by a problem. Then, facts and information will either be unwelcome and resisted or will drastically interfere with the student's problem-solving process. Later in this chapter and in the next we will show why facts, when given while a student is immersed in feelings and emotions, usually act as a strong roadblock to his working through the problem.

What about praise? Teachers almost universally resist the idea that praise could be one of the roadblocks. After all, praise is so commonly accepted in our schools, homes, and places of work as a potent motivator ("Praise 'em and they'll work their heads off"). In recent years this idea has received strong scientific support from psychologists of the school of behavior modification who train teachers to reinforce "good behavior" (usually determined by the teacher) by systematically dispensing rewards, and among these are praise, positive evaluation, or kind words of support.

From our own theory of effective teacher-student relationships, we arrive at the following assertions about praise:

1. When a student has a problem with himself, which usually means unhappiness or dissatisfaction with himself or his behavior, praise

either falls on deaf ears, makes him feel his teacher simply does not understand, or provokes in him an even stronger defense of his existing low evaluation of himself.

2. When the teacher-student relationship is in the No-Problem area, praise might not be a roadblock, *provided it comes from the teacher as a spontaneous, random (unplanned or unscheduled), and genuine (not pretended) verbal response to the student's performance.*

3. When praise is employed consciously and deliberately by teachers as a *technique* for the purpose of influencing students to choose some behavior deemed "desirable" by the teacher in lieu of below-the-line behavior, chances are students will perceive such praise as manipulative and insincere, intended primarily to meet the needs of the teacher ("You're only praising me because you want me to act this way all the time").

4. In the classroom, praise bestowed on one student (or a few) often will be felt as negative evaluation of the rest. Even a single student who has become accustomed to receiving frequent praise (or other rewards) may feel negatively evaluated when he does not happen to get praised ("You haven't said anything nice about my painting, so you must not think it's good").

What about the third question that teachers in T.E.T. ask? What is wrong with using questions?

Professional helping agents (counselors and therapists) have discovered that questioning and probing, *when the other person owns the problem,* often acts as a roadblock or communication stopper. Why this happens can be understood, first, because people feel threatened when they think someone is probing too deeply into feelings they are unprepared to share with another. When their inner private world is invaded, people often close up in self-defense.

Secondly, questions can be very derailing if they are irrelevant and not on target, as is so often the case. How often have you shared your feelings with another who persists in asking questions that seem to be "fishing expeditions"—casting into water without knowing where the fish are lurking? The questioner is often guessing, so a high percentage of his questions will be off-target, which requires the person with the problem to detour and respond in some way or deal with the irrelevancy. ("No, that's not why I'm feeling bad," or, "It has nothing to do with my parents.")

Finally, most questions severely limit the range of subject matter or feelings or topics the person with the problem can communicate. "Ask a person a question and you may get an answer, but that's probably all you'll get," an opinion pollster once said. He meant that questions do not usually open people up or give them a chance to carry the conversation wherever they may want to go. Instead, questions literally direct the speaker to confine the conversation narrowly to the answer called for by the listener's specific question, and that question may well be off the point.

A student says to his teacher, "I'm really confused about whether to go to college or get a job—I can't make up my mind." The teacher asks, "Is it a matter of finances?" By that question the teacher is controlling or "programming" the student to talk about money. The critical issues underlying the student's dilemma may be quite different—such as uncertainty about whether he is smart enough for college, reluctance to leave a girl friend behind, inability to select a major field of study, boredom with school, wanting to get out of an unhappy relationship with parents, etc.

The point, again, is that questions do not leave the respondent free to explore and/or communicate what the real issues may be. They limit and restrict. In effect, the questioner takes over the direction of the discussion; he does not enable the problem's owner to assume responsibility for the problem solving.

WHY THE LANGUAGE OF ACCEPTANCE IS SO POWERFUL

The Twelve Roadblocks are the language of Unacceptance because they so often communicate to the troubled person that he *must* change, had *better* change, or *should* change. They can also communicate that merely having the problem is unacceptable and that something must be wrong with the problem owner. Some of the roadblocks even make the troubled person feel that you couldn't care less about his problem. Because of these effects, the Twelve Road-blocks are very ineffective responses in the helping relationship.

But why is the *language of Acceptance* more effective? How do you communicate acceptance and the desire to help another? What do you say to a troubled person that will be helpful? If you avoid using the Twelve Roadblocks, what are alternative ways of responding?

When a person is able to feel and communicate genuine acceptance of another, he possesses a capacity for being an effective helping agent. Acceptance of the other, just as he is, is an important factor in fostering a relationship in which the other person can grow, develop, make constructive changes, learn to solve problems, move in the direction of psychological health, become more productive and creative, and actualize his fullest potential. It is one of those simple but beautiful paradoxes of life: When a person feels that he is truly accepted by another, as he is, then he is freed to move from there and to begin to think about how he wants to change, how he wants to grow, how he can become different, how he might become more of what he is capable of being.

Acceptance is like the fertile soil that permits a tiny seed to develop into the flower it is capable of becoming. The soil only enables the seed to become the flower. It *releases* the capacity of the seed to grow, but the capacity is entirely within the seed. Like the seed, a young person contains entirely within his organism the capacity to develop. Acceptance is like the soil—it merely enables the youngster to actualize his potential.

Why is adult acceptance such a significant positive influence on children and young people? This is not generally understood. Most parents and teachers have been brought up to believe that if you accept a youngster he will remain

just the way he is; and that the best way to help him become something better in the future is to tell him what you
don't accept about him now.

Therefore, most adults rely heavily on the language of Unacceptance. They believe this is the best way to help young
people. The soil that most teachers provide for students is
heavy with evaluation, judgment, criticism, preaching, moralizing, admonishing, and commanding—messages that convey
unacceptance of the student as he is. This is illustrated by the
words of a thirteen-year-old girl who was just starting to rebel
against adult values and standards:

They tell me so often how bad I am and how stupid my ideas are
and how I can't be trusted that I just do more things they don't
like. If they already think I'm bad and stupid, I might as well go
ahead and do all these things anyway.

This bright girl was wise enough to understand the old
adage, "Tell a child often enough how bad he is and he will
most certainly become bad." Young people often become
what adults tell them they are—day after day.

The language of Acceptance opens kids up. It frees them
to share their feelings and problems. Professional therapists
and counselors have shown just how powerful such acceptance can be. Those therapists and counselors who are most
effective are the ones who can convey to the people who
come to them for help that they are truly accepted. This is
why one often hears people say that in counseling or therapy
they felt totally free of the counselor's judgment. They report
that they experienced a freedom to tell him the worst about
themselves; they felt their counselor would *accept them* no
matter what they said or felt. Such acceptance is one of the
most important elements contributing to the growth and
change that takes place in people through counseling and
therapy.

Conversely, we also have learned from these "professional

change agents" that unacceptance closes people up, makes them feel defensive, produces discomfort, makes them afraid to talk or to take a look at themselves. Part of the secret of success of the professional therapist's ability to foster change and growth in troubled people is the absence of unacceptance in his relationship with them and his ability to talk the language of acceptance so it is genuinely felt by the other.

In working with teachers in our Teacher Effectiveness Training course, we have demonstrated that they too can be taught these skills used by professional counselors and thereby drastically reduce the frequency of messages that convey unacceptance in the classroom.

When teachers learn how to demonstrate through their words an inner feeling of acceptance toward a student, they are in possession of a tool that can produce some startling effects. Teachers can help a student learn to accept and like himself and to acquire a sense of his own worth. They can greatly facilitate his developing and actualizing the potential with which he was genetically endowed. They can accelerate his movement away from dependence and toward independence and self-direction. They can help him learn to solve for himself the problems that life inevitably brings, and they can give him the strength to deal constructively with the usual disappointments and pain of childhood and adolescence.

To accept another "as he is" is truly an act of love; to feel accepted is to feel loved. And in psychology we have only begun to realize the tremendous power of feeling loved: It can promote the growth of mind and body, and is probably the most effective therapeutic force we know for repairing psychological and physical damage.

Specific skills are required to do this. Yet most people think of acceptance only as a passive thing—a static state of mind, an inner attitude or feeling. True, acceptance does originate from within. But to be an effective force in influencing another, it must be actively communicated or demonstrated. A person can never be certain that he is accepted by another until he sees it demonstrated in some active way.

The professional counselor or psychotherapist, whose effectiveness as a helping agent is so greatly dependent on his ability to demonstrate his acceptance of the client, spends years learning ways to put across this attitude through his own habits of communication. Only through formal training and experience do professional counselors acquire specific skills in communicating acceptance. But first they learn that *what they say* makes the difference between their being helpful or not.

We would like to emphasize once again: Talk can cure, and talk can foster constructive change. But it must be the right kind of talk. How teachers talk to their students will determine whether they will be helpful or destructive. The effective teacher, like the effective counselor, must learn how to communicate acceptance, must acquire some specific communication skills.

In our T.E.T. classes teachers skeptically ask, "Is it possible for a nonprofessional like myself to learn the skills of a professional counselor?" Ten years ago we would have said, "No." But meanwhile we have demonstrated in our classes that it *is* possible for most teachers to learn how to be effective helping agents for their students. We know now that it is not knowledge of psychology or an intellectual understanding about people that makes a good counselor. It is primarily a matter of learning how to talk to people in a constructive way.

Psychologists call this "therapeutic communication" because certain kinds of messages have a therapeutic or healthy effect on people. They make people feel better, encourage them to talk, help them express their feelings, foster a feeling of worth or self-esteem, reduce threat or fear, facilitate growth and constructive change.

Other kinds of talk are nontherapeutic or destructive. These messages tend to make people feel judged or guilty; they restrict expression of honest feelings, threaten the person, foster feelings of unworthiness or low self-esteem, block growth and constructive change by making the person defend more strongly the way he is.

While a very small number of teachers possess this therapeutic skill intuitively and hence are "naturals," most teachers must first unlearn their destructive ways of communicating and then learn the more constructive ways.

MORE CONSTRUCTIVE WAYS OF HELPING
STUDENTS WHO HAVE PROBLEMS

One of the most difficult ideas for teachers (or anyone else) to comprehend and accept is that a person can help another merely by listening. Silence is golden, so the old expression goes. It is also potent. Effective professional counselors spend a lot of their time just listening. Through experience they have learned that listening is one of their most effective tools—it *invites* a troubled person to talk about what is troubling him; it *facilitates catharsis and release* of his feelings and emotions; it *keeps the ball with the person* who owns the problem; it fosters his *exploration into deeper and more basic feelings*; it tells him of your *willingness to be a helper*; and it *communicates acceptance of him as he is*, troubles and all.

Is it any wonder that listening is considered the most valuable tool of effective counselors? Yet most teachers, as well as most parents, or for that matter most people, think that it's the counselor's job primarily to *tell the troubled person something*—talk *to* him; send him messages; give him advice, facts, warnings, sympathy, insights, solutions; ask him questions; offer him evaluations and judgments.

Teachers are surprised and disbelieving when they learn in our T.E.T. classes that one of the best ways to help a person with a problem is to *just be there*. Expert counselors sometimes say that their success depends primarily on getting the person started and then "staying out of his way" by listening.

In the remainder of this chapter you will be shown *four different ways to listen to students* and thereby become more effective in helping them when they have problems.

Passive Listening (Silence)

Saying nothing actually communicates acceptance. Silence —"passive listening"—is a powerful nonverbal message that can make a student feel genuinely accepted and encourage him to share more and more with you. A student cannot talk to you about what is bothering him if you are doing the talking.

Acknowledgment Responses that Work

While silence certainly avoids the communication road-blocks that so often tell the student his messages are unacceptable, it does not prove for sure that you are *really* paying attention. It therefore helps, especially at pauses, to use nonverbal and verbal cues to indicate that you are actually well tuned-in. We call these cues "acknowledgment responses." Nodding, leaning forward, smiling, frowning, and other body movements, used appropriately, let the student know that you really hear. Verbal cues like "Uh-huh," "Oh," "I see"—what counselors humorously refer to as "empathic grunting"—also tell a student that you are still attentive, that you are interested, and that it is acceptable for him to go on.

What Door Openers Can Do

Occasionally students need additional encouragement to talk more, to go deeper, or even to begin. Such messages are called "door openers." Some examples are: "Would you like to say more about that?" Or, "That's interesting, want to go on?" Or, "Sounds like you have some strong feelings about that." Or, "I'm interested in what you are saying." Or, "Do you want to talk about it?" Notice that these messages are open-ended questions and statements. They contain no evaluation about what is being said.

A teacher in a T.E.T. class describes her first try at using these techniques with a student:

One student in my fifth-period class kept waiting around after class like she wanted to talk but didn't know how to begin. Yesterday I decided to try a door opener and see what happens, so I said, "Is there something you want to talk about?" At first she sort of stumbled around not knowing where to begin and I bit my tongue and stuck to some "Uh-huhs" and "go-ons." Finally, she opened up and for about ten minutes just talked her head off. I had no idea she was carrying around such a load. It was awfully hard for me to keep from asking questions but I didn't. That little ten-minute talk seemed to make her feel a lot better and I felt really close to her. At the end, she squeezed my hand. I can't believe how helpful to her it was for me simply to listen.

This teacher's experience in listening is not unique, nor are her feelings about what happened in the process. Rather universally, teachers experience (1) difficulty in refraining from the use of roadblocks, (2) surprise at the problems students are having, (3) a sense of relief when the student begins to talk unhampered by outside direction, and (4) a feeling of closeness with the student.

One never knows where a dialogue might go if, instead of roadblocks, the more facilitative techniques of silence and acknowledgment are used, as in the following example:

STUDENT: I'll never get the paper out. I think I'll quit.

TEACHER: (*Silence, nods*)

STUDENT: I've been here since three this afternoon. Everybody else split. They seem to think because I'm the editor that I have to do all the work. That's a bummer.

TEACHER: *Uh-huh.*

STUDENTS Ellen didn't get the typing done and Maryanne still has to do those layouts—and look at that mess over there that Steve calls the sports page.

TEACHER: (*Nods*)

STUDENT: (*Pause*) The problem is that everybody is waiting for somebody else to do something. We need a list of things that have to be done and the order they must be done in. That way everybody will be able to see what the next job is and who has to do it.

TEACHER: I see.

STUDENT: I can make the list at home tonight. See you tomorrow.

TEACHER: Right.

The Need for Active Listening

Silence, acknowledgment responses, and door openers do have limitations; they do not provide much interaction—the speaker is doing all the work. In addition, the speaker has no way of knowing whether the teacher *understands;* he only knows that he is listening. Such responses often fail to foster "going deeper," getting away from the superficial or surface problem to underlying causes and feelings. Also, the student may not know whether the teacher is *accepting* him and his message. He only knows that the teacher is tuned in.

In short, these three ways of listening are relatively *passive* and do not prove that the listener has understood. Such an inactive role is much like an observer watching a drama unfold on a stage—the actors know you are there and you seem to be willing to hear their words, but that is about all they can be sure of.

Effective listening requires far more interaction and a lot more proof that the counselor has not only heard but has also understood accurately. The competent counselor therefore extensively uses a fourth kind of listening response, which we call "active listening."

In order to appreciate fully the significance of active listening, most teachers need a brief introduction to the relatively obscure theory of human communication—what really does go on when Person A talks to Person B. In the T.E.T. course the most useful way to acquaint teachers with this communication process is through a model or diagram developed and explained in the next section. Once you have grasped this model, we will introduce you to the fourth kind of listening: active listening

WHAT COMMUNICATION IS REALLY ALL ABOUT

Why do people talk? What causes a person to want to communicate? The communication process begins when one person talks to another because he has a need—something going on inside him. A person lives his life, in a sense, "trapped" inside his physical self, within his own "bag of skin." Talk is an attempt to communicate to the outside world what is happening inside. In Figure 11 we use a circle to represent a person—call him Terry. His "bag of skin" is the circumference or boundary of the circle.

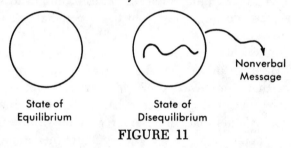

State of
Equilibrium

State of
Disequilibrium

Nonverbal
Message

FIGURE 11

In the diagram to the left Terry is working away contentedly at a task he enjoys in a state of relative equilibrium—no unmet needs, no problem. As it gets later in the morning, Terry begins to experience mild hunger, represented by the diagram on the right. Because he is enjoying his work, he ignores his hunger or may not even be aware of it. But his body may begin to send out nonverbal messages in the form of fidgeting, restlessness, looking around the room.

Now, in Figure 12 we will have Terry become *very* hungry, so that he is in a more severe state of disequilibrium. Such a state motivates Terry to get rid of the disequilibrium—i.e., to get his hunger need satisfied somehow. This is when he may use conscious verbal communication.

But how? It is impossible to communicate what is actually going on inside us—e.g., hunger, frustration, tiredness, or other such feelings. These are physiological processes or bodily conditions that cannot be communicated—literally, they must remain inside one's skin. To communicate how we feel inside or what is bothering us, we must select a *code*— what communication experts call the process of "encoding." All verbal messages are codes—language equivalents of our feelings, not the feelings themselves.

Now a very hungry Terry is a circle with a greatly amplified wave (his severe disequilibrium). The process of encoding is shown as a box, and the code or message that Terry might send ("I'm hungry") is shown as an arrow, directed toward a receiver (or listener).

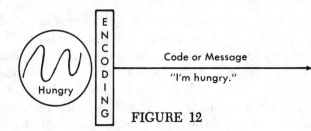

FIGURE 12

Sometimes coded messages are fairly clear. "I'm hungry," is easy to understand. Unfortunately, clear, easily understood messages are relatively rare. Most messages people send are uniquely coded. This means that the content of the message may be *related* to the feeling, but the feeling itself is not clearly expressed. Instead of saying, "I'm hungry," Terry will more likely say something like, "When do we eat?" or "What time is it?" Taken literally, these coded messages can be misleading. For example, a listener might interpret "What time is it?" merely as a request to know what time it is. A teacher who responds by saying "You know how to tell time" misses the message completely.

Below are examples of student messages not easily understood by a teacher because they are uniquely coded—i.e., the
code does not clearly identify what is going on inside the
student, what is bothering him, or what he is feeling.

The Student is feeling:	*His coded message:*
1. Anxious about the upcoming exam.	"Why do we have to learn all this stuff about the Constitution and Bill of Rights?"
2. Afraid of not being chosen to be on one of the baseball teams.	"Do I have to go out to P.E. today?"
3. Overwhelmed by the amount of homework assigned.	"This stuff is too hard—I just can't understand it."
4. Rejected and not liked.	"Marcia is a stuck-up snob."
5. Disappointed in the results of an art project.	"I hate art—it's for sissies."

Because most young people's messages are uniquely coded
and therefore difficult to understand, it is foolish for teachers
to *respond only to the code*. To do so results in misunderstanding the real meaning of the youngster's message. This usually
means that the teacher fails to help the student, because she
never learns what is bothering him. Furthermore, responding
to the code communicates to the student that his teacher
doesn't understand him, which causes even further deterioration of the teacher-student relationship.

HOW TO LEARN ACTIVE LISTENING

The most effective method for preventing such break-
downs in communication is active listening, a way of listening that all but insures understanding what students
communicate. Active listening, as opposed to passive listening
(silence), involves interaction with the student, and it also
provides the student with proof (feedback) of the teacher's
understanding.

A typical classroom situation will serve to illustrate active listening and how it differs from passive listening.

One of your students is feeling a lot of anxiety about his work because he is far behind in his reading and realizes how much work it is going to take to catch up. He has a problem and wants to try to solve it.

Obviously, he cannot show the teacher the anxiety inside his organism, so he must go through the process of encoding, selecting some verbal symbols to represent his inner state. Suppose (as in Figure 13) he selects this code: "Are we going to have a test real soon?"

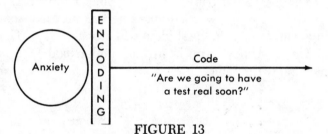

FIGURE 13

Now, when you receive that message your mind must go through a *decoding process* (illustrated in Figure 14) to enable you to understand the meaning of the student's message (what is going on inside him). The decoding process must be a guess or an inference, because you as the receiver

SENDER   RECEIVER

FIGURE 14

cannot see inside the student's skin. If you guess right, your decoding process will produce (inside you) "He is worried." An incorrect decoding might produce "He wants a test soon," or "He forgot the test was scheduled for next week."

While the decoding process is critical in the communication process, *you do not know whether you are right or wrong.* Equally important, *the student cannot know whether you have decoded his message correctly or incorrectly.* He cannot read your mind any better than you can read his.

Suppose, therefore, you decide to check up on the accuracy of your decoding effort before you respond to his message. All you need to do is to *feed back* (or mirror) the results of your decoding. (See Figure 15.) Using your own words, you mirror back, "You are worried about getting an exam soon." Hearing your feedback, the student will probably say, "That's right." He now knows you heard and understood him, and you now know the same.

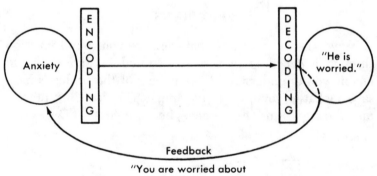

FIGURE 15

This process of "feeding back" is what we call "active listening." It is the last step that completes an *effective communication process.*

But suppose the student was feeling anxiety because he

was afraid the test was going to be an essay test on which he usually performs poorly.

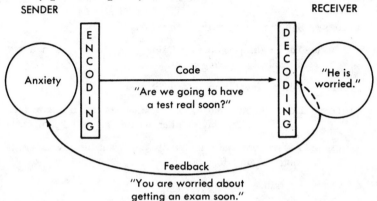

FIGURE 16

In this case your decoding was off target (as illustrated by Figure 16). Your consequent feedback told the student you did not guess correctly. He will most likely correct you and the conversation might go something like this:

STUDENT: No, it's just that I don't know what kind of a test you're going to give and I'm afraid it'll be an essay type.

TEACHER: Oh, you're worried about the *kind* of test we are going to have.

STUDENT: Yes. I don't do well on essay tests.

TEACHER: I see, you feel you can do better on objective tests.

STUDENT: Yeah, I always botch up essay tests.

TEACHER: It'll be a multiple-choice test.

STUDENT: What a relief! I'm not so worried now.

In this case the teacher's first feedback was not on target so the student knew he had to restate or re-encode his message until ultimately he was understood.

Here are some additional examples of effective active listening with students sending messages that are cues and clues revealing that they are experiencing problems:

1. STUDENT: Sally tore up my drawing. (*Sobs*)

   TEACHER: You're disappointed at losing your drawing and angry at Sally for tearing it up.

   STUDENT: Yeah. Now I'll have to do it over!

2. STUDENT: I don't know what to take next semester. I'd like to take woodshop, but my mother wants me to take algebra.

   TEACHER: You're torn between what you want and what your mother wants for you.

   STUDENT: Uh-huh.

3. STUDENT: Richard always cheats. I'm not going to play with him anymore.

   TEACHER: You hate the way Richard treats you so much that you're going to quit playing with him.

   STUDENT: Yes, I'll play with Tommy and David instead.

4. STUDENT: This school sure isn't as good as my last one. The kids there were friendly.

   TEACHER: You feel pretty left-out here.

   STUDENT: I sure do.

5. STUDENT: Why does it have to rain all the time? We never get to do anything fun like swing on the swings or climb on the monkey bars when it rains.

   TEACHER: You're pretty bored having to stay in the room.

   STUDENT: Yes, I wish we could go outside.

In each of these illustrations the teacher accurately decoded the message and learned what was going on inside the student. In each case, the teacher checked out the accuracy of his decoding and elicited verification—the student's positive response of "Yes" or "Uh-huh." Notice also that in each case the teacher focused on how the student was *feeling* about the external situation, not on the external situation itself, keeping the responsibility with the student, not on the outside world. For instance, in the situation where the student says: "Richard always cheats. I'm not going to play with him anymore," the teacher focuses on how the sender *feels about the situation*. He does not place the focus on Richard by saying, "Richard is really a bad guy, huh?"

Here is a dialogue with a sixth-grade boy and his elementary-school principal. Note how the principal's active listening helped the student move away from the surface "presenting problem"—his difficulty with his teacher—to the underlying problem, concern about his older brother:

STUDENT: (*Hesitantly*) I . . . I thought I wanted to tell you about Mr. Larson.

PRINCIPAL: Sounds like you're not too sure now, like you're changing your mind about talking to me.

STUDENT: Well, if he ever found out I talked to you he'd really be mad.

PRINCIPAL: I see. You're worried about what Mr. Larson would do if I told him about this conference.

STUDENT: Yeah.

PRINCIPAL: I won't tell anyone what you talk about here unless you say it's okay.

STUDENT: (*Relieved*) That's cool, 'cause I'm already in enough trouble with him. You know what he did? Look at this shirt. (*Points to front of shirt where a button is missing and a triangular tear shows around the buttonhole.*) He grabbed me and ripped it. Boy, wait until my mom sees that! Oh, wow!

PRINCIPAL: You're afraid that she'll really be mad at you.

STUDENT: Yeah, she's always yelling at me about tearing up my clothes or getting all dirty. She'll never believe that Larson, uh, Mr. Larson, tore it. She'll say, "Well, why would a teacher do that?" and I'll have to tell her about the fight with Steve and then she'll say, "That's all you ever do anymore, just fight and argue." I'll never hear the end of it. Over and over, "You just fight and argue."

PRINCIPAL: You're pretty sick of hearing that.

STUDENT: (*Nods*) It wasn't so bad until Alex got back from Nam. Do you know Alex? He used to go here, but I guess that was before you came. Well, anyway he came back and moved in my room and he took all my stuff and crammed it in a box in the corner of the closet, and you know, took over. He really thinks he's boss, like he orders me and my sister around all the time and mom won't do anything about it. She says, "Somebody has to straighten you two out and your father's not here to do it." It's not my fault dad split.

PRINCIPAL: You feel like things have really changed for the worse since Alex came back. You've lost your privacy and you get bossed around more.

STUDENT: Right, it's not the room so much. Alex has got to have someplace to stay while he's looking for a job or till he goes back to school or whatever he does, but it's sure not like it used to be.

PRINCIPAL: It's different since Alex came back.

STUDENT: No, I mean when dad was there and Alex was okay. (*Pause*) I think Alex is on something.

PRINCIPAL: Drugs, you mean.

STUDENT: Yes. Sometimes he's really neat, you know, like he used to be, but sometimes he's sort of wild and then he goes out and he'll be gone for a long time and when he comes back he's all goofed up, you know, kind of out of it.

PRINCIPAL: You have some evidence that makes you suspicious.

STUDENT: Yeah, like the money I've been saving to buy a new mitt for Little League is gone.

PRINCIPAL: You think Alex took it to buy drugs.

STUDENT: I don't really care about the money. My old mitt is okay.

PRINCIPAL: You're more worried about Alex.

STUDENT: What'll I do? (*Begins to cry*) He'll get busted or O.D. [overdose] or something.

PRINCIPAL: You're scared of what is going to happen to Alex.

STUDENT: Yes, and I can't tell mom. She'd freak out and call the cops or something and that'd made it worse.

PRINCIPAL: You're pretty sure your mother wouldn't be able to handle it.

STUDENT: She wouldn't. I was wondering if you had the phone number of that guy from the drug center that was over here talking to our class.

PRINCIPAL: You feel he might be able to help you or tell you how to help Alex.

STUDENT: Yeah, but I lost the paper he gave us with the address and stuff.

PRINCIPAL: I'll get you another one. (*Gets it from the file*)

STUDENT: Thanks. Can I have a tissue? (*Blows nose, wipes eyes*) I guess I'd better go. (*Starts to leave*) Oh, about the shirt. Mr. Larson didn't tear it, not on purpose. He was just holding me and Steve to break up the fight and I tried to pull away and that's when the shirt got torn.

PRINCIPAL: You're not really mad at Mr. Larson—you feel it wasn't his fault.

STUDENT: No. He's okay. I've got to go now. Uh, you won't say anything?

PRINCIPAL: Not unless you say it's all right.

STUDENT: Okay. See you tomorrow.

The principal reported that the total time for this particular conference was less than ten minutes. While it is not unusual for active listening to make a session flow from beginning to conclusion as easily as this one did, teachers must realize that some conferences might end in ambiguity and apparent confusion as in the following counseling situation with a high-school senior:

STUDENT: You know, I'm going to graduate this spring and I just wish I didn't have to. It'd be really neat if I could go here another year.

TEACHER: You really hate to see it end.

STUDENT: Yeah. It's not that I like school so much, it's just that I don't know what to do next year, you know? I'd like to go on to college, but it costs a lot of money and my dad can't afford it. I could get a job, but the kind I can get don't pay much. They're really a drag.

TEACHER: You're pretty discouraged about the choices you see for yourself after you graduate.

STUDENT: Yes, I am, except if I went to State. My boy friend goes there and I could live with him, you know, and share expenses for the apartment and food and stuff. (*Pause*) The only problem is my dad would kill me if he found out.

TEACHER: You're afraid of how he'd react to your living with your boy friend.

STUDENT: Oh, I know how he'd react. He'd come and drag me home or call the police. That's another problem. My dad doesn't like Jim, that's my boy friend. Mostly he doesn't like him because he has long hair and he's really into art and music. Dad's more the rugged type, you know?

TEACHER: They're really very different from each other.

STUDENT: Well, not that much. Dad's sweet under all that he-man stuff, kinda like Jim. . . . I think they are a lot alike in many ways. It's just that daddy has very strong ideas about what a guy is supposed to do to be a man—like play football and drink beer and join the army. I guess he's really a male chauvinist 'cause he doesn't think a girl can do anything and he says Jim's like a girl because he just paints and writes music and stuff.

TEACHER: He really puts that stuff down as not proper for boys.

STUDENT: Yes, he does. (*Pause*) I think he wanted a boy.

TEACHER: You think he was disappointed you weren't a boy.

STUDENT: Yeah, he wanted me to be a boy instead of a girl. My mother died when I was born, and my grandmother lived with us when I was little. I remember him telling her that it sure would be easier to raise me if I was a boy, that he'd know what to do. I think that's why he doesn't like Jim. If I had been a boy he'd have taught me to play football and be tough like him. I guess he thought when I started dating I'd go out with guys like that, and I never have. Well, Jim's the only guy I've ever really gone out with, you know, seriously. I went out with one guy on the football team once 'cause I thought it'd make dad happy, but he was gross.

TEACHER: That was a bad experience for you.

STUDENT: It sure was! I found out that I can't go out with guys to please daddy. I've got to go out with the kind I like, even if they've got long hair and fangs like Dracula. There's this one guy in my government class that's really a fox. I'd go out with him in a minute, but I don't think he'd give me a second look.

TEACHER: You don't think you have a chance with him, huh?

STUDENT: Not since I gained all this weight. You know, since Jim's been gone all I do is sit around the house and eat till I look like a balloon. I'm pretty disgusted with myself but I don't seem to be able to do anything about it. I look at myself in the mirror and get so upset I go out and eat something. That's dumb, isn't it?

TEACHER: You really feel you're defeating yourself by your own behavior.

STUDENT: Yes. I don't understand myself.

This rambling, inconclusive interaction illustrates that counseling cannot insure clear and dramatic results. But active listening at least started the process of problem solving, provided cathartic emotional release, and strengthened the student's view of the teacher as someone she can talk to.

WHAT'S REQUIRED FOR EFFECTIVE ACTIVE LISTENING

For active listening to be effective, teachers must have certain attitudes or "sets." Without these, teachers will come across as insincere, patronizing, or manipulative, and even their accurate active listening will seem mechanical, unnatural, and wooden to students.

1. The teacher must have a deep sense of trust in students' ability ultimately to solve their own problems. When students do not

find solutions quickly, and they ramble and sound inconclusive as in the above example, teachers need to have faith *in the process,* and remember that the purpose of active listening is to facilitate solution finding—a process that might take days, weeks, even months.

2. The teacher must be able to *genuinely accept* the feelings expressed by students, however different they may be from feelings the teacher thinks students "should" have. Students free themselves from troublesome feelings when these feelings can be openly expressed, examined, and explored.

3. The teacher must understand that feelings are often quite transitory. They exist only *as of the moment.* Active listening helps students move from momentary feeling to momentary feeling; feelings get "defused," dissipated, and released. "This, too, shall pass" applies to most human feelings.

4. The teacher must *want* to help students with their problems and make *time* for it. In a later chapter we will suggest ways to organize time so that teachers who *want* to help students with their problems *can,* without sacrificing their own needs.

5. Teachers must be "with" each student who is experiencing troubles, yet maintain a separate identity, not get caught up in the feelings of the student to the point that the separateness is lost. That is, teachers must experience the feelings *as if* they were their own, but not let them *become* their own (and trouble them).

6. Teachers need to understand that students are seldom able to start out by sharing the real problem. Active listening helps students clarify, go deeper, and get away from the initial presenting problem. Teachers who are uncomfortable with real-life "gutty" problems will show this discomfort. When that happens, it is only fair to say, "I'm uncomfortable," and offer to help the student contact another person who might feel more at ease and accepting of the kinds of real-life problems students so often experience.

7. Teachers must respect the privacy and confidential nature of whatever the student reveals about himself and his life. Too often, teachers gossip about students and openly discuss the young peoples' problems with other teachers. Nothing will destroy the counseling relationship more quickly.

Active listening is not a gimmick that teachers can pull out of their bag of tricks to patch up students when they have problems. It is a specific method for putting to work a set of attitudes about students, about their problems, and about the role of the teacher as a helping person.

"WHY COUNSEL STUDENTS? I'M A TEACHER!"

When they first learn about active listening in a T.E.T. course, some teachers ask questions like these:

"Why listen to kids? Is this going to help me teach?"

"We have counselors to do counseling. Why should I do their job?"

"I have enough to do without counseling. How can I find time to listen and teach, too?"

"That's all very well, but I have thirty-five students. How can I listen to all of them?"

"Is active listening going to help my students learn more?"

"Active listening isn't my style. Won't the kids think I've flipped out if I start feeding back?"

These are understandable reactions. After all, active listening puts teachers in a role which is new and strange for some of them. Most teachers are accustomed to lecturing, probing, telling, judging, and evaluating. They accept only the specific task of "teaching" assigned to them, and that task seems to require a lot of lecturing, probing, telling, and evaluation. So it is natural for teachers to question whether it will be worth their time and trouble to learn and use active listening.

In a discussion of these questions in a T.E.T. class, one teacher related his own classroom success with active listening:

I think one of the things that may be hanging us up here is that we aren't viewing active listening as a teaching tool. In my department we have been urged to use all kinds of new inquiry approaches and to hold discussion groups. We have been given special training in these techniques for two years. But only in the last few days, after I learned about active listening, has any of these approaches ever worked for me. Now I see why my discussion groups always turn into bull sessions or I end up lecturing as usual—the only difference being that the students are seated in a circle instead of rows. In other courses they told us we had to be "nonevaluative" but never showed us how. Since I've been trying active listening, discussions are really *discussions*. I'm enjoying it, and the kids in my classes are really turned on.

Active listening is a powerful tool, as this teacher pointed out, for facilitating learning—for clarifying, promoting inquiry, creating a climate where students feel free to think, discuss, question, and explore. Teachers already trained in teaching strategies to promote thinking processes grasp and appreciate the significance of the "minimal evaluative feedback" quality of active listening and use it regularly to enhance their own teaching performance.

Another teacher reported back to his T.E.T. class a different successful experience in his-fifth grade classroom:

I decided to try active listening in my class. I'm not good at it yet, but the class is really different in spite of my goofs. Not just different—better. I started by taking five of the worst boys in my class off in a corner for a few minutes, one at a time. I'd start with a door opener like, "You seem to be having a lot of fights lately. Would you like to talk about it?" That's all it took to get them talking like mad, especially when they found out that I wasn't going to tell them they were wrong to fight or give them a lecture about shaping up. It's strange how just those few minutes alone with each of those kids have changed their attitudes. They're not picking on each other as much, and we haven't had a fight for several days in my room. Now all the other kids want a "rap session," as they call it.

Teachers who try active listening discover that, rather than being a time waster, it acts in many ways to *free up more time for profitable teaching and learning*. Here's how:

1. Active listening *helps students deal with and "defuse" strong feelings*. Expressing strong, troublesome feelings helps students to free themselves from them so they can then get back to the task

of learning. Active listening invariably fosters this kind of cathartic release.

2. Active listening helps students understand that they need not be afraid of their own emotions and helps them understand that feelings are not "bad." With active listening, teachers can *help students understand that "feelings are friends."*

3. Active listening *facilitates problem solving* by the student. Because active listening is so effective in helping students talk, it promotes "talking it out," "thinking out loud," "working it through."

4. Active listening *keeps the responsibility with the student* for analyzing and solving his problems. Teachers who try active listening are often amazed at the creativity and energy students bring to tackling problems and finding their own solutions.

5. Active listening *makes students more willing to listen to teachers.* When a teacher listens to them, students know that their points of view, opinions, feelings, and ideas have been understood, so it's much easier for them to open their minds to the teacher's ideas, opinions, and points of view. When teachers say their students never listen to them, it is a good bet that these teachers aren't doing an effective job of listening to the students.

6. Active listening *promotes a closer, more meaningful relationship between a teacher and a student.* Students who are heard by their teachers invariably experience a sense of greater self-worth and importance. The satisfaction of being understood, coupled with this increased self-esteem, causes students to feel warmly toward the teacher who listens. The teacher feels a similar warmth and closeness, for teachers who listen empathically get a broader understanding of their students and begin to see what it's like to be in their shoes for a little while. Listening empathically, walking a few steps with a student on his life journey, is an act of caring, respect, and love. This is why we say teaching can be a form of loving. Furthermore, when relationships between teacher and students develop mutual caring, respect, and love, "discipline" problems decrease significantly. Kids don't hassle and make trouble for teachers they respect and care for. So the time formerly spent handling disciplinary cases can be used for teaching and learning.

TWO TYPES OF VERBAL COMMUNICATION AND THEIR EFFECTS ON STUDENTS: A Catalogue

TEACHERS may find this catalogue useful as a summary of this chapter. Some may use it as a review; others may wish to share it with other teachers or their principals. Its primary purpose is to analyze in greater depth the risks involved (and the possible effects on students) in each category of verbal response.

COMMUNICATION ROADBLOCKS

1. Ordering, Commanding, Directing

These messages tell a student that *his* feelings, needs, or problems are not important; he must comply with what the *teacher* feels or needs. Example: "I don't care if you're thirsty; sit down and stay there until you're excused."

They tell the student that he is unacceptable as he is at the moment. Example: "Stop whining, you're no baby."

They produce fear of the teacher's power. Students hear a threat of being punished by someone bigger and stronger than themselves. Example: "Get out of the halls" (the "or else" is implied).

They may make students resentful and angry and may

cause them to express hostile feelings—fight back, resist, test the teacher's will, throw a temper tantrum.

They can communicate that the teacher doesn't trust the student's competence or judgment. Example: "Make a study schedule tonight and bring it in to me tomorrow."

2. *Warning, Threatening*

These messages are very much like ordering, commanding, and directing, but the consequences for refusal to comply are added. Example: "Stop whining or I'll give you something to whine about."

They tell the student that the teacher has little respect for his needs or wishes. Example: "If you don't get that paper finished you can stay here until you do."

They can make a student feel fearful and submissive. Example: "If you don't straighten up I'm going to call your parents."

Like orders and commands, such warnings and threats evoke hostility.

Students sometimes respond to warnings or threats by saying, "I don't care what happens, I still feel this way." In addition, they sometimes are tempted to do something they have just been warned not to do just to see whether the consequences promised by the teacher will materialize.

3. *Moralizing, Preaching, Giving "Shoulds and Oughts"*

These messages bring to bear on students the power of outside authority, duty, or obligation. Students commonly respond to "shoulds and oughts" by resisting, and defending their postures even more strongly.

Moralistic messages convey to students that the teacher does not trust their judgment, that they had better accept what others deem right. Example: "You ought to do the right thing, tell the dean what you know."

They cause feelings of guilt, convince students that they are "bad." Example: "You shouldn't do things that are going to bring shame on you and the school."

They imply that the teacher has no faith in the student's ability to form opinions, make judgments, or hold values of his own. Example: "You must respect your elders."

4. Advising, Offering Solutions or Suggestions

Such messages are heard by students as evidence that teachers don't have confidence in students' ability to solve their own problems.

They sometimes influence students to become dependent on teachers, to stop thinking for themselves, to turn to outside "authorities" for answers in every stressful situation.

Advice communicates an attitude of superiority (I know what's best for you), which is especially irritating to adolescents struggling to assert independence. Since advising implies superiority on the part of the advisor, students sometimes spend excessive time reacting to this attitude instead of developing ideas of their own.

These messages frequently leave students feeling that they have been misunderstood; that if the teacher had understood, he wouldn't have suggested the solution he came up with. The feeling is, "If you really understood how I feel, you wouldn't make such a dumb suggestion."

5. Teaching, Lecturing, Giving Logical Arguments

Though teaching, lecturing, and giving logical arguments are legitimate functions in the No-Problem area of the teacher-student relationship, they are regarded by students as illegitimate at other times. Students experiencing problems may react to "teaching" by feeling inferior, subordinate, and inadequate.

Logic and "facts" often evoke defensiveness and resentment since they imply that the student is illogical and ignorant.

Students, like adults, seldom relish being shown that they are "wrong." Consequently, they tend to defend their positions to the bitter end. They think, "I'm right, you're wrong, and I'll prove it if it kills me."

Lecturing has always been an inefficient method of teaching. When it is used inappropriately, it is not only inefficient, it is hated. Students feel "hassled" and quit listening.

Students sometimes resort to desperate methods of discounting teacher "facts." They write off teachers' views not only on out-of-school topics but in matters of teaching as well. A familiar student reaction is: "You're square—too old to know what's happening today."

Students often have more facts and more relevant information about their problems than their teachers have, which is why a teacher's factual arguments are often interpreted by students as power plays to get them to "do it my way."

6. Judging, Criticizing, Disagreeing, Blaming

More than any others, these messages make students feel stupid, inadequate, inferior, unworthy, bad. To a large extent the self-concepts of students are shaped by the evaluations and judgments of their parents and teachers, the most significant adults in their lives. These negative evaluative statements chip away at student self-esteem.

Negative criticism provokes countercriticism. Students often react by thinking (and sometimes saying), "Well, you're not so hot yourself!" Often teachers who are the most prolific users of negative evaluative statements are the very ones who complain the loudest about the lack of respect they get from students.

Evaluation strongly influences students to hide their feelings, play it safe, and go elsewhere for help.

Students respond with defensiveness and anger to these messages because they need to protect their own self-images. Telling a student that he is lazy will usually make him angry and almost never make him ambitious.

About the only thing worse than negative evaluation is *frequent* negative evaluation. Students subjected to a great deal of negative input about themselves come to think of themselves as no good, undeserving, and unlikable. There is a great deal of evidence that it is exactly this kind of self-image that promotes high risk taking that is most likely to be self-defeating and injurious.

7. *Praising, Agreeing, Giving Positive Evaluations*

While teachers easily understand the terrible hurting power of *negative* evaluation, they are often shocked to learn that, contrary to commonly held belief, praise is not always beneficial to students and often has very negative effects. A positive evaluation that does not fit a student's self-image may evoke anger ("I am *not* a good student"). Students interpret these positive messages as attempts to manipulate them, a subtle way of influencing them to do what the teacher wants ("You just say that so I'll work harder").

Students correctly infer that if a teacher judges positively, he can also judge negatively at another time. They also correctly infer that to judge implies superiority.

The absence of praise in a classroom where praise is frequently used can be interpreted by students as criticism ("You didn't say anything good about my drawing so you must not like it").

Praise is also frequently embarrassing to students when given publicly. Most students despise being held up as the "good example" as much as being exposed as the "bad example."

Students who are praised a lot may grow to depend on it, even demand it. ("Look, teacher, look at *my* paper!" Or "Isn't this a good drawing?" Or, "Look, teacher, I'm sharing with Bobby").

Finally, students sometimes infer that teachers who praise them don't really understand them, that the positive evaluation is used to save the teacher from having to take time to understand what the students are feeling.

8. *Name-Calling, Stereotyping, Ridiculing*

Name-calling, stereotyping, and ridiculing are forms of negative evaluation and criticism, and, as such, have the same devastating effect on the self-images of students.

The most frequent response of students to such messages is to give one back to the teacher. Example: "Well, you're too bossy," or "Look who's acting like a baby now."

Teachers who use such messages in attempts to influence students are invariably disappointed. Instead of looking at themselves realistically, the students are able to use the teacher's unfair message to excuse themselves ("I am not a baby; babies don't act like this. *I* act like this").

9. *Interpreting, Analyzing, Diagnosing*

Such messages tell students that the teacher has them "figured out," knows what their motives are or why they behave the way they do ("You're just doing that to get everyone's attention"). This amateur psychoanalysis can be threatening and frustrating to students. If the teacher's analysis is correct, the students feel exposed, naked, and embarrassed. If the analysis is wrong, as it usually is, students feel angry at being falsely accused.

Students often see these messages as evidence that the teacher feels he is the wiser, that from his position of superiority he can see through the students and, like God, know their inner thoughts and feelings. These "I know why" and "I can see through you" messages often cut off any desire on the part of students to say more. They teach students to refrain from sharing information with the teacher. It's too risky.

10. *Reassuring, Sympathizing, Consoling, Supporting*

On the surface, these messages seem to be helpful to students struggling with problems. In fact, they are not as helpful as they appear. To reassure a student when he is feeling disturbed about something may simply convince him that you don't understand him.

Teachers reassure and console because they are not comfortable with the strong negative feelings students may have (and express) when they are troubled. Reassuring and supportive messages, at these times, tell students that the teacher wants them to stop feeling the way they do ("Don't feel bad, things will turn out all right. You'll feel better tomorrow").

Students see through teachers' attempts to get them to change—and distrust them.

Sympathy and other devices often used to discount student feelings stop further communication because students sense that the teachers want them to stop feeling the way they do.

No one likes to be told that he is not in touch with reality. All forms of reassurance imply that the troubled person is exaggerating, doesn't understand how things *really* are, is in a sense "crazy." This is why students sometimes react with hostility to attempts by teachers to make them feel better with support and sympathy.

11. *Questioning, Probing, Interrogating, Cross-Examining*

To ask questions when students have problems may convey a lack of trust, some suspicion or doubt. Example: "Did you do your homework last night like I told you to?"

Students interpret some questions as attempts to entrap, to get them out on a limb, only to have the limb sawed off by the teacher. Example: "How long did you study? Only an hour? Well, you don't deserve a good grade."

Students often feel threatened by questions, especially when they don't understand why the teacher is questioning them. Notice how often students respond to a question with one of their own. ("Why do you want to know?")

When teachers question a student who is sharing a problem, the student may infer that the teacher is trying to get information in order to solve the problem for him, rather than let him solve his own problem ("Your Aunt Emma has come to live with you? How do you feel about that?").

When a question is asked of a student sharing a problem, each question limits the student's freedom to talk about what he wants to talk about. In a sense, each question dictates the student's next message. If you ask, "When did you first notice this feeling?" the student must talk about the onset of that feeling, nothing else. Lawyers learn the techniques of cross-examination in order to extract the truth from unfriendly witnesses. The lawyer directs. The recalcitrant witness tells as little as possible. Interrogation is therefore a poor method for facilitating open and constructive communication.

Questions are most frequent when the teacher's desire to know more—his natural curiosity—gets in the way of his ability to be helpful.

12. *Withdrawing, Distracting, Being Sarcastic, Humoring, Diverting*

Such messages can communicate to a student that the teacher is not interested in him, doesn't respect his feelings, and may even be rejecting him.

Students are generally quite serious and intent when they need to talk about a problem. Responding with kidding, teasing, sarcasm, or humor can make them feel hurt, rejected, put down.

Putting students off, diverting them from their feelings of the moment, may appear successful at first. But a person's feelings tend to reappear until dealt with. Problems put off are not problems solved.

Students want to be heard and understood respectfully. Teachers who use sarcasm, humor, and distractions teach students to take their problems elsewhere. These teachers are written off by students as helping agents and, unfortunately, as persons students might trust and have a relationship with.

COMMUNICATION FACILITATORS

1. *Passive Listening (Silence)*

Encourages students to talk once they have started, but does not meet students' needs for interactive and responsive two-way communication.

Silence does not "interrupt students," but students never

know if the teacher is paying attention. Nor do they get any proof that the teacher understands.

It may communicate some degree of acceptance, but students may guess that the teacher is evaluating while being silent. Silence does not communicate empathy and warmth.

2. Acknowledgment Responses

Somewhat better than silence in demonstrating to students that the teacher is paying attention. Such responses do communicate some empathy. They indicate that the teacher is at least awake and attentive.

Facilitate further communication from students, but only weakly.

Communicate acceptance to some degree, but do not prove teacher acceptance.

Do not prove to students that the teacher really understands.

3. Door Openers, Invitations to Talk

Very effective in showing students that the teacher wants to listen and take the time to be a counselor.

Particularly useful at the start, right after the student sends a cue or clue that a problem exists. They can help a student who bogs down or gets stuck while he is sharing the problem.

Are not effective in demonstrating acceptance, understanding, or warmth. Invitations open the door but do not keep the door open. If used too often, door openers may sound repetitious.

4. Active Listening (Feedback)

Makes students feel their ideas and feelings are respected, understood, and accepted. Fosters further communication. Defuses feelings and provides cathartic release. Helps students accept their feelings as natural and human—teaches them that feelings are friends.

Facilitates identification of the underlying or real problems. Starts the problem-solving process going, but leaves the responsibility with students to be their own problem solvers.

Puts students in the frame of mind of being willing to listen to the teacher. Brings teacher and student into a relationship of greater mutual understanding, mutual respect, mutual caring.

Carries the risk of being mechanical and sounding phony or manipulative if used as a gimmick without underlying attitudes of worth, empathy, trust, and acceptance.

IV. THE MANY USES OF
ACTIVE LISTENING

W HENEVER more open and honest communication is required, active listening will help. It fosters effective class discussions about specific subject matter. It counters students' resistance against learning new things. It aids very dependent and submissive students. It helps a class ventilate feelings generated by disruptive school events or happenings in the world outside of school. It facilitates more effective parent conferences or teacher-parent-student conferences.

As teachers become more skilled in active listening, they will experiment with it in many other kinds of situations in the school, in their own family life, and in all their human relationships.

HOW TO FOSTER EFFECTIVE
CONTENT–CENTERED CLASSROOM DISCUSSIONS

Teachers who want to break away from the "lecture model" of teaching are often as frustrated as the teacher we quoted earlier who told of finding his class discussions degenerating into "bull sessions." Some teachers stop using class discussions because they cannot get the students to open up and talk. Active listening will help these teachers to become expert facilitators of group discussions on the academic subject being studied by a class. Here is a sample of a group discussion where the teacher relies entirely on active listening to clarify and restate:

TEACHER: You've been reading about the Spanish-American War. I'm wondering what you've learned and what your reactions are to your reading.

BRET: I thought it was going to be dull, but it wasn't. Henry and I were talking on the bus yesterday about how surprised we were that the book told the truth. Most of the history books I've read before made the United States out to always be, you know, good guys. . . .

HENRY: (*Interrupting*) Like the ones we had on the Civil War that said Lincoln freed the slaves and all that bull.

TEACHER: These books seem different to you. You don't feel you're being lied to by these authors.

MARCIA: I don't think the other books exactly lied. They just told one side of the story or left out some things that happened. . . .

HENRY: If that's not lying, what is? If I told people that our football team scored two touchdowns, gained a hundred and eighty-five yards, intercepted a pass, and blocked a punt last Friday against Central, they sure wouldn't get the whole picture, right? [Central won the game 45–15.]

GROUP: (*Laughter*)

TEACHER: Henry, you maintain that withholding information is the same as lying and that some of the references we have had seemed to do that.

HENRY: Yes. It's *true*! When we compared some of the different books you'd think they were talking about different wars.

NANCY: Well, how does anybody get to be an historian anyway? After all, they're just people who write books about things that happened a long time ago. They're bound to be prejudiced.

VICKY: You're right. My sister says that historians are all male chauvinist pigs writing stuff like "brave *men* traveled west and some even took their families." Nobody ever wrote about brave *women*, or if they did, it was like they were surprised that women could shoot a gun or put up with hardships.

TEACHER: If I understand, you are all questioning the ability of *anyone* to write an unbiased history—you're saying that writers' opinions will influence their views of history.

NANCY: That's the problem, so why even bother to read the stuff?

BRET: You're missing the point, Nancy. The point is not to believe something just because it's written in a book. I think we ought to read more books, not less.

NANCY: Fewer. Say "fewer" books, not "less" books.

BRET: Chalk up one for you. Anyway, get more books.

HENRY: Yeah. I wonder what Spanish history books say about the Spanish-American War?

VICKY: If they were written by men they're probably just as chauvinistic as ours.

MARIE: Who ever heard of a woman historian?

VICKY: Nobody. That's why all the books talk about history as if the only important things that happened were done by men and the only important people were men. One book I had, I think it was in eighth grade, had about three pages called "Great Women in American History." It made me sick.

TEACHER: It's your experience, Vicky, that women have been treated pretty lightly by historians.

VICKY: Yes.

HENRY: Well, what did women do in the Spanish-American War? I don't see what this thing about women has to do with what we're talking about.

MARCIA: I think it has a lot to do with it. You were the one that was griping about not telling the whole story, Henry. Well, not telling about the things women did is like leaving out part of the story.

HENRY: Yeah, but women never *did* anything. They never wrote treaties, or formed governments, or were captains of ships, or explorers, or *anything*.

VICKY: That's just the attitude I was talking about. You read the books that *men* write and you get the idea that *men* do everything. I don't claim that women were generals or anything. It's just that women are put down in the books. You know, the things they *have* done are sort of sneered at.

TEACHER: You seem very interested in how history is written, especially how biases, like the one Vicky sees regarding women, show up in what you read. This seems a change from the general feeling I got earlier that you liked the books you were reading on the Spanish-American War.

VICKY: It was Henry and Bret that said that.

BRET: Said what?

VICKY: That you liked the books. You were talking about how they gave a fair description of the war and didn't try to make the U.S. look good when they didn't deserve it. Well, these same books aren't so fair to women. My sister is taking a women's studies course at the university and she's got some materials that show how to evaluate the language of books to see how slanted they are against women. I'll get her to help me look through these books and then next week I'll show you.

BRET: Okay, but how about other slants?

TEACHER: You're interested in finding out how to read between the lines and get the real truth when you read history—not just about women, but about any bias that happens. Is that right?

HENRY: Yes. How do we evaluate the stuff we read?

TEACHER: Vicky has promised to share some ways to evaluate. Bret, you suggested reading a variety of books, and, Henry, I believe it was you who suggested getting foreign books so we could compare. Are there any other ideas?

MARIE: I think we need an expert. We could get a historian to come here and tell us what to do or answer questions. My neighbor teaches history at the university and maybe he'd come to our class.

VICKY: Another male historian. (*Shrugs*)

MARIE: I think he's fair. In fact, we could ask him about sexism in history books.

NANCY: You could get us some of the references listed as source books in the bibliography.

TEACHER: You mean in the textbook we're using?

NANCY: Yes.

MARCIA: I think we ought to put off talking about the Spanish-American War until after we do this other stuff. It blows my mind that maybe all the stuff I've read could be, you know, not true. When Vicky was talking I got to thinking, and she's right, none of the books I ever read ever made women out to be important even when they were, so how do I know about the rest of the things they wrote?

TEACHER: You can see some advantage to studying the writing and evaluating of history books before doing any more reading.

MARCIA: Yes.

GROUP: (*Agrees*)

TEACHER: Okay. Let's set a time schedule for who is going to do what kinds of things. I'll get the source books from the library by next Tuesday. Vicky, when will you be able to make your report? (*Arrangements are made to define the tasks of the members of the study group.*)

In less than ten minutes this discussion radically changed the direction of the class to an exploration of historical source materials and the development of a set of criteria for evaluating the texts and other books used in history courses at the school.

Did you notice that the teacher used none of the twelve roadblocks and relied almost entirely on active listening? This is the key to effective discussions.

Teachers who use active listening to foster discussion usually find out about special interests, talents, strengths, and weaknesses of the group members. The strengths and special talents can then be used to help the entire class (or group) learn. Deficits or weaknesses can be noted for later curriculum enrichment.

A special note: nothing so inhibits discussion as evaluation, or the threat of evaluation. Teachers must make it clear that discussion groups are for the purpose of extending and enriching learning and not for grading or judging. Notetaking by the teacher, unless shared openly or written on a chart pad or chalkboard for everyone to see, can be threatening.

Fear of peer evaluation is also a block to participation. Here is a brief excerpt from a class discussion in which a teacher used active listening to handle negative evaluative statements by a member of the class:

MARGARET: . . . So I feel that offshore drilling for oil must be stopped.

STEVE: That's a dumb thing to say. What do you know about it?

MARGARET: (*Defensively*) Well, if you'd listen once in a while you'd find out. I just finished explaining it.

TEACHER: You feel you've made a good case for your point of view, Margaret, and you're upset when Steve disagrees with you.

MARGARET: Right! He's the one that doesn't know what he's talking about.

TEACHER: You question Steve's facts.

MARGARET: (*Nods*)

TEACHER: But, Steve, I hear you expressing strong feelings about what Margaret has reported. You really disagree.

STEVE: Right. (*Goes on to offer information about the need for greater petroleum production*)

TEACHER: You see the problem from a different angle from the one presented by Margaret.

MARGARET: Well, I agree with Steve that we need more oil, but we can't endanger the ocean with leaks like the ones in Texas and California.

STEVE: They didn't have to leak.

TEACHER: Your disagreement is about oil leakage in the ocean, not whether offshore drilling should or should not occur.

BOTH: (*Agree*)

By avoiding evaluative roadblocks himself, the teacher helped these students clarify their positions and arrive at a new definition of the problem. Compare this with a reconstruction of the same discussion—this time with the teacher using the same disagreement to teach a lesson about good manners, through lecturing and logic. Here is how it might go:

MARGARET: . . . So I feel that offshore drilling for oil must be stopped.

STEVE: That's a dumb thing to say. What do you know about it?

MARGARET: (*Defensively*) Well, if you'd listen once in a while you'd find out. I just finished explaining it.

TEACHER: Wait a minute, you two. It's not very helpful to argue and call names. Steve, if you disagree just say, "I disagree." You don't have to say Margaret is dumb because you don't agree with her. And, Margaret, maybe Steve did listen. Just because he disagrees doesn't mean he didn't listen to you. Okay, now go ahead.

MARGARET: I'm finished.

STEVE: (*Silence*)

Unfortunately, it is often assumed that subject-matter class discussions can be employed only after children reach the higher grades in school. This could not be farther from the truth. Students at any grade level have untapped capacity for carrying on productive discussions, with almost no probing, direction, or guidance from their teacher.

A teacher* in a Chicago suburb submitted to us a taped recording of a classroom discussion involving nine boys in the third grade who had been placed in a special group because

---

* Marlene Anderson, Hinsdale, Illinois.

of their slow reading. Seven had failed either the first or second grade, and one boy had been in an E.D. (emotionally disturbed) class for two years. All had difficulty expressing themselves orally and in writing. Following is a transcribed tape-recorded session of this group, immediately after they had been shown a TV program in the classroom. Notice how the teacher uses active listening almost exclusively, plus some door openers.

TEACHER: Let's think about the TV program we saw. Is there someone who could review for us what happened?

MARK: There was this girl who wanted to be a good ice skater, and when she went to the rink she'd fall down and everyone would laugh at her.

JERRY: Yeah, the teacher fell down once, too, and people laughed at her.

JACK: Then later on the teacher lied 'cause she didn't want to get laughed at again.

MARK: They laughed so much at the girl that the next time the kids went skating she put a big bandage around her knee and said she couldn't skate 'cause she was hurt.

TEACHER: She lied so others wouldn't laugh at her.

JACK: Yeah, and remember the teacher did, too. She told the kids she couldn't go skating 'cause she had a meeting and the kids saw her after school and she wasn't at a meeting.

TEACHER: It surprised you that a teacher would do that.

OTHERS: It sure did.

JERRY: But that wasn't nice to laugh.

MARK: They laughed at the girl again when she went to the chalkboard and she didn't know how to spell a word.

JERRY: That was sad.

TEACHER: Becky on the TV show asked, "How can you do anything when others laugh at you?"

MARK: She must have felt terrible.

TOM: Like she was afraid to do anything because they might laugh.

TEACHER: She was fearful of doing things.

KEN: And she gets so afraid that she has to fake things.

TEACHER: Sounds like some of you have been in situations where someone has laughed at you.

OTHERS: Oh, boy, sure have.

TOM: I remember when I did something once and kids laughed and I felt horrible.

JERRY: I've had that happen to me, too.

MARK: It hurts.

TEACHER: It is very painful.

TOM: It hurts so much that it gets you right in the guts.

MARK: Or right in the heart.

JERRY: It hurts so much that you want to go up to them and punch them.

MARK: Or beat them up.

KURT: I was playing ball once at a friend's house and some bigger boys were there and when I threw the ball they took it and started laughing. How do you expect me to punch bigger kids?

TEACHER: It's even more frightening and painful when the people are bigger.

KURT: I just ran home.

TEACHER: People do many things to avoid being laughed at.

JERRY: Some fight and punch.

MARK: Yeah, and some lie.

TOM: How about those who fake?

MARK: I guess you just have to learn to be an expert at what you're going to do so no one will laugh.

KURT: But you can't be an expert at everything.

TEACHER: It's a pretty impossible task for you to be that good all the time.

KURT: Sure it is.

MARK: I practice roller skating a lot to be good. I don't care if they laugh, I just go ahead and practice.

KURT: Maybe they'll laugh at you when you do something besides roller skate. Like when you try to do schoolwork and you don't understand.

TOM: Then you have to lie or fake.

TEACHER: I wonder if there is a difference between a little lie and a big lie?

MARK: Sure there's a difference. A little lie can turn into a big one, and if you do it often then you become a big liar.

TEACHER: It can become a habit.

OTHERS: Yup.

KURT: A little lie doesn't get you into as much trouble as a big lie.

JACK: I lied once to my mother. I came home late and told her I had to stay after school when I didn't.

TEACHER: You felt you had to get out of a situation so you lied.

JACK: I'd never lied before and I wanted to see what it was like.

TEACHER: It was a new feeling for you when you lied, and you wanted to discover something.

JACK: It was pretty bad 'cause my mom found out and I couldn't play for a week.

JERRY: I feel guilty when I lie.

MARK: I get embarrassed.

JERRY: It's better to tell the truth.

TEACHER: People sometimes tell little lies in order to save face. Does anyone know what that means?

TOM: Maybe people won't like you sometimes if you tell the truth.

TEACHER: It's important to you then that people like you; and you're afraid if you really tell the truth sometimes they may not like you, so you end up telling a little lie.

TOM: That's about it.

TEACHER: I wonder which is more important, what your friends think of you, what you think of yourself, or what adults think of you?

JERRY: What adults think of you 'cause if they don't like you they can give you away or sell you. They think, "He's no good, I'll throw him away and get someone else."

KURT: You can't sell a person.

JERRY: But they can whip you if they don't like you.

TEACHER: Then it's important to you what adults think of you so they will not turn away from you and hurt you.

JERRY: Sure.

MARK: I think it's more important what you think of yourself 'cause if you didn't like yourself that would be a shame, 'cause others may like you and you'd be unhappy if you didn't like yourself.

TOM: I think you should have all three. 'Cause you want friends and you want to like yourself or you might do daring things and almost kill yourself. And you gotta have parents or else you won't be able to eat or anything.

JERRY: Yeah, I think so, too.

TEACHER: You agree with Tom now.

JERRY: Yup.

MARK: I guess if you could have all three, people wouldn't laugh at you.

TOM: Then you could all laugh.

JERRY: Yeah, I don't get upset anymore. I just ignore it when they laugh at me, or we laugh together.

TEACHER: You think pretty well of yourself now.

JERRY: Sure.

TEACHER: Well, boys, our time is up. This has been an interesting discussion.

JERRY: I like talking like this.

TEACHER: You appreciate the time we spend together like this.

OTHERS: Yes, we do, too.

The teacher reported the following incident that happened after this fascinating discussion:

When we were finished, Jerry asked if he could listen to the tape of the discussion. I agreed, and Jerry went to the art center, got a large piece of paper and crayons, and returned. He turned the tape on, and as he listened, with the volume turned as loud as could be, he started to scribble with large sweeping strokes using bright colors of yellow and orange, green and purple. When he was almost finished I said:

TEACHER: You have many bright, happy feelings today.

JERRY: Yup, the yellow and orange are gay feelings *we* had today, and the green and purple are floating feelings.

He then took a black crayon and covered much of the paper, leaving some bright colors showing through.

TEACHER: On top of those warm floating feelings are some pretty bad feelings.

JERRY: This is our reading group. There are lots of real bad feelings yet, but some of those good feelings are starting to come through.

In this teacher's classroom discussion, we watched eight- and nine-year-olds delving rather deeply into two problems of vital importance to children: criticism of others and lying. Active listening enabled them to be open and honest. By avoiding evaluation, the teacher kept full responsibility with the children for the direction of their own discussion. *This is education at its very best.*

Not apparent in the transcript is the effect of this type of "nondirected discussion" on the children themselves. According to the teacher, Jerry, who did a great deal of talking, had never before participated in group work in the classroom; and Jack, who normally stuttered so badly that he would not talk much, not only opened up and talked frequently but did it *without a bit of stuttering*.

HOW TO USE ACTIVE LISTENING TO HANDLE RESISTANCE

All teachers sometimes run into resistance: students don't always want to learn what the teacher wants to teach. This resistance can take many forms, from passive inactivity to open refusal to cooperate. Unfortunately, most teachers fail to decode this resistance as a clue that the students are having difficulty. Instead of listening to the resistance, they move in with roadblocks. Here are some actual classroom examples:

Situation: Elementary-school teacher asks students to draw six balls.

MATT: I can't make very good balls.

TEACHER: Oh, balls are easy to make. Yours are fine. (*Reassuring, Supporting*)

MATT: Not to me, they're not.

Situation: First-grade class is drawing pictures.

TODD: Teacher, my picture turned out real ugly, so I'm not handing it in. You don't want to see it.

TEACHER: I'm sure that it's fine, and I *do* want to see it, so please hand it in. (*Reassuring*)

TODD: (*Keeps his paper turned face down on his desk.*)

TEACHER: Right now, Todd! Hand it in! (*Ordering, Commanding*)

Situation: First day of school. Eddie is gazing out the window of his second-grade classroom.

TEACHER: What are you doing, Eddie?

EDDIE: Nothing. (*Pause*) Do we have to go to school all day?

TEACHER: Certainly we go all day. You went all day last year. Whatever made you think we didn't have to go all day? (*Using Logic; Probing; Questioning*)

Situation: High-school English class is reading assigned material. Cory has his head down on his desk with his eyes closed.

TEACHER: What's the matter, Cory, bored? (*Interpreting*)

CORY: No, I'm sleepy.

TEACHER: (*Laughs*) Would you like us to bring in a bed for you and sing you a lullaby? (*Everybody laughs except Cory*) (*Sarcasm*)

Situation: Paul has taken all morning doing an assignment that the other fourth-grade students finished in only a few minutes. It is almost recess time and he is still not done.

PAUL: I can't finish this.

TEACHER: Paul, you are going to do that even if you have to miss recess, so I suggest you get to work. (*Threatening; Suggesting*)

Resistance against learning is almost invariably an indication that the student has encountered some kind of problem in his life that is interfering at that moment with his ability to function in the Teaching-Learning area of our rectangle. At these times, rather than punish him for experiencing a problem, it is a teacher's job to help the student return to the learning function as rapidly as possible.

Here is how one of the previous situations might have developed if the teacher had acceptingly heard the student out instead of using probing questions and logic:

Situation: First day of school. Eddie is gazing out the window of his second-grade classroom.

TEACHER: What are you doing, Eddie?

EDDIE: Nothing. (*Pause*) Do we have to go to school all day?

TEACHER: You really wish you were out there instead of sitting here in the classroom.

EDDIE: Uh-huh. There's nothing to do in here. You just have to sit in a seat all day and do papers and read.

TEACHER: You miss being able to play outside like you did all summer.

EDDIE: Yes. Playing games and swimming and climbing trees.

TEACHER: That was fun, so it's hard to give all that up and come back to school again.

EDDIE: Yes. I hope summer comes back soon.

TEACHER: You're really looking forward to next summer.

EDDIE: Yes, when next summer comes I can do what *I* want to do.

The teacher now hears Eddie's question about going to school all day as a *code for some problem he is having.* Instead of answering quickly, the teacher listens for the feelings behind the question. "Uniquely coded" questions are excellent clues that students are experiencing problems. We call questions uniquely coded when they ask the obvious; seem out of place; don't fit what you know about the student; or jar you with their incongruity.

Here are some questions that may not be requests for answers at all. They are highly coded messages, and under them lie problems:

"How does it feel to die?"

"Are we going to have a test on this stuff?"

"Why do we have to dress for P.E.?"

"Is math more important than science?"

"Why does this school require four years of English?"

"Is it time for recess yet?"

"Why do boys always have to show off?"

"Do you have to take a lot of math to be an engineer?"

"Did you ever have acne?"

"Why learn this stuff?"

These and thousands of other questions transmit many cues and clues, including the cue that active listening is needed. Sometimes these questions will be phrased as statements—e.g., "I'll bet you had acne when you were my age," or, "It must feel horrible to die." Whether they surface as questions or as assertions, such messages require an active-listening response in order to get to the real problem.

Sometimes the resistance may be less subtle, as in the following exchange:

TEACHER: . . . So the United Nations was created to give nations a forum to solve their problems by negotiation instead of war.

STUDENT: That's a lot of bull. You don't know what you're talking about!

TEACHER: You're angry when you hear that.

STUDENT: You bet! It's more propaganda from the Establishment to keep the peons in line while the big powers rip them off.

TEACHER: You don't trust the United Nations. You see it as a device to oppress people, not help them.

STUDENT: (*Calming down*) Yes. It was started during World War II, right? Well, look at the world today. Wars, famine, energy crises, pollution, overpopulation. The same problems we had without the United Nations. The U.N. is no better than the governments of the big powers let it be, and they're all corrupt.

TEACHER: You're pretty discouraged about the ineffectiveness of the U.N.

STUDENT: Yeah. It's not the fault of the U.N., though. It's the governments that are letting industry ruin the planet and they're the ones that start the wars . . . and all they do is blab away at the U.N.

TEACHER: You're disturbed about the pollution and wars and disappointed that the U.N. hasn't been more effective in stopping them.

STUDENT: Right. We've got to do something to clean up our own government first. Then maybe the U.N. can take a lesson from that and start helping worldwide.

TEACHER: So, you see us first having to improve our government, *then* working on wider problems.

STUDENT: Right.

In many ways, overt and hostile resistance is easier to handle than the more covert kind. Many times teachers will say or do things that "push students' buttons." Then students have a need to spout off, to rid themselves of their inner anxieties. Having done so, like the student who railed against the United Nations, they may be ready to return to learning and listening. Teachers taking our Teacher Effectiveness Training course are encouraged to view these situations as *opportunities* to bring out into the open the feelings, attitudes, ideas, biases, and concepts held by students.

T.E.T. instructors say, *"Think of the student who 'takes you on' as your best friend in the class. He is probably speaking for others who hold similar views but haven't said so."*

Because students don't openly disagree, it does not follow that they agree. One teacher in a T.E.T. class related this experience:

The administration in my district hired some consultants to help us teach drug education. One of the seminars was led by a person from the State Department of Education who gave the kids a lot of facts and figures that didn't make sense to me. Nobody said anything in the seminar, but you should have heard the kids in the parking lot!

Tuning in to the subtle clues, verbal or nonverbal, that students send when they resist your teaching will help open up the classroom environment, increase productivity, and enrich learning; and it will decrease the "parking lot" underground gripe sessions, whatever form they may take.

HOW TO USE ACTIVE LISTENING
TO HELP DEPENDENT STUDENTS

The almost universal use of roadblocks by parents and teachers causes students to adopt certain ways of coping. Probably the most common way for students to try handling the stream of adult messages that warn, order, threaten, command, moralize, teach, instruct, evaluate, diagnose, sympathize, patronize, reassure, praise, question, humor, stereotype, and blame is to become submissive, dependent, and uncommunicative.

An elementary-school teacher with over two decades' experience talked about the problem of the submissive child:

The longer I teach, the more worried I get about the quiet child. Oh, I have a few that I wish were more quiet, but I'm talking about the youngster who can't do anything without my constant attention—the one who, when left alone, goes off into a dream world or who can't take a chance on being wrong or cries if he makes a mistake. The ones that really scare me are the ones that are always polite, say, "Yes, ma'am," do everything I tell them, but inside they're seething. I've been around long enough to watch some of these youngsters grow up, and, believe me, the quiet ones sometimes have the worst problems.

Jerry Farber, in his article *The Student As Nigger*, points out how disabling this coping mechanism can be at the college level:

. . . They haven't gone through twelve years of public school for nothing. They've learned one thing and perhaps only one thing during those twelve years. They've forgotten their algebra. They've grown to fear and resent literature. They write like they've been lobotomized. But, Jesus, can they follow orders! Freshmen come up to me with an essay and ask if I want it folded, and whether their name should be in the upper right-hand corner. And I want to cry and kiss them and caress their poor tortured heads.

While Farber's inclination to "caress their poor tortured heads" is understandable, dependent students have a far greater need—namely, to acquire independence and autonomy.

To help students increase their ability to rely more on their own resources and less on the resources of others requires that teachers clearly define ownership of problems. Once again, locating the student behavior correctly in the rectangle is the first step.

Suppose a second-grader says to her teacher: "I don't know how to draw the tile roofs on my mission."

Many teachers incorrectly identify that problem as their own. ("I've got to go over and solve this problem.") In effect, they place that behavior in the bottom part of the rectangular window (see Figure 17):

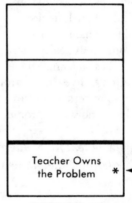

Teacher Owns
the Problem   ✱ ◄────── Child is upset with
                          inability to draw
                          tile roofs.

FIGURE 17

By placing that behavior in the area of teacher-owned problems, the teacher sows the seeds of dependence. Once the teacher assumes ownership, the next step is usually to use one of the roadblocks in an attempt to make the student change his feelings or to "try, try again"; or, what is even worse, to show the student how he should draw tile roofs. Result—further dependence.

The drive toward independence and self-responsibility is strong within each of us. It is much like a block of granite. Chiseling away at that source of independence will eventually reduce it. Each time a teacher makes a student submit to outside direction of his life in those areas that affect him and him alone—each time the student gives in to pressures to conform to his teacher's blueprint for his behavior when his behavior affects no one else—a little more of his block of independence is chiseled away and it becomes a little easier to submit the next time.

Here are some examples of how teachers, by incorrectly defining problem ownership and then using roadblocks, chip away at student independence:

1. TEACHER: Charles, you are too quiet. You've got to enter more into our class discussions.

(In this case the teacher placed Charles's quietness into the Teacher-Owned-Problem area even though rarely would a teacher in any way be tangibly affected by quietness. Then the teacher sent a *negative evaluation* followed by a *solution*.)

2. STUDENT: Math is too hard for me.

   TEACHER: Math isn't hard, Randy. Your problem is that you give up the first time you run into anything tough. Now, give it a try.

(This time, the teacher failed to decode Randy's message and instead *disagreed* with him, then *analyzed* why Randy was feeling as he was. Finally, the teacher *handed a solution to* the child.)

3. STUDENT: (*Fourth trip to teacher's desk in ten minutes*) Is this answer right?

   TEACHER: You know that answer is right, Cindy. Why do you keep coming up and asking me?

(This teacher placed Cindy's unsureness and need for approval into the Teacher-Owned-Problem area, *analyzed* her, and then asked a *probing question* about her motives.)

4. TEACHER: (*Sees shy Alfred doodling on a piece of paper instead of doing the assigned work.*) What are you doing, Alfred?

   ALFRED: Nothing. (*Slides paper into a notebook*)

   TEACHER: Aren't you interested in what we're doing in class?

   ALFRED: (*Whisper*) No.

   TEACHER: Speak up! Are you bored with this class?

   ALFRED: *No.*

   TEACHER: Well, why are you just wasting your time? If you know what's good for you, you'll get busy and turn in this assignment.

ALFRED: (*Goes back to doodling as soon as the teacher leaves.*)

(This teacher incorrectly defined Alfred's disinterest and boredom as a teacher-owned problem, and then asked *probing questions* followed by a *threat*.)

5. TEACHER: (*Observes Eloise with her head on her desk, sobbing.*) What's the matter, Eloise?

ELOISE: (*Muffled*) I don't know.

TEACHER: You're crying about something. What made you cry?

ELOISE: (*Between sobs*) Nobody likes me.

TEACHER: (*Pulls up chair next to Eloise and puts arm around her shoulders.*) It just *seems* that way. Everybody likes you! You're so sweet and pretty, except when you cry like this. Now, cheer up. (*Pats cheek*) Feel better now?

(This teacher refused to allow Eloise to feel bad, used *probing questions, analysis, positive evaluation* followed by *negative evaluation*, and finally gave a *command* that Eloise feel differently.

It is the repetition of these kinds of interactions, day after day, week after week, that ultimately causes students to distrust their own feelings, to develop dependence on the "safer" course of feeling and behaving the way others tell them to feel and behave.

All students are going to have feelings that trouble them, and from time to time they will behave in ways that create problems for themselves. It is then that teachers can be most helpful by refusing to take over the ownership of these feelings and problems. Instead, if they use the skill of active listening to promote the student's *internal* resolution of these *internal* conflicts, they will *add* to the youngster's granite block of independence and self-responsibility, not reduce it.

Here are some common student-owned problems that teachers often respond to as if they were teacher-owned:

Bruce can't seem to get his homework done.
Alice thinks she is ugly.
Hal can't decide on a vocation.
Terri hates her parents.
Lawrence is afraid of bigger boys.

Gayle thinks she is pregnant.

Robert is disappointed at being cut from the team.

Margo doesn't have any friends.

Emily hates to take piano lessons.

Ken is angry because he has lost an important tennis match.

Bill is afraid people will laugh at him if he makes a mistake.

Donnie is afraid of the dark.

Karen thinks she is dumb.

Grace is shocked at the behavior of other students.

Phillip is frustrated by long-division problems.

Manuel is afraid of fire.

Molly is afraid to go to kindergarten.

Students naturally encounter such problems in their daily lives. These problems *belong* to them. As they grapple with and solve these problems they learn how to handle negative feelings and find solutions. To the extent that they learn to rely on their own resources, trust their own feelings, and live with the consequences of their own decisions, they will develop self-confidence, autonomy, and independence.

The greatest disservice teachers perform for students is rushing in to protect youngsters from their problems, thus denying them a crucial experience: dealing with the consequences of their own solutions.

Here is what happened between a teacher* and a student who forgot to bring her math materials to school. Note how the teacher, skillfully relying on active listening, lets the student *own her problem*. And how quickly the student comes up with her own solution!

STUDENT: I forgot my math things at home.

TEACHER: Hmm, you have a problem.

STUDENT: Yeah, I need my prescription sheet and math book and the paper I was working on.

* Marlene Anderson, Hinsdale, Illinois.

TEACHER: Wonder what kind of solutions we could come up with.

STUDENT: I could call my mother and have her bring them . . . but she doesn't hear the phone sometimes.

TEACHER: That may not work out then.

STUDENT: I could get a book from the math center to use and take a fresh piece of paper because I know what page I was on.

TEACHER: Sounds like you have the problem all solved.

STUDENT: Yeah.

Most teachers in a similar situation would have given the student a lecture or perhaps a scolding, ending with a solution: "Go home right now and get that work."

HOW TO MAKE THE MOST OF
STUDENT–CENTERED DISCUSSION GROUPS

During the course of a school year many events so arouse, frighten, stimulate, or capture the thoughts of students that it is impossible for them to concentrate on schoolwork. At the elementary level it could be a new student, unusual weather, a fight in the playground, fire engines going by the school, an approaching holiday—all may temporarily disrupt the learning routine. At the secondary level the static may come from pep rallies, basketball tournaments, the "big game," a drug arrest, threats of violence, an important social event, a national tragedy. The emotional stability of students becomes upset. It is difficult for them to work. To pretend that these student feelings don't exist, or to ignore them, is to invite frustration for everyone.

Teachers who learn to pick up the cues and clues that tell them their students are diverted or preoccupied can help students handle their feelings by first setting aside, temporarily, all plans for learning activities. Then they can conduct a class discussion to enable the students to talk about their feelings. Once again, the needed skill is active listening.

When teachers try out these student-centered discussions

they universally report that feelings get "de-escalated." A further outcome of such discussions is that students explore feelings and attitudes and thereby inevitably come to grips with value issues. This promotes real intellectual growth.

Many teachers schedule student-centered discussions as a regular part of curriculum offerings and allow students to talk about what *they* wish to discuss. These sessions usually start with the teacher asking an open-ended question. The question may be rather broad: "What would you like to talk about today?" Or it could be more specific: "There have been a number of fights on campus lately. What are your feelings about these incidents?" After such door openers the teacher uses active listening exclusively. The idea is to clarify, restate, and communicate to students that their ideas and feelings are understood and accepted.

A teacher of upper elementary-grade students told about his experiences with student-centered discussions:

They were really helpful. I'd forgotten how hard it is for eleven- and twelve-year-olds to make sense out of the world. I was surprised at the amount of nonsense they believed in, and, at the same time, how much insight they have. Some of the things they talked about have been low-level things like how the food in the cafeteria could be improved. But they tackled a few really tough issues, too. Things like "What is honesty?" and "Do people ever have the right to control other people for their own good?" Really heavy stuff, things I didn't work on until I was in college, or later. I don't know a better way to let kids sort through all the conflicting information and feelings than these class meetings.

A rather dramatic and disturbing incident took place in the classroom of a teacher enrolled in a T.E.T. class* in a Boston suburb:

The class was beginning a penmanship lesson and several parents were visiting. As I was writing on the board, I turned and saw

* Submitted by T.E.T. instructor Katherine Pigott Newman, Sharon, Massachusetts.

Vic go over to Mike and punch him several times. As I tried to separate them, Vic resisted my restraints and was angry and had lost all self-control. After sending him out of class for a cooling-off period, I continued the lesson. Within a short time the principal brought Vic back to class and he sat at his desk, both fists clenched. I asked him if he was ready to do the work, but he indicated he was not, so I left him alone. First I decided to wait until the parents were no longer visiting, but I decided the need to help Vic was greater than the parents' need to see a regular class in progress. I asked the class to place their chairs in a circle. Vic did not join us. I suggested leaving a space for his chair so he could join us any time he was ready to do so. Someone suggested I start, so I told them I was upset when Vic started hitting Mike and embarrassed because parents were there. I also said I was very unhappy that Vic was so angry, and I wondered how Mike was feeling. Various class members shared similar feelings—only six out of the twenty-three children didn't speak as we went around the circle asking about feelings. Mike passed, but he had a bit of a smile on his face. Then Bob came up with a statement, saying that Vic was not solely to blame because Mike had been bugging Vic at snack time, prior to the penmanship period.

TEACHER:	(*To Bob*) Mike did something that upset Vic?
BOB:	Yes. He went over to Vic's desk and took his pretzels. (*At this point Vic joined the circle.*)
MIKE:	No, I didn't.
SEVERAL CHILDREN:	Yes, you did!
VIC:	He did. Jan gave me some pretzels and Mike ate them.
TEACHER:	Mike came over to your desk and took the pretzels without asking if he could have them.
VIC:	Yes.
TEACHER:	Mike, Vic says you took the pretzels Jan had given him.
MIKE:	I thought Jan said I could have them.

JAN: I gave Vic some pretzels and Mike took them so I gave Vic some more. Mike took those, too.

DICK: He's always doing that. He does little things to you. He goes by you and bumps you or trips you. Then he acts so innocent.

RAY: He says things, too.

TEACHER: What Mike did today is not unusual.

CLASS: Yeah!

TEACHER: Mike does things that irritate you.

DICK: He sure does, and then when we do something about it, we're the ones who get caught.

TEACHER: Mike, the class seems to feel you often do things that upset them.

MIKE: (*No response*)

TEACHER: It sounds like others often get into trouble when they get angry because of things you do to upset them.

MIKE: I don't get them in trouble. They just don't like me.

TEACHER: You feel no one in the class likes you.

MIKE: Some of them like me.

TEACHER: Some of the class like you and some of them don't.

MIKE: Yeah. They don't let me play at recess.

TEACHER: You'd like to play with them in the games at recess.

MIKE: I'd like to play soccer and kickball, but Dick and Vic say I can't play.

TEACHER: When you ask if you can play, Dick and Vic tell you you can't.

MIKE: They say I'm not good enough.

DICK: We don't say he can't play. It's just that we have enough.

TEACHER: Some of you decide how many can play in the recess games.

DONALD: They say, "No newcomers."

BRUCE: Tom and Curt cheat.

SID: Yeah. They make up rules they like and then don't follow rules they don't like. They say they never heard of them.

TEACHER: Tom and Curt are in Room Nine, right?

SEVERAL: Right.

TEACHER: It sounds as if we have several problems here. I'd like to go back to the problem Mike and Vic had first. It'll soon be lunchtime. After lunch we can talk about what we might do to make it possible for everyone to have a chance to play. It sounds as though others besides Mike would like a chance to play. Is there anything else you, Vic and Mike, would like to say about what happened at snack time?

VIC: He just better not take my stuff again.

TEACHER: If Mike takes something of yours without asking, you'll be angry.

VIC: I'll punch him in the mouth!

TEACHER: You'll feel angry enough to want to punch him in the mouth.

VIC: Yeah!

TEACHER: It's okay to feel angry, but since we have a school rule that says no fighting, you'll have to find another way to handle your anger. Can you think of something you might have done instead of hitting Mike?

VIC: I guess I have a problem. My parents say I should fight, and the school says I can't fight.

TEACHER: It sounds like it's hard for you to know just what to do.

VIC: I guess in school I can't fight. I get into trouble if I do.

BETH: He could tell the teacher.

LINDA: He could give Mike some of his snack so Mike wouldn't have to take it.

BILL: He could tell him nicely to leave him alone.

VIC: He can have some of my snack if he stops bugging me and asks first.

TEACHER: Mike, Vic says he'll share his snack with you if you ask first. He'd like you to stop bugging him.

MIKE: I don't really care about the snack. Maybe I can play in the kickball game next recess.

TEACHER: You feel you'd be happier if you could play with Vic and the others. You wouldn't want to bug them if you could be friends with them.

MIKE: Yeah. I'd like to be a part of the team.

In this one discussion a great many highly significant things went on: the de-escalation of Vic's anger; what Mike learned from his classmates; the benefits to the entire class from the problem solving; what the students learned from the teacher's nonevaluative approach; the class members' increased understanding about Mike's feeling left out; etc.

Obviously, this incident disturbed the entire class. Teaching and learning were interrupted. Everyone's attention was riveted on the emotion-packed and violent incident. The teacher wisely (and courageously, in view of the parents' presence) called the classroom meeting, obviously with a lot of faith in the students' ability to handle the problem. Her trust was vindicated.

Again, active listening proved to be the teacher's principal tool; and the outcome, unpredictable to everyone, was nothing short of remarkable.

HOW ACTIVE LISTENING HELPS
PARENT–TEACHER CONFERENCES

Most school districts recognize the value of conferences between teachers and parents and make provisions for them. Usually, the stated purpose of these meetings is discussion of the academic progress of students. But any teacher who has participated in these conferences knows how far the discussion can stray from academic matters and how disturbing and frustrating this can be.

School districts seldom provide adequate training for handling the nonacademic problems that often arise during parent-teacher conference periods. Here are just a few of the many subjects and feelings that parents bring up:

Objections to other teachers.

Neighborhood gossip.

Intimate marital and family problems.

Threats of severe punishment of their youngsters for poor academic progress.

Anger directed at the teacher for their youngsters' lack of achievement.

Questionable or even illegal acts.

Condemnation of the school, school district, or educational system.

Strong opinions about some teaching methodology they want the school to adopt or eliminate.

Threats of reprisals against the teacher for real or imagined insults or slights.

"Overprotectiveness" and overconcern for their children.

Lack of parental concern.

Expression of strong emotions—crying, yelling, shouting obscenities.

These and hundreds of other problems that may come up during a parent-teacher conference find many teachers unprepared, and leave them stunned and helpless, or defensive and hostile.

Teachers trained in T.E.T. know how not to overreact or underreact to these situations. They know how to act more appropriately.

First, they determine who owns the problem. They ask themselves, "Does this parent's problem, his expression of feelings or his behavior, tangibly or in any concrete way affect me? Is it this parent who is feeling bad, or do I feel bad?"

If the teacher finds that it is the parent who owns the problem—as it so often is—another set of questions must be asked: "Do I have the time to help this troubled parent? Do I feel like helping? Can I allow him to find his own solutions, solve his own problem? Can I genuinely accept the parent's feelings?"

When the teacher mentally constructs a "rectangle window," locates the behavior in the Parent-Owned area, and decides to try to be a helping person, then his principal tool is active listening. If the parent's behavior is tangibly and concretely affecting the teacher, active listening will not be appropriate.

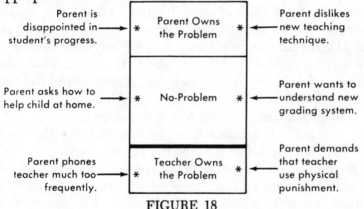

FIGURE 18

Figure 18 may be helpful in visualizing this sorting-out process. Each statement represents a parental question, statement, or problem, and we have located each in the appropriate part of the teacher's rectangular window through which he is viewing the parent.

Most problems in a parent-teacher conference will be owned by the parent. If the teacher has the time, feels accepting, and wants to help, active listening is appropriate. If there is no time because the problem seems complex or

LIBRARY ST. MARY'S COLLEGE

lengthy, the teacher can suggest another conference when more time can be made available. If the conditions for effective active listening are not met, for any reason, and the teacher is feeling unaccepting, he must say so rather than make the error of communicating acceptance verbally when he feels he is unaccepting. (In the next chapter we will explain how to handle situations when the teacher is feeling unaccepting—when *his* needs are unmet, when *his* rights are threatened, or when he feels that interference is keeping him from doing *his* job.)

Notice that in the middle area (No-Problem area) the teacher may appropriately respond to requests for information or help by providing data, suggestions, alternatives. If the parent asks "How can I help my child learn at home?" this *may* be a clear request for information. The parent simply *may* be asking for techniques he can use to aid his child's attempts to do homework or for ways to reinforce at home the skills the child is taught at school. Then, the teacher should feel free to share what knowledge he has that may help this parent.

But it is sometimes wise to check out such a message to see if it really is a clear request for information rather than a code for some other message the parent is trying to send. The teacher may first want to use active listening to help the parent say what he really means, such as, "You're puzzled about how to be most helpful to Johnny." If the parent says no more than, "Yes," the teacher can give whatever helpful information he has. If the parent responds with more messages about the problem ("Well, no. I just feel that he's got to learn more, and he doesn't seem to be doing it here."), additional active listening is in order.

Here is a dialogue of a parent-teacher conference submitted by a teacher enrolled in a T.E.T. class in Boston.* It

---

* Submitted by T.E.T. instructor Katherine Pigott Newman, Sharon, Massachusetts, and taken from a paper written by the teacher involved in this parent-teacher conference.

took place following a grade-level meeting for parents and teachers where a relatively new type of report card was discussed. Note how active listening helped drain off the parent's initial hostility:

PARENT: (*Waving report card while entering the classroom*) I don't mind telling you that I'm coming in here steaming about this thing!

TEACHER: You're upset about the report card.

PARENT: Yes! I don't like it, and I don't know anyone else who does either.

TEACHER: You prefer the old system of reporting grades.

PARENT: Yes, and when we were asked to evaluate these things last year, I really spent a lot of time and wrote down just what I thought about them. Other parents I've talked to said that they wrote evaluations criticizing them, too.

TEACHER: You expressed your feelings, but you don't think that it did any good.

PARENT: No good at all. This fall I read in the paper that the cards had been evaluated, and the response was so good that they were going to continue with this system. I don't know who likes them so much, but I sure don't. Who did this evaluation anyway?

TEACHER: Well, the evaluation forms were sent home to the parents of all the elementary students in town.

PARENT: Well, I was at that meeting last night, and I heard *some* parents saying that they liked them. I guess they're all right for *some* kids, but I want to know more about my daughter's progress.

TEACHER: You don't feel that the changes made in the cards this year are enough to give you what you really want to know about your child.

PARENT: Well, these are a lot better than last year, I must say. There's a lot more room for comments, and the comments are much more specific. At least I feel as if I have an idea of what she's doing in class. But I still can't tell if there's one area where she shows a really strong interest or aptitude. All of the comments are so good. I know that she's a good student, but I wonder just how good.

TEACHER: You want to know just how well she is doing in specific subject areas.

PARENT: Yes, and if there is any area in which she does especially well.

(There followed a rather long and detailed explanation of this school's program, how it is departmentalized, what is covered in each subject area, and how this child is progressing.)

PARENT: I really feel better. I feel as if I really know what she's doing now. I hope you know that I was not blaming you personally for this situation. I know that you people were given these to work with and you just have to do the best you can with them.

TEACHER: I wasn't at all offended. I think it's important to say what you think. That's the only way to come to an understanding.

WHAT THREE–WAY CONFERENCES CAN ACCOMPLISH

Many more teachers are beginning to appreciate the value of including the student as a third member of the parent-teacher conference. After all, they reason, the student's progress is the topic of discussion, and who knows more about it than the student? This is especially true if the teacher and the student are planning, agreeing upon, and assessing the student's learning progress.

Parent-teacher conferences can be very threatening to students if they are excluded from these sessions. They often feel that parents and teachers are meeting in secret to plot against them, to reveal information that might be embarrassing, or to make important decisions about them without their participation.

Generally, teachers who have tried three-way conferences report positive results. The benefits seem to be:

Greater feelings of security on the part of students.

Better use of time; less wandering from the topic.

More complete information for the parent.

Opportunity to facilitate the resolution of parent-student disagreements.

Less chance of misunderstanding; everyone hears the views of the others directly.

Better planning for future learning.

Greater feelings of parent-child unity.

Educative process is more likely to be regarded as cooperative rather than competitive.

Increased desire by the student to carry out decisions, since he participated in making them.

Increased feelings of cooperation by all participants.

When they first try three-way conferences, teachers occasionally encounter some parental resistance, although most teachers report overwhelming support for the idea from those who agree to such conferences. Any parental resistance should be responded to with active listening, and as the parent feels understood, his disappointments, expectations, anxieties or other feelings can be sorted out and dealt with individually. (Teachers report that one common cause of parental resistance to including the student in these meetings is the parent's need to talk privately about *his* own problems. Such resistance disappears if arrangements are made for another meeting with the parent alone.)

SUMMING UP

Active listening is an invaluable skill for helping other people work through the problems they encounter as they live their lives. It promotes growth, independence, confidence, and self-reliance. It relieves teachers of the impossible task of assuming full responsibility for students' learning. It substitutes for that impossible task the freedom to teach—in the noblest sense of that noble undertaking. Active listening is an essential element in the increasing movement to turn classrooms into places of warmth, understanding, security, and growth—a way to make a reality of the maxim "Teaching is a way of loving."

V. WHAT TEACHERS CAN DO WHEN STUDENTS GIVE THEM PROBLEMS

MANY teachers feel overwhelmed and frustrated by the task of trying to manage a classroom learning environment. When a large number of youngsters are simultaneously trying to get their needs met, some are bound to become annoying, boisterous, stubborn, loud, aggressive, forgetful, selfish, inconsiderate, absentminded, or capable of destructive behavior.

When teachers hear parents complain about how hard it is to handle their children at home, they are understandably tempted to ask, "What would you do if you had thirty of them at a time, in one room, with the added responsibility of trying to teach them something?"

Without a doubt, teachers have a difficult job; and most of them experience many hours of irritation, frustration, and exasperation, as expressed so honestly by the junior-high-school teacher who said:

About halfway through the day I begin to look forward to the end of the last period. By the time it arrives I'm emotionally drained. I can hardly drag myself home. When I get there I just want to be left alone. It's ruining my marriage. I really don't think teaching is worth it. The kids take too much out of me.

Although teaching is indeed difficult and emotionally exhausting, this teacher's tiredness is not so much due to hard work as to frustration. Working hard at something satisfying is generally exhilarating. In this chapter we will examine why teachers end the day as this one did—exhausted, discouraged, defeated.

WHAT TO DO ABOUT TEACHER–OWNED PROBLEMS

Chapters III and IV focused on situations where students experienced problems in their own lives; the responsibility for change rested within them. For such problems, active listening is the skill of choice for keeping responsibility where it belongs and for helping students resolve their own problems. We emphasized then that it is important for the teacher to recognize that *the student owns these problems.*

It is just as important that teachers learn to locate problems *they* own. The clues that should tell them that they own these problems are the teachers' own feelings: annoyance, frustration, resentment, anger, distraction, irritation. Quite another set of clues are the physical manifestations of their inner feelings: tension, discomfort, upset stomach, headache, jumpiness. Teachers must own—and take responsibility for —these feelings and reactions. The penalty for not doing so is the frustration and weariness described above by the discouraged teacher.

Here are some common situations where the teacher owns the problem:

A student is scratching a new desktop.

Several students interrupt your conference with another student.

A student leaves reference books he has used unshelved.

A student repeatedly comes late and disturbs the class.

A student wastes art paper.

A student doesn't check in the lab materials he checked out.

Several students smoke in the darkroom of your photo lab.

A student takes up a lot of your time tattling about other students.

A student uses materials from your desk without asking.

A students eats candy and leaves wrappers all over the floor.

Several students argue loudly enough to interrupt you and the rest of the class.

A student is about to spill paint all over a cabinet.

Several students whisper loudly while you are giving directions.

These and hundreds of other such student behaviors either actually or potentially interfere with teachers' legitimate needs. In some tangible and concrete way they prevent (or threaten to prevent) teachers' getting their needs met. No teacher wants desks scratched, wants to be interrupted, wants reference books to be lost, wants to clean up after others, etc. Teachers are human; teachers have their legitimate needs; and teachers will encounter hundreds of student behaviors they cannot accept. Such behaviors belong in the bottom section of the teacher's rectangular window—below the "Acceptance Line."

Unacceptable behaviors that have a tangible or concrete negative effect upon teachers cannot be handled effectively by using active listening; nor can teachers ignore them and continue to function in the No-Problem area. Something has to be done about those behaviors, for the sake of teachers.

The differences between a teacher's posture when the student owns the problem and when the teacher owns the problem are shown in Table 1. In the T.E.T. classes, this table convinces most teachers that helping with students' problems is an entirely different task—a different kind of interaction or process—from helping themselves when stu-

When the Student Owns the Problem	When the Teacher Owns the Problem
Student initiates the communication.	Teacher initiates the communication.
Teacher is a listener.	Teacher is a sender.
Teacher is a counselor.	Teacher is an influencer.
Teacher wants to help the student.	Teacher wants help for himself.
Teacher accepts the student's own solution.	Teacher has to be satisfied with the solution.
Teacher is primarily interested in the student's needs.	Teacher is primarily interested in his own needs.
Teacher is more passive in the problem solving.	Teacher is more active in the problem solving.

TABLE 1

dents cause them problems. As Table 1 shows, the two tasks require exactly opposite postures.

The lessons of this table are immediately obvious to most teachers:

1. You must first locate the student's behavior in the appropriate section of the rectangular window.

2. If it is in the area of student-owned problems, it's appropriate to become a counselor, and the language of acceptance will be effective.

3. If it is in the area of teacher-owned problems, the counselor posture is inappropriate and language of acceptance will be ineffective and phony.

What can teachers do when they correctly identify a student behavior as unacceptable to them and locate that behavior in the area of teacher-owned problems?

Look at it this way: You have three variables to work with when you try to modify unacceptable behavior to get your own needs met—the *student*, the *environment*, and *yourself*. That is, you can direct your influence toward:

1. Attempting to modify the student's behavior

2. Attempting to modify the environment

3. Attempting to modify yourself

Consider the following example: Miss Williams is repeatedly interrupted by one of the students in her class who seems to be unable to go ahead with an assignment without constant checking and reinforcement. This is unacceptable to Miss Williams, so *she owns the problem*. What can she do?

1. Miss Williams can confront the student, sending some message that will cause the student to stop interrupting her. (*Modify the student.*)

2. She can provide the student with programmed self-checking materials. (*Modify the environment.*)

3. She can say to herself, "He's just a dependent student and he'll outgrow it soon," or, "He obviously needs more of my time than the others." (*Modify the self.*)

This chapter will deal only with the first of these three alternatives: modifying the student. The other two will be dealt with in later chapters.

WHAT TYPICAL INEFFECTIVE CONFRONTATIONS DO

In the T.E.T. course, the word "confront" has been chosen consciously to describe the act of standing up to another to tell him that his behavior is interfering with your rights. It is an active posture—an act of courage, of assuming responsibility for seeing to it that your needs are met. Confrontation is behavior motivated by the self-preservation need—an act of necessary selfishness, in the purest sense of that term.

In our T.E.T. classes, instructors present teachers with typical unacceptable behaviors of students and ask them to demonstrate how they might confront each student. With amazing consistency, ninety to ninety-five percent of the teachers send confronting messages that have been shown to have a high probability of producing one or more of these effects or outcomes:

1. Causing the student to resist changing
2. Causing the student to feel that the teacher thinks he is stupid, or at best hopelessly incapable
3. Making the student feel that the teacher has little consideration for him as a person with feelings and needs
4. Making the student feel guilty or ashamed or embarrassed
5. Chipping away at the student's self-esteem
6. Causing the student to feel that he must defend himself
7. Provoking anger and feelings of "That does it—I'm justified in getting revenge!"
8. Causing the student to withdraw, give up, quit trying

Not that teachers want such results. Universally they feel, "I just want to get *my* needs met, too!" Most teachers have simply never thought about the full impact of their messages on students. They say just what has always been said to *them*, mouthing words of their parents and their former teachers. One teacher expressed his feelings about his classroom confrontation habits this way:

The thing that blows my mind is that since I started to listen to myself talk to students I hear the very words I used to hate from my own teachers. Why is that? Why would I say the very things, almost word for word, that used to make me hate school and despise my teachers?

Like everyone else, this teacher, especially under stress, responds as he has been conditioned or "programmed" to respond. He cannot readily resort to any other way.

The typical messages teachers send when confronting students fall into three general categories:

1. Solution messages
2. Put-down messages
3. Indirect messages

WHY SOLUTION MESSAGES FAIL

Solution messages tell a student exactly how to modify his behavior—what he *must do, had better do, should do,* or *might do.* In these messages the teacher hands out solutions to *his* own problems and expects the student to buy them.

Participants in the T.E.T. classes, when asked to recall how their former teachers confronted them, report that their teachers often "pushed their solutions." They remember the negative impact of these "solution messages." One teacher put it this way:

My own teachers were always ordering me around or threatening to send me to the principal or to call my parents. I hated that. Sometimes I was "bad" just to get even with them. I used to sneak into the room and glue the pages of their grade books together or something mean like that. You know, I *still* think some of them had it coming.

Another teacher recalled:

I always felt so stupid or bad when my teachers yelled at me. The only thing I could do was give in and do it their way—or be bad.

If they reacted like this to their former teachers, it is little wonder that teachers in our T.E.T. classes are dismayed when they discover how frequently they use solution messages themselves. Why should their students respond differently than they did themselves?

There are five different kinds of solution messages:

a. *Ordering, Commanding, Directing*
   "Spit out that gum."
   "Sit down this minute."

b. *Warning, Threatening*
   "If you don't line up, I'll leave you standing out there all day."
   "One more time, young man, and you'll stay after school."

c. *Moralizing, Preaching*
"You should know better than to do that."
"Fourth-graders should know what is right."

d. *Teaching, Using Logic, Giving Facts*
"Assignments don't get finished when you dawdle."
"Books are for reading, not marking."

e. *Advising, Offering Solutions*
"If I were you, I'd get back to work."
"Visit during recess, not in class."

Such messages sound pretty familiar because classrooms from coast to coast are filled with them, as if each teacher were somehow molded into a perpetual solution=message-sending machine. The analogy of a sending machine is not too far from fact. Teachers are so strongly programmed by their own parents and former teachers to respond with this kind of "script" when a situation requires confrontation. Hence, students are all but compelled to regard them as sending machines spewing out solutions, day after day.

To most teachers, solution messages seem to be the quickest and most efficient way to get their own needs met. If a student is doing something that is "bugging" the teacher, what is wrong with telling him or pressuring him to stop doing it?

What is wrong is that it so often does not work. Even when it does, the price may be too high, because solution messages all contain a secret, hidden message: *"You're too dumb to figure out how to help me."* Students hear and resent this hidden message.

Solution messages also contain other hidden messages: "I am the boss, the authority" and "You change because I say so." No wonder students resist and retaliate.

Solution messages are bound to carry a high risk of back-firing on teachers, because the best that can be hoped for is submissive compliance and, frequently, a positive behavioral change accompanied by a negative attitudinal change. The student may spit out his gum as ordered, but will resent the

LIBRARY ST. MARY'S COLLEGE

teacher's directive and resolve to chew gum more secretively in the future.

As with other forms of ineffective confrontation that we will examine, solution messages contain information only about the student, *never about the teacher*. The student has no way of knowing how his behavior is affecting the teacher. He knows only that the teacher has decided that he, the student, must change in a specific way. At these times students are apt to make incorrect inferences about the teacher, such as: The teacher is cranky, unfair, uncaring, mean, unjust, hard-nosed, bossy, on a power trip, uptight, unfeeling, pushy, narrow-minded, etc. Having made such inferences, students are not likely to be motivated to care a great deal about the teacher's welfare. On the contrary, they are usually motivated to fight back, rebel, or develop other strategies to defeat the teacher's attempts to impose his solutions.

WHY PUT–DOWN MESSAGES FAIL

Even worse are put-down messages which denigrate the student, impugn his character, or chip away at his self-image. Put-down messages carry evaluation, criticism, ridicule, judgment. We have classified them into six separate categories:

a. *Judging, Criticizing, Disagreeing, Blaming*
   "You're always the one who starts trouble here."
   "You're being naughty."
   "You're a pest."

b. *Name-calling, Stereotyping, Ridiculing*
   "You're acting like wild animals today."
   "You're a bunch of hippies."

c. *Interpreting, Analyzing, Diagnosing*
   "You have problems with authority."
   "You're doing that to get attention."

d. *Praising, Agreeing, Giving Positive Evaluations*
   "You have the brains to be a good student."
   "When you put forth the effort, you do such good work."

e. *Reassuring, Sympathizing, Supporting*
   "It's hard to sit still on such a hot day, isn't it?"
   "I realize the game is tonight, but let's not forget you're in school until three o'clock."

f. *Probing, Questioning, Interrogating*
   "Just why are you out of your seat?"
   "How do you expect to pass this course when you talk in class so much?"
   "Why didn't you put your materials back in the cupboard?"

These six kinds of teacher messages are heavily loaded with negative judgments the teacher has made about the student—put-downs. Did these samples have a familiar ring?

Such messages, and the thousands of variations heard daily by students, have the effect of placing blame and responsibility on students for causing the teacher a problem. They clearly point out that the student is somehow a problem student. As with solution messages, the student hears no data about the teacher and his problem; the student is denied learning that the teacher is human, with human needs and human feelings.

The rare students who already have a positive concept of themselves will usually discount put-down messages, infer that the teacher is out of touch with reality, and proceed basically unchanged. Unfortunately most students are struggling to find even some small degree of worth in themselves. Their self-evaluation is already one of "I'm not okay." Negative evaluation of these students further reinforces their poor self-image.

So put-down messages may be either: (1) discounted (no positive behavioral change occurs, and the student makes inferences about the character of the teacher); or (2) internalized by the student as additional proof of his own inadequacy. Either way, the student hears the teachers sending the hidden message *"There's something wrong with you or you wouldn't be causing me this problem!"* The student is forced to defend himself against what appears to be an attack. He may resist, argue, try to prove the teacher's assessment wrong; or he may develop strategies to shift blame. Many students develop an attitudinal shield of "I don't care, go ahead, do your worst!" A really healthy response by students to put-down messages would be to find them ludicrous and laugh. Unfortunately, too few students have the strength to confront teachers this way.

WHY INDIRECT MESSAGES FAIL

Included in the *indirect message* category are kidding, teasing, sarcasm, digressions, and diverting comments.

"Your shoes *look* better than they *sound*."

"I've never taught a class of monkeys before."

"I suppose I'd be foolish to call on you today."

"Could we wait for our little clown to stop showing off?"

"When did they make you principal of our school?"

"I hope you grow up to be a teacher and have a hundred students like you."

"We'll go on now that the comedy hour is over."

Teachers sometimes resort to such indirect messages because they know that the risks of solutions and put-downs are so great. They seem to hope that students will get the point of the indirect message even though it is pretty well hidden. Because of the relative gentleness of indirection (compared to solutions or put-downs), it is tempting for teachers to send these messages.

They seldom work. Indirect messages are often not understood. Even when they are, students learn from them that the teacher is not direct and open, but indirect and sneaky. The hidden message is: "If I confront you directly you may not like me," or, "Its too risky to be open and honest with you." Students then feel that the teacher is untrustworthy and manipulative. With the exception of sarcasm, which can be withering, students look at indirect messages as attempts by teachers to "gentle" them into acting differently. Too frequently, the message is so gentle or humorous that it has no impact at all.

By now you have undoubtedly recognized that the list of ineffective confrontation messages turns out to be identical to our list of ineffective counseling messages described in Chapter III—the twelve roadblocks to communication—because these roadblocks are just as ineffective for helping students with problems they own as for solving problems *you* own.

An amazing paradox! Since the typical twelve roadblocks are in fact the "language of unacceptance," they might seem okay to use when student behaviors are unacceptable to you. In reality they seldom accomplish what you want—a change in students' behavior—and they carry a high risk of damaging students' self-esteem and your relationship.

We will now demonstrate how to confront students with a higher probability of influencing them to modify their behavior and a lower probability of damaging either their self-images or your relationship with them.

YOU–MESSAGES VERSUS I–MESSAGES

In teaching the T.E.T. course over the years, we discovered another way of thinking about and classifying confrontation messages. Most teachers find it easy to understand and extremely helpful as they try to change their own confronting habits in the classroom.

Notice that all of the twelve roadblocks either contain the pronoun "you" or, due to the structure of our language, the "you" is implied, as in, "Empty the trash," a message which carries the message, "*You* empty the trash." Teachers are usually surprised to discover that almost all their confrontation messages are "you-messages."

You stop that! (*Ordering*)
You had better quiet down or else! (*Warning*)

You ought to know better! (*Moralizing*)
You can do it if you try. (*Logic*)
(*You*) Do it the way I showed you. (*Providing Solutions, Ordering*)
You're not thinking maturely. (*Criticism*)
You're acting like a baby. (*Name-calling*)
You're trying to get even. (*Analyzing*)
You're usually a very good student. (*Positive Evaluation*)
You'll feel better tomorrow. (*Reassurance*)
Why did *you* do that? (*Probing Question*)
You're another Albert Einstein. (*Sarcasm*)

None of these you-messages reveals anything about the teacher—the focus is all on the student. If the teacher said something about how he *felt* about the behavior or how it tangibly *affected* him, the message would have to come out as an I-message rather than a you-message:

I can't work when I have to first clean up a lot of materials that have been left around.

I'm frustrated by this noise.

I'm really annoyed when people get pushed around in this room.

Notice how I-messages put responsibility for what is happening where it belongs—within the teacher, inside the person experiencing the problem. Another name for I-messages might be "responsibility-taking messages."

WHAT'S WRONG WITH YOU–MESSAGES

To appreciate fully the difference between you-messages and I-messages, teachers need to relate both types of messages to Figure 15 in Chapter III as the model for communication when one person talks to another.

Suppose you are feeling very frustrated because one of your bright students repeatedly interrupts you while you are working individually with students having difficulty with fractions. His behavior (interrupting) is giving you a problem—you *own* the problem. You are feeling frustration (inside your skin).

To encode this feeling for the student, chances are you will probably select a code that becomes a you-message, as in Figure 19.

TEACHER

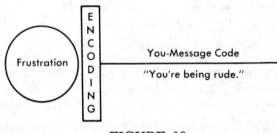

FIGURE 19

If you had selected a code that accurately matched what was going on inside you, it would inevitably have been an I-message (or an "I-am-feeling message"), as, "I am frustrated."

When you send a you-oriented message you are in effect blaming the student for having whatever need prompted him to contact you. You thereby avoid responsibility for your own feeling of frustration, even though a you-message is a (very murky) code for what is happening inside you.

A clear code about your own inner condition would always be an I-message: "I'm frustrated trying to work with this group when I am interrupted so frequently." Such a message communicates something the teacher is experiencing; the you-message is a negative judgment about the student.

Take a look now at Figures 20 and 21, which contain contrasting messages, and try to determine how they would be received by the student.

In the first example the student hears an *evaluation of him*. Such you-messages are almost always heard by students as

TEACHER   STUDENT

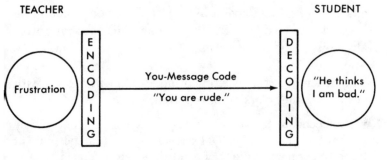

FIGURE 20

evaluations of how bad they are (put-downs). The second message is decoded as a *statement of fact about the teacher.*

WHY I–MESSAGES ARE MORE EFFECTIVE

I-messages can be called "responsibility messages" on two counts: A teacher who sends an I-message is taking responsibility for his own inner condition (listening to *himself*) and assuming responsibility for being open enough to share this assessment of himself with a student; secondly, I-messages leave the responsibility for the student's behavior with the student. At the same time, I-messages avoid the negative impact that accompanies you-messages, freeing the student to be considerate and helpful, not resentful, angry, and devious.

I-messages meet three important criteria for effective con-

TEACHER   STUDENT

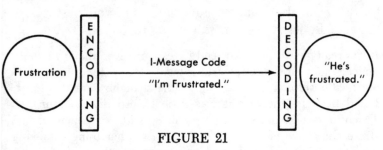

FIGURE 21

frontation: (1) they have a high probability of promoting a willingness to change; (2) they contain minimal negative evaluation of the student; and (3) they do not injure the relationship.

One teacher, after experimenting for the first time with I-messages in her classroom, reported:

I was reluctant to try an I-message with the kids I have. They are so hard to manage. Finally, I screwed up my courage and sent a strong I-message to a group of children who were making a mess with water paints in the back of the room by the sink. I said, "When you mix paints and spill them all over the sink and table, I have to scrub up later or get yelled at by the custodian. I'm sick of cleaning up after you and I feel helpless to prevent it from happening." I just stopped then and waited to see what they would do. I really expected them to laugh at me and take that "I don't care" attitude they've had all year. But they didn't! They stood there looking at me for a minute like they were amazed to find out I was upset, and then one of them said, "Come on, let's clean it up." I was floored. You know, they haven't turned into models of perfection, but they now clean up the sink and tables every day whether they've spilled paint on them or not.

This teacher's experience is not unique. Most teachers have to screw up their courage to confront directly and openly—it means revealing the self. Yet, almost without exception, once having taken the risk, teachers find that students who were thought to be "bad" or "inconsiderate" respond with more consideration than expected.

Another teacher pointed out how difficult it was for him to shift from the blaming, guilt-producing you-messages to the actually less risky I-messages:

It was really hard for me to send I-messages, even though I could understand what my you-messages were doing to the students and our relationships. I kept having trouble changing. For one thing, I had been taught that it was rude to use the pronoun "I." Teachers used to mark my papers all up with red pencil when I wrote about myself in the first person. Another thing, probably worse, was that as a child I had been taught not to expose my feelings, that it was unmanly and a sign of weakness to let people know how I was feeling. Even though I've been working on it, I still have trouble *knowing* how I am feeling. It seems like I'm upset all the time and I know I've got to get past the upset and find out what's *really* bugging me.

Students will look at this teacher as a real person, because he is developing the inner security to expose his feelings, first to himself and then to others—to show himself as a person *capable* of feeling disappointment, hurt, anger, fear. He will be seen by students as genuine, someone with weaknesses, a vulnerable person, even at times a person who feels inadequate and frightened—someone very like the students.

For many teachers this realness is a threat. It destroys the image they thought was expected of them, a monument of godlike infallibility, fearlessness, and imperturbability. They worry that their students might not respect them if they reveal themselves as they really are. You-messages seem comforting to such teachers because they help them to hide feelings, to put the blame on students rather than taking responsibility for revealing their own humanness.

We often ask teachers in our T.E.T. classes to list the names of their own former teachers. As a rule there are blank spots in their memories, teachers whom they cannot remember. How is it possible to forget completely a very significant person with whom you spent as much as a thousand hours? One hypothesis is that there was never any *intimacy* in the relationship. The forgotten teacher was a cardboard cutout, not a real person in the life of the student, someone easily forgotten.

I-messages foster intimacy. They reveal teachers as transparent, honest, real people—people with whom students can have meaningful relationships. One teacher reviewing the list of her own former teachers said:

I'll never forget Mrs. Miller. She was so honest with us. She never pretended or put us on. She used to say, "Say what you mean and mean what you say." Taking this T.E.T. course has made me realize that what she did was send I-messages instead of you-messages like my other teachers. I loved Mrs. Miller. I still do.

HOW TO PUT AN I–MESSAGE TOGETHER

Teachers find that sending I-messages isn't easy. To have the greatest impact on students, an I-message must have three components. First of all, students must find out from it *what* is creating a problem for the teacher. If the student doesn't have to guess why the teacher is confronting him, the message is bound to be more effective. A nonblaming, non-judgmental description of what is unacceptable is a good start for an I-message.

"When I find papers left on the floor . . ."
"When I see new books with torn pages . . ."
"When I can't find materials I left on the table . . ."
"When I get interrupted while I give instructions . . ."

Notice that these statements all refer to *conditions resulting from behaviors of a student* (or students). These conditions are the cause of the teacher's concern.

Sometimes the *specific behavior* of the student is the concern of the teacher. In the following examples the pronoun "you" does appear. However, unlike you-messages, they contain no blame, evaluation, solution, or moral.

"When you jump up and down . . ."
"When you push Johnny on the playground . . ."
"When you interrupt me . . ."

Every reporter knows the difference between reporting only what happened (the facts) and editorializing (evaluating). A good I-message is a factual report without editorial characterization. Look at the difference it makes if evaluation creeps into the description of an event:

"When I find I can't trust certain troublesome people in here . . ."
"When you are inconsiderate of each other . . ."

"When you are sloppy and leave messes on the floor . . . "
"When you act like a bully . . . "

While these are true you-messages, even the first one, they start out as descriptions of behavior but become evaluations or judgments. We call I-messages that begin with judgments "disguised you-messages."

Notice that each of the good I-messages begins with "When." It is important to let students know that it is just at the particular times when *specific* behaviors occur that you experience a problem. You are not *always* upset. It is when you have to deal with a specific behavior or condition that you get upset. This helps the student understand that you are focusing on a particular situation or behavior, not on his general character or overall personal acceptability. He *can* help you out by changing a specific behavior. If he hears your message as generalized unacceptance he will be puzzled: Where should he begin? What can he do to gain your acceptance?

The second component of a three-part I-message is generally the hardest for teachers to send. It pins down the *tangible* or *concrete* effect on the teacher of the specific behavior described in the message's first part.

"When you leave the door unlocked *[nonjudgmental description]* things of mine sometimes get stolen. . . ." *[tangible effect].*

"When the paints are not returned to the cupboard *[nonjudgmental description*), I have to waste a lot of my time collecting them and putting them away. . . ." *[tangible effect].*

What exactly do we mean by "tangible or concrete effect"? Our experience has shown that I-messages generally fail to have impact unless the claimed effect on the teacher appears real and solid in the eyes of the student. A student thinks to himself, "Yes, you may very likely have your things stolen." Or he might think to himself, "Having your things stolen seems very improbable." Still, when a student understands (or "buys") that his behavior now causes (or might in the future cause) the teacher a real problem, he will be more motivated to change. Most students are reluctant to be thought of as "bad guys." Most students want their teachers to like them. And students often don't know just how their behavior is affecting others. Their intent is to get their own needs met. For the most part they are blissfully unaware that in doing so they may be causing problems for others. When they are told about the effect of their behavior, the most common reaction is "Gee, I'm sorry about that, I didn't realize. . . . " or some variation of that.

Teachers sometimes have trouble incorporating this important second component into an I-message because they have been so long accustomed to sending messages to change behaviors that have no tangible or concrete effect on them. Teachers have strong ideas of what is "good" or "bad," "right" or "wrong," even though they are in no way affected by the behaviors. But such attempts at exercising influence fail to demonstrate to the satisfaction of the student that the teacher is being tangibly affected. This is why the student has little or no motivation to modify that behavior. Example: "I can't stand to look at your long hair."

So when teachers first learn to send I-messages they have to sort student behaviors into two categories: those that do have a tangible effect; and those that do not. We tell teachers to expect results only from I-messages in the first category. Students are people, and people seldom modify behavior unless they are convinced that their behavior in some way has a *tangible and concrete* undesirable effect on another.

The third part of the I-message must state the feelings generated within the teacher because he is tangibly affected.

"When you have your feet in the aisle [*description of behavior*], I'm apt to trip over them [*tangible effect*] and I'm afraid I'll fall and get hurt [*feeling*]."

This teacher is saying that the behavior may create a possible effect (tripping), and this effect is producing the feeling of fear. The sequence (behavior→effect→feeling) communicates that the feeling is being blamed on the possible *effect,* not on the student's *behavior.* Now the student will be far less defensive than if he felt that the teacher's fear was related directly to the behavior. After all, the teacher is not afraid of being hurt by the student's *feet;* the teacher is afraid of being hurt by *falling.*

This logical sequence is important but not sacrosanct. An I-message in any order (or even with one part missing) automatically achieves a high probability of being heard by students as an honest, open statement by the teacher about "where he's at." Any reasonable I-message is always far preferable to a blaming you-message or a weak "indirect message."

HOW TO SHIFT GEARS AFTER SENDING AN I–MESSAGE

While I-messages produce less defensiveness from students than you-messages, it's obvious that nobody welcomes hearing that his behavior is causing someone else a problem, no matter how the message is phrased. Even the best-constructed I-message may cause a student to feel hurt, sorry, surprised, embarrassed, defensive, argumentative, or even tearful. After all, he has received a message, loud and clear, that his behavior is unacceptable, troublesome, or hurtful to his teacher. Frequently the student's initial response will be a cue or a clue signaling that his teacher, by confronting him, has now caused the *student* a problem. *He* now owns a problem.

In T.E.T. we coach teachers to stay alert to these cues and clues, and we stress the necessity of shifting gears—from confrontation back to active listening. This shifting from confronting to counseling helps the student deal with his newly created problem. It also demonstrates the teacher's understanding and acceptance of the student's reactions.

The following private conversation illustrates confrontation *without* shifting gears:

TEACHER: Allan, your being late to class is causing me a problem. When you come in late I have to stop whatever I'm doing. It's distracting to me and I'm frustrated.

STUDENT: Yeah. Well, I've had a lot to do lately and sometimes I just can't get here on time.

TEACHER: That's all well and good, but I just can't go on ignoring it. I just can't continue to be interrupted. (*Second I-message*)

STUDENT: I don't see why you're making a big deal out of it. So I'm a few minutes late. Big deal!

TEACHER: When you say things like that I feel really unappreciated. (*Third I-message*)

STUDENT: Don't take it so personally. Just ignore me when I'm late and it won't be a problem.

TEACHER: Don't tell me what to do! You get here on time from now on! (*You-message*)

STUDENT: (*Stalking out*) What a grouch!

In this scenario the teacher failed to hear the defensive reaction of the student after the first I-message. This escalated his own and the student's anxiety. The predictable result was a standoff with angry feelings on both sides.

Here is how the same scene might go when the teacher listens to the student's reaction to the I-message and shifts gears.

TEACHER: Allan, your being late to class is causing me a problem. When you come in late I have to stop whatever I'm doing. It's distracting to me and I'm frustrated.

STUDENT: Yeah. Well, I've had a lot to do lately and sometimes I just can't get here on time.

TEACHER: I see. You're having some new problems of your own lately. (*Active listening*)

STUDENT: Right. Mr. Sellers asked me to help in the chem lab after third period—you know, setting up for fourth period. It's a good deal.

TEACHER: You're really pleased he asked you. (*Active listening*)

STUDENT: Right on! I can probably get to be the lab assistant next year and I could sure use the job.

TEACHER: There may be a good payoff for you and that's pretty important. (*Active listening*)

STUDENT: Yeah. I know you're upset about me being late. I didn't think it would be such a problem. You know, I've tried to sort of slip in quietly.

TEACHER: You're a little surprised that it's such a problem to me even when you try to be quiet. (*Active listening*)

STUDENT: Well, not really. I can see your point. You do have to stop and change the attendance record and stuff. Mostly I'm late because Mr. Sellers and I get to talking too long. I'll tell him it's a problem for you and I'll just split a few minutes earlier, okay?

TEACHER: That would sure help me. Thanks, Allan.

STUDENT: No sweat.

In this re-run, the teacher laid out his problem with his initial I-message but then shifted to active listening to enable Allan to work through his own problem to the point where he was able to come up with an acceptable way to help the teacher with his problem.

HOW TEACHERS MAKE THEMSELVES ANGRY

Teachers in our T.E.T. classes often can't wait until they can get back to their classes and begin confronting their "troublemakers." But in their eagerness they end up simply venting their anger, and not infrequently they scare students half to death or make them even more aggressive and reactive. We have learned a lot from our in-depth analyses and discussions of such angry I-messages.

When anger is the feeling part of a teacher's three-part I-message, the confrontations are perceived by the students as blaming, put-down messages. Instead of revealing the inner feelings of the teacher, anger seems to point the finger of blame at the student. The I-message "I am angry" is usually interpreted by the student as "I am angry at *you*" or "*You* made me angry." In our T.E.T. classes we try to help teachers understand first of all that anger comes *after* experiencing some earlier feeling. Anger is a *secondary* feeling. It always follows a primary feeling. Here is how it works.

Mr. Jones is on yard duty at an elementary school. One of the children throws a rock, narrowly missing Jones's head. His primary or "gut-level" reaction is fear; but then he runs across the playground and "acts angry," shouting some threatening you-messages like "Don't you *ever* throw rocks on this playground when I'm around!" The purpose of his acting angry is to punish the rock thrower or make him feel guilty for having scared the supervisor out of his wits. He may also act angry hoping it might scare the child enough so he won't throw rocks again. He hopes to teach the child a lesson he'll never forget.

Teachers admit in T.E.T. classes that their anger messages are generally attempts to punish or teach a lesson to a student because he has done something that caused some other feeling.

Anger can be looked at as a posture or an "act," not a true emotion or feeling. Frequently, shortly after a person acts angry he may get very real physiological sensations—rapid heartbeat, trembling, etc. These physical manifestations may be reactions to the violence of his own behavior. In a sense, a person can be said to manufacture his own internal reactions, which then feel like an emotion.

Here are examples of teachers *making* themselves angry as a result of experiencing a primary feeling:

Student almost falls through a window while hanging display materials. Primary feeling is *fear*. Teacher acts angry and says, "Get down right now—I can see you can't be careful."

Student gets lost on a field trip. Primary feeling of the teacher is *anxiety*. Teacher acts angry when child is finally found, and yells, "Never, never leave the group! Why can't you learn to follow rules?"

Teacher has gone out of her way to prepare an interesting demonstration. Students are restless, bored, passing notes to their neighbors. Teacher's primary feeling is *disappointment*. Teacher angrily says, "I feel like I will never again try to make this subject interesting for this ungrateful class. Look how much it is appreciated!"

Student cannot grasp the concept of adding fractions. Primary feeling of the teacher is *frustration*. Teacher angrily shouts, "You're not even trying—it's so simple a third-grader would get it before you do!"

Teachers readily admit that angry attempts to punish or teach a lesson don't work. If they did, the entire world's problems would have been solved generations ago.

How can teachers learn to behave differently?

In our T.E.T. classes we try to help teachers learn to recognize their angry you-messages for what they are (secondary feelings) and to concentrate instead on sending the primary feeling as an I-message. When sending a primary (rather than an angry secondary) feeling, teachers discover a remarkable difference. The primary feeling is almost always much less intense than anger. When teachers pick up this difference it helps them to realize that anger is much like a witch's brew, bubbling and fermenting inside the teacher until it spews forth, powerful and withering in its effect. It is excessive—a case of overkill.

One T.E.T. class participant talked about his experience with a particular student and the angry feelings he had about their relationship:

I was always mad at Charles even though I couldn't ever put my finger on exactly what he was doing to make me angry. I just wrote it off as "one of those things," you know. Charles was just one of those people who rubbed me the wrong way. Yet, I was constantly upset. When we began looking at anger in this class, I thought, "What's my primary feeling about Charles?" I almost hate to admit what I found out because it makes me look like I'm a lot more insecure than I feel I really am, but my primary feeling was fear. I was afraid that Charles with his brilliance and sharp tongue was going to make me look stupid in front of the other students. Last week I asked him to stay after class and I just told him how threatened I get when he pins me down on some minor point or when he asks me technical questions that I have no way of knowing answers for. He was kind of stunned, and said he wasn't trying to make me look bad, that he was really trying to score "brownie points" with me. We ended up laughing about it and I'm not threatened by him anymore. When he forgets and pins me down now, I just laugh and say, "Hey, that's another brownie point for you."

The experience of this teacher in getting in touch with his primary feeling of fear and telling the student about it illustrates what frequently happens. He discovered that he had no really serious basis for the primary feeling and, therefore, no need to use punishing, angry you-messages.

A school counselor courageously spoke up in his T.E.T. class about his struggle to uncover the cause of his anger toward his own son:

This whole thing about anger being a secondary emotion was hard for me to accept, mainly because it meant examining *myself* instead of blaming my son for where I was at. For the last several months my son, Gary, and I have been in a sort of yelling match. He's been running around with a bunch of guys that I know about, and believe me they're pretty rough. Well, maybe you wouldn't call it *rough* exactly, but they smoke a little grass, drink some beer, and some of the girls they hang around with don't get their pictures in fashion magazines. As I look at it now, I see that I was coming down on Gary pretty hard with a lot of you-messages, stuff like "Show me a man's friends and I'll tell you what he's like." Then Gary would tell me to get off his back and I'd really get mad. Well, after last week's class I drove around for a while before I went home, just thinking about what might be under my anger. As I said, I was afraid you were really right and I'd find out that Gary was all right and the problem was really me, so I tried to pick holes in your theory. A couple of days later, though, I thought, "The reason I'm trying to punish Gary with you-messages is that I'm disappointed in him." That felt pretty good for a while, but then I thought, "Okay, what's under the disappointment?" You know what the *real* primary feeling is? Fear. I was afraid of what people at the school were going to say about me if they found out my son is running around with the people he's with, that they would think, "Some counselor! His own kid is running around with bums!" Once I got a hold on that I didn't even have to confront Gary. Hell, that was a trip I was laying on myself. I did tell Gary that I found out I was yelling at him about something I had going inside me and that I was going to quit. He sort of said, "Yeah," but the last couple of days we're beginning to talk to each other again. In fact, I'm finding out that he doesn't really think too much of that bunch either.

Like many of us, this father allowed his own fear of being evaluated by his peers to generate anger and resentment toward his son. It threatened to damage the relationship. After he discovered his primary feeling, he was able to take complete ownership of (and responsibility for) it. He then felt no need even to confront his son; only to share the fact that he had decided to behave differently toward him. The counselor who told this story agreed in the class that his son might very well appreciate being told the whole story, just as he told it to the class. Later he told his son.

SENDING I–MESSAGES CAN BE RISKY

We have emphasized the high risk of you-messages, but sometimes teachers ask, "Are there any risks with I-messages?" The answer is yes. They have already been mentioned, either directly or by inference, but a review may be in order.

Probably the greatest risk most people feel, at least when they first try I-message confrontation, is the risk of self-disclosure. I-messages are statements about the self, revelations of inner feelings and needs, information not possessed by others. Their risk is that others will know you more intimately, more as you really are. Rejection by others after you make such a disclosure might be more painful; it would be rejection of the real you, not of some role you might be playing. Obviously, someone who holds himself in low esteem will feel less like sharing his real self than someone who has a higher opinion of his personal worth.

The opposite side of this coin also entails risks. Lack of self-disclosure results in lack of intimacy—superficial relationships, playing games, acting out roles. Teachers who try I-messages report almost without exception that the benefits of being "real" far outweigh the risks.

The second major risk is the possibility of self-modification. Teachers who begin to send I-messages often report that they have had to analyze situations more carefully than they did before, and that sometimes (as in the case of the school counselor whose son was running around with the "wrong" crowd) they end up modifying themselves, not the youngster. Since you-messages always place the fault or blame outside the sender, self-modification is never an issue. Also, after confronting, the switch to active listening frequently results in the discovery of new information that sheds new light, thereby promoting more self-modification by the teacher.

The third major risk is responsibility. One of the most difficult (and yet rewarding) acts for most people is to assume responsibility for themselves; it's more comfortable to define everything that is wrong as someone else's fault. You-messages place the *locus of responsibility* outside the self, while I-messages keep responsibility with the teacher for his own human condition. But teachers have pointed out to us that another way of looking at the risks of I-messages is to view them as opportunities for personal growth. They cite changes in their own lives as evidence that risk and growth often go together, and that change toward a richer, fuller, more rewarding way of being is worth the risk.

One teacher put it this way: "With I-messages I can now get my own needs met and the kids still like me. . . . Some risk!"

WHAT EFFECTIVE I–MESSAGES CAN ACCOMPLISH

Teachers report some startling results of confronting students with I-messages. Most frequently they find that students are surprised upon learning how their teachers feel—and feel free to say so:

"I didn't know I was upsetting you."

"I didn't think you noticed."

"We didn't know we could be getting you in trouble."

People of all ages are often unaware of how their behavior affects others. But once they are told about it (in a nonblaming, honest way), even youngsters of any age will respond, more frequently than teachers imagine, simply out of consideration for their teachers' needs. We have seen it happen time again: *I-messages can turn thoughtlessness into thoughtfulness.*

Mr. G., the principal of a continuation school (special school for rebellious and troublesome students), gave this dramatic account of what I-messages can do:

For weeks I had been resentfully tolerating the behavior of a group of boys who were continually ignoring some of the school regulations. One morning I looked out my office window and saw them casually walking across the lawn carrying Coke bottles, which is against school regulations. That did it. Having just attended the session in the T.E.T. course that explained I-messages, I ran out and started sending some of my feelings: "I feel so darned discouraged with you guys! I've tried everything I can to help you get through school. I've put my heart and soul into this job. And all you guys do is break the rules. I fought for a reasonable rule about hair length, but you guys won't even stick to that. Now, here you've got Coke bottles and that's against the rules, too. I feel like just quitting this job and going back to the regular high school, where I can feel I'm accomplishing something. I feel like an absolute failure in this job."

That afternoon I was surprised by a visit from the group. "Hey, Mr. G., we've been thinking about what happened this morning. We didn't know you could get mad. You never did before. We don't want another principal down here; he won't be as good as you've been. So we all agreed to let you take the electric clippers and cut our hair. We're also going to stick to the other rules."

After recovering from his shock, Mr. G. went into another room with the boys, and each submitted to his barbering until their hair was short enough to conform to the regulation. Mr. G. told our class that the most significant thing about this incident was how much fun they all had during the volunteer hair-cutting session. "We all had a ball," he reported. The boys got close to him and to each other. They left the room friends, with warm feelings and the kind of closeness that so often results from mutual problem solving.

This story illustrates how kids can be responsive and responsible if adults level with them. Too often in schools, teachers and administrators underestimate students' willingness to accommodate to the needs of adults.

Teachers also report that their use of I-messages eventually influences students to start sending honest messages themselves—to other students and to teachers. Students model themselves after their teachers; it is probably the most significant way for students to learn effective (and ineffective) interpersonal behavior.

Three weeks after completing the T.E.T. class, a beaming St. Louis teacher* reported hearing this message sent by her star eighth-grade student to the school principal: "Mr. Wilson, when you stand around outside our door and listen in, the kids get suspicious and aren't sure what to think."

The proud teacher commented, "I knew for sure that my

---

* Submitted by T.E.T. instructor Patrick Sobota, St. Louis, Missouri.

I-messages were not only paying off for me but the modeling effect on the kids was bringing in dividends."

And what was the effect of the student's confrontation on the principal?

The teacher answered, "We never saw him stand outside *anyone's* door the rest of the year."

VI. HOW TO MODIFY
THE CLASSROOM ENVIRONMENT
TO PREVENT PROBLEMS

Teachers can prevent many unacceptable behaviors of students with relative ease just by modifying the classroom environment. This means confronting the physical and psychological characteristics of the classroom, rather than the student.

Why does this method work? Because, as teachers know from experience, most classrooms unfortunately are designed, constructed, and furnished in ways that make it difficult for students to stay motivated and involved in the learning process; and when students are distracted and bothered by the classroom environment, many of their coping mechanisms turn into behaviors unacceptable to teachers and interfere with efforts to teach.

In this chapter we will suggest specific things teachers can do to modify the classroom environment to prevent or eliminate many unacceptable student behaviors. By focusing directly on the environment, teachers can further enlarge the No-Problem area and greatly increase teaching-learning time, even beyond what can be accomplished by confronting with I-messages.

THE INADEQUACIES OF THE TYPICAL CLASSROOM

Despite recent efforts to improve school-building de-sign, the typical classroom in the United States remains a rectangle of approximately 960 square feet with a wooden or asphalt-tile floor, hard wall surfaces, large glass windows, chalkboards and bulletin boards. Lighting and ventilation are frequently inadequate, seating is usually so uncomfortable as to be unthinkable for use in homes or modern business offices. Hard surfaces and parallel walls often cause severe acoustical problems. Storage is invariably a problem; it's either inadequate, inconvenient, or both. And, in many class-rooms, adequate control of the temperature is impossible or prohibited.

Into this physical setting are crammed up to forty-five (or even more) human beings, including one or more adults who are expected to teach certain skills or subject matter in a prescribed length of time.

Impossible? Well, not entirely. Teachers and students have been overcoming these severe handicaps for years by sheer determination, creativity, energy, and drive. But as the focus of teaching has changed from rote memorization toward pro-cesses of learning and creative thinking, the task has become much more difficult. Today's teachers are finding that, as a result of changes in teaching approaches, physical limitations of classrooms create special problems. The switch from large group lecturing to small groups and individualized instruc-tion has made a great difference in itself. In a word, *teachers are expected to teach differently but are given much the same setting in which to do it.* Students are expected to learn in a new style, but in a setting designed for the old. No wonder that the classroom environment fosters many of the student behaviors that teachers find unacceptable.

A teacher working in an elementary school built in the early 1900s talked about the problem in a T.E.T. class:

I hear people talking about how much we Americans value education, but I don't know if that's true. My room is dark and dingy, the chairs are splintering oak, the floors creak, and you can hear a pin drop even if it's in the next room. I'm supposed to keep thirty squirming seven-year-olds interested and eager for learning, but also *quiet*, because the noise level gets louder as it travels down the halls. I'm sure any group of adults who had to do what these children do every day would organize, join a union, and go out on strike for better working conditions.

Even in newer, modern buildings, where carpeting and acoustical materials soften noise, where air-conditioning units keep the temperature at a steady seventy-two degrees, and the walls are brightly painted, the grouping of large numbers of people in a relatively small space can create environmental problems—and behavior problems.

For teachers to be effective in modifying the classroom environment they need the ability to think creatively about possible changes, using a systematic model for classifying various types of environmental modification. With this help, most teachers in our T.E.T. classes have been able to find rather innovative ways to reduce unacceptable behaviors.

HOW TO THINK CREATIVELY ABOUT CHANGE

More than most of us realize, our ability to think creatively about how we might change things is limited by self-imposed restrictions. It is not easy to depart from the usual, from the traditional, what we are accustomed to. The late Dr. Boyd Lane, a truly creative educator, once developed his own list of 165 surefire ways to stop the creative process in schools. The list included such inhibitors as:

We tried it once and it didn't work.

The administration won't buy it.

The community won't understand.

We don't have enough money.

It's too radical.

It's too conservative.

The teachers' union will fight it.

The people aren't ready for it.

It's too late.

It's too soon.

We need more involvement.

There are too many people involved.

It will get bad press.

All of Boyd Lane's "creativity stoppers" are evaluative statements, and, as we pointed out in Chapter III, nothing so inhibits the creative process as evaluation (or the threat of evaluation). Most people need procedures or methods that stimulate creative thinking—guidelines or rules that social scientists have found helpful in releasing the creativity of individuals or groups.

In T.E.T., teachers are taught "creative brainstorming," a tested procedure for generating new and creative ideas. Here are eight guidelines for brainstorming alone or in a group:

1. Select a place where outside interference will be at a minimum, a place where concentration is easy.

2. Decide what the specific problem is—e.g., "How can we improve the handling and storage of classroom materials?"

3. Set a time limit for the brainstorming session.

4. Tape-record or write down all ideas generated.

5. Quantity, not quality, is desired, so get out as many ideas as possible.

6. Use the "blue skies" approach. Do not limit thinking to practical, pragmatic, or rational ideas—the wilder the better!

7. No evaluations are permitted. The time to evaluate is *after* all the ideas are generated, not during the process.

8. Shift the frame of reference from time to time—e.g., "How would a student solve this? How about an expert materials handler in a plant? Or an efficiency expert?"

When a group is involved in this process, the obvious advantage is that members can "piggyback" on each other's ideas. The old adage that "two heads are better than one" seems to fit the creative process. In the T.E.T. classes the instructors get teachers to use this method to generate fresh thinking about modifying the classroom environment. Then, back in their schools, teachers find they can use the same process with their students or peers in a group.

HOW TO THINK SYSTEMATICALLY
ABOUT THE CLASSROOM ENVIRONMENT

When we ask teachers to think creatively about modifying the classroom environment, they usually find it difficult to zero in on such an abstraction as "the environment." What parts of the environment? What elements can be changed? Where do we start?

To make the job less vague and imposing, here are eight way to think about making environmental changes:

1. Enriching the environment

2. Impoverishing the environment

3. Restricting the environment

4. Enlarging the environment

5. Rearranging the environment

6. Simplifying the environment

7. Systematizing the environment

8. Planning ahead for the environment

In the following pages we offer teachers specific ideas in each of these eight categories.

HOW TO ENRICH THE ENVIRONMENT

Most teachers are quite aware of possibilities for *enriching* the learning environment; they have had training in how to do it, and they have spent more time on trying to do it than on any other way of modifying the environment. But few teachers have looked at environmental enrichment as a means to eliminate or prevent unacceptable student behaviors; they are only familiar with it as a teaching technique. Many unacceptable behaviors arise from sheer frustration and boredom, perhaps just from being so long in one environment that it has become dull and uninteresting. Enriching the classroom environment so that students have available a multitude of stimulating alternatives, choices, or electives can reduce boredom and its inevitable consequences—unacceptable and troublesome behavior. With little effort teachers can try out many of the following ideas for increasing students' sensory input:

Use colored light.

Play music.

Put in "learning centers."

Add a library section.

Install an art center, for construction, fingerpainting, clay, watercolors, oils, wood sculpturing, metal sculpturing, etc.

Use audio-visual materials.

Decorate in bright colors.

Set up displays.

Give demonstrations.

Put in a "rap session" area.

Make a puppet stage, stage puppet plays.

Install a "creative-writing corner."

Invite guest speakers.

HOW TO IMPOVERISH THE ENVIRONMENT

Sometimes students behave inappropriately and unacceptably because the environment is providing *too much stimulation*. Overstimulation at times can be just as frustrating as too little stimulation. Students can be overwhelmed by an environment that offers too many choices, much like a child on Christmas day who faces so many presents that he cannot enjoy any of the ones he opens just because of the anxiety of not knowing what is in the next box. This is especially true for students who have the central-nervous-system dysfunction called "hyperkinesis."

Teachers in T.E.T. come up with ideas like the following to impoverish, at least temporarily, the environment of classrooms:

Darken the room.

Put down pieces of carpet where noisy activities take place.

Put away all materials except those to be used in the present activity.

Schedule the use of materials, limit their availability.

Schedule "quiet times."

Install study carrels.

Use earphones on audio-visual equipment.

Install room dividers, partitions.

Have students (teachers, too) remove shoes.

Use a "focusing" technique, such as television, films, filmstrips.

Install a "meditation corner."

HOW TO RESTRICT THE ENVIRONMENT

Sometimes behaviors are unacceptable only because they happen in the wrong place or at the wrong time. For instance, restricting the use of paints to one corner of the room may prevent many problems.

The very nature of school is environmentally restricting because it requires attendance at a certain place at a certain time. Most students can handle such limitations on their freedom if the limitations are reasonable and if students understand the reasons for them. Out of a need for control over their own complex lives, students often accept appropriate restrictions on their freedom in the classroom.

These are a few of the ideas teachers may want to consider for restricting the environment when appropriate:

Designate areas for certain activities—e.g., art, music, study, discussion.

Limit the number of students who may be in one place at one time.

Use sign-up sheets for activities.

Assign places for students during special activities.

Use study carrels.

Require that noisy activities be performed in only one area.

Design traffic patterns to restrict movement.

Rotate schedules for the use of equipment.

HOW TO ENLARGE THE ENVIRONMENT

Undesirable behaviors sometimes occur because the environment is too limiting, too restricting, or when it is limiting for too long a time. The usual classroom is terribly restricting. In some ways it can become like a prison cell. Sensitive teachers can create ways to extend this environment into the outside world. Here are a few feasible suggestions:

Study trips

Visits to off-campus areas and events

Visits to on-campus areas and events

Use of library facilities

Use of multipurpose rooms: gymnasiums, cafeteria, etc.

Use of outside resources—people and things

Combining classrooms occasionally

Team-teaching to permit smaller groups

Cross-age tutoring (students teach other students)

Expanding the classroom into the halls or adjacent lawns on occasion

Use of aides or paraprofessionals to free the teacher to work in different ways with different groups

Use of specialists, consultants, experts

HOW TO REARRANGE THE ENVIRONMENT

Sometimes students make problems for themselves and others because the environment is poorly arranged. In some classrooms even walking across the room requires dexterity. One primary-grade teacher, after repeated unsuccessful I-messages to one of her students, discovered that the traffic patterns in the classroom required everyone to pass by this student's desk. He was very much in the same advantageous position of ancient trade pirates who controlled access to a narrow mountain pass and were able to extract a toll from passing caravans. When the traffic pattern was changed in this room so other students could sharpen pencils, get materials, and move from one group to another without going through the "pass," the problem disappeared; the one student's unacceptable behavior became acceptable, and no more I-messages were needed.

Here are some rather obvious ways for teachers to rearrange the classroom environment to prevent problems:

Put away unused materials.

Design effective traffic patterns.

Rearrange furniture or desks in a circle for discussion.

Get rid of unused furniture.

Keep electrical equipment away from water outlets.

Put all materials for a project in one area.

Get additional pencil sharpeners, wastebaskets, etc.

Keep materials in inaccessible locations (high shelves, cupboards) if they require close supervision when used by students.

Put equipment and machines that are for individual use in study carrels or other areas, to be used by only one person at a time.

Remove doors from much-used cabinets.

Arrange for clothing and lunch-box storage near the entrance.

HOW TO SIMPLIFY THE ENVIRONMENT

More and more people are becoming concerned about the negative impact of our environment because it is becoming so complex. The classroom environment, too, can become unnecessarily complex and difficult for students to manage. This is especially true for small children trying to function in an environment built for people six feet tall. Virginia Satir, the noted family therapist, asks adults to try functioning in a family environment while on their knees; this helps them relive the perspective of a small child. The same exercise might prove valuable for teachers of small children.

The environment can be complicated for kids in many more ways. Complex rules, regulations, procedures, and rituals can create great frustration and hostility, as anyone knows who has tried to fill out a federal income-tax form or tried to understand an insurance policy.

Here are some ways that effective teachers have suggested for simplifying the classroom environment:

Put materials, books, tools and equipment where students can reach them.

Review procedures and rules, and substitute simple ones for those that are complicated.

Post rules, policies, and regulations where students can see them easily.

Lower doorknobs, handles, and hooks.

Put a small step-stool by high cabinets.

Design storage for playground materials so that they can be managed by the students themselves.

Put operation rules and instructions on machines and equipment used by students.

Label drawers, cabinets, files, storage areas—using color code when possible.

Eliminate unused or seldom-used equipment, furniture, materials.

HOW TO SYSTEMATIZE THE ENVIRONMENT

One of the easiest ways to eliminate confusion and duplication of effort is to develop systems for getting things done. The danger of over-systematizing to the point that the system becomes more important than the task (as occurs in some bureaucracies) always exists. But the small size of the group and the relative intimacy of classroom activities make this unlikely.

Here are typical ideas for systematizing that teachers generate when they brainstorm this problem in T.E.T. classes:

Assign certain tasks to certain people.

Develop a check-out procedure for books and other materials.

Use the meat market's "take a number" technique for scheduling time with the teacher.

Alphabetize, color-code, set up filing systems, use check-out trays containing everything needed for a project.

Use "in-basket" and "out-basket" technique for handling assignments.

Use "round-robin" assignments for routines like attendance-taking, opening-and-closing tasks, handling money collections, form-filling, handling visiting "dignitaries," cleanup, materials inventory, etc.

Develop check lists (similar to preflight checklists used by pilots) to assure completion of tasks.

Develop flow charts to illustrate complex operations such as laboratory setups or takedowns.

HOW TO PLAN AHEAD

Advance planning can often prevent trouble in the classroom, as everywhere else. Sharing plans for upcoming events and discussing what is expected from students; discussing state laws or school policies *before* problems arise; planning in advance for ways to handle commonly faced problems (e.g., tardiness, oversleeping, teacher absences, substitute teachers, unusual weather conditions, assignments turned in late, emergencies and emergency drills)—all these steps help students to know ahead of time what to do. Result: Troublesome behaviors don't arise when the youngsters encounter such unusual situations.

T.E.T. instructors sometimes ask groups of teachers, "What are the behavior problems you know you are going to face this year in your school or classroom?" The teachers list most of the chronic problems that plague them year after year. By planning ahead and putting out information, a surprising number of these problems can be eliminated beforehand.

Here are some ideas that teachers have suggested for preventing problems by planning ahead:

Hold training sessions to show students how to operate new equipment and machines.

Have "dry runs" or rehearsals for unusual or complicated procedures.

Hold discussions of grading and evaluation procedures at the beginning of the year.

Plan (and rehearse in advance) how to be helpful to substitute teachers.

Share verbally (and post lists of) known important dates and events.

Develop and use individual calendars of events, using duplicate copies, one for the student to have at home and one at school.

Discuss openly those school rules and policies over which the teacher and class have no control, and let students know in advance the penalties for violations of these rules and policies.

Advise students of the costs for (and limits on) use of books, materials, equipment.

Especially useful for young students or students new to the school are orientation walks, tours of facilities, guided trips around the school.

Schedule time for special people, such as school counselors, psychologists, bus drivers, administrators, curriculum specialists, librarians, nurses, coordinators, so they may talk to the students about how they can be of help.

These and countless other procedures and techniques help students know what is expected, and provide information to aid them in doing their jobs acceptably. Students are remarkably flexible and able to function smoothly if they know the "whats" and "hows." Many teachers have had satisfying results when they shared with their students the eight ways to modify the environment and asked the youngsters for their ideas for changes.

Such innovative teachers recognize that the classroom isn't just *theirs*; it belongs to everybody who comes together in it. It really is unfair to expect students to do all the changing to fit "the teacher's room." Students who are given the chance to participate in designing their own living and learning environments have a greater investment in it, an increased sense of ownership and responsibility. Such feelings pay big dividends for teachers who foster them.

HOW TO UPGRADE THE QUALITY OF TIME IN THE CLASSROOM

Another way of planning for a better learning environment is to examine how people function together in the classroom, what their needs are, and how they get met.

Experienced teachers know that problems sometimes occur even in the so-called No-Problem or Teaching-Learning area of the rectangle. Even though teacher-student and student-student relationships seem to be problem-free, something can happen to create problems. One student hits another for no apparent reason; or another starts yelling at his peers to leave him alone; or the teacher suddenly becomes aware of annoying noises or disturbances that previously went unnoticed. It isn't until we examine the *quality* of the teaching-learning environment that these behaviors begin to be understood and handled constructively.

Within the No-Problem area—those times when teaching and learning become possible—three different kinds of available and usable time exist: (1) Diffused Time; (2) Individual Time; and (3) Optimum Time.°

Why Diffused Time Causes Problems

Classrooms are active places! It is literally impossible, if not inhuman, to crowd twenty or thirty or more human beings into the relatively small space of a classroom and wind up with quiet, immobility, and inactivity. Teachers and students are tuned in to their environment with all five senses. Incoming stimuli are constantly received, monitored, processed. What does this mean to a typical teacher and his students? Here is a situation common to elementary-school classrooms:

The teacher is seated with six students at a small table conducting an oral reading lesson. Each of the six students has some materials employed by the teacher to work on diction, pronunciation, and vocabulary skills. They read aloud in turn. Elsewhere in the room another group of students is working on an art project, arguing quietly about the placement of cutouts on the mural they are constructing. Another group is using math materials at the math center, noisily dropping some of the objects and exclaiming in surprise and excitement as they discover how things work. Other students are reading books, walking over to the library shelves, sharpening pencils, groping in their desks for materials, shuffling feet, coughing, whispering, exchanging crayons ("Let me use your red one, mine's broken"), or helping each other with tasks and projects.

Every person in this room is being flooded with incoming stimuli—the smell of human bodies and freshly sharpened pencils; the sights of moving persons, colors, shadows; the sounds of voices or moving chairs or heavy breathing; the

° Credit for this important concept belongs to T.E.T. instructors Michael Lillibridge and Gary Klukken, Tampa, Florida.

clatter of things being manipulated, played with, moved; the feel of the hard chair and cramping muscles, the texture of construction paper, crayons, paints, the sharpness of scissors as they cut along the lines. These and thousands of other sensory inputs are being received and processed by each person, continually, almost without surcease.

As students grow and develop they learn how to screen incoming stimuli—which noises, feelings, sights, or tastes to pay attention to, and which to ignore. *Not* paying attention (or suppressing awareness) also takes energy. Concentration, for the most part, is the use of energy to suppress awareness of all incoming stimuli except one or two. Studies indicate that even well-motivated adults are seldom able to do this for more than twenty minutes at a time, and the attention span of younger people is usually much less. Ultimately, any student's supply of energy that is used to suppress awareness becomes exhausted. He suddenly becomes aware that he is perspiring, or that his legs ache from sitting in one position too long, or that others are crowded too closely around him, or that the group at the math center is too loud. He finds others *unacceptable to him,* so he starts yelling at them: "Get away!" "Leave me alone!" Or: "It's too hot in here!" He has reached the limit of his ability to handle *diffusion* (and confusion). He now has another need to be met—relief from being overloaded with signals, relief from Diffused Time.

Consider again our familiar rectangular window in Figure 22. Within the No-Problem area (Teaching-Learning area) we have located Diffused Time in area (1). Areas (2) and (3) represent the two other kinds of time experienced by teachers and students in the classroom: Individual Time (2), and Optimum Time (3).

Why Individual Time Is Vital—And How To Get It

The time represented by area (2) in Figure 22 has the quality of decreased sensory input. When the stress of relating to other people—or the use of energy in suppressing

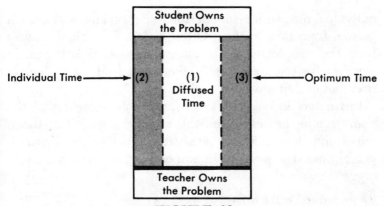

FIGURE 22

awareness of numerous stimuli—becomes overwhelming, people have a need to escape from their environment into one requiring less energy, less management, less involvement. Students and teachers alike sometimes have a need to be alone, to be in an environment where incoming stimuli are significantly reduced, where there are no other persons with whom to cope.

If their need for individual time is frustrated, people get edgy, oversensitive, cranky, hard to get along with; or they seek "illegitimate" ways to get individual time, such as daydreaming or fantasizing in class, behaving so badly that they get sent out of the room or sent home or to the counselor's office. Teachers frequently report that the worst time of day is toward the end, late in the afternoon. At this time most students, *and* teachers, have depleted their supply of energy and can hardly bear to have to relate to each other or to the confusion of the classroom any longer.

It is important to recognize the legitimacy of this important need: Each person in a learning environment must be able to get some time alone, time away from the maddening crowd, time to think, to process, to turn off, to recharge, to be neither responsive to (nor responsible for) any person other than the self.

As with every other human characteristic, the need for

individual time varies from person to person and, within each person, from time to time. Often, only a few minutes away from the complexity of the classroom environment can do wonders for the ability of teachers and students to handle stretches of diffused time.

Instructors in our T.E.T. classes involve teachers in the brainstorming process to generate creative ways to help themselves and their students satisfy the crucial need for individual time. The possibilities are endless, but here are a few suggestions:

"Quiet corners" in the room

Individual study carrels

Designated "alone places" outside the classroom

Use of closets or large storage areas

By prearrangement, use of libraries, office space, storage rooms, when not in other use

Vision screens, cubicles, and retreats constructed from cardboard cartons

By prior arrangement, released time from the classroom

Use of headphones and tape recorder to shut out all other sounds

Use of a section of the classroom or space outside designated the "elbow room" where a student or teacher can go to be away from physical contact with others

Use of sleep masks (blindfolds) and earplugs

Use of designated "walking paths," trails or walks on the campus

Use of quiet "meditation spots" in grassy areas, under trees, in deserted bleachers, etc.

Cooperative or team-teaching to allow teachers to get away from time to time

Why Optimum Time Is Vital—And How To Create It

Area (3) in Figure 22 represents Optimum Time periods, best described as "interpersonal" or "one-to-one." There is some evidence that human interpersonal transactions occur only in diads (two persons) or, at most, in triads. You can verify this hypothesis by observing people in group situations. Notice that one-way communication from a speaker, entertainer, or lecturer can be tolerated by a large group, but when close communication is needed people either pair off, or interact in threes.

Observe a group of four or more people around a dinner table. Usually they either pair off into twosomes carrying on separate conversations, or they form a triad with one person left out.

Since the need to communicate is strong within each of us, we seek small groups to enable us to meet that need. The most important person with whom students can relate, the most significant person to them in the classroom, is surely their teacher. When students are denied gratification of this need for time with the teacher in the Teaching-Learning area of the rectangle, they tend to concoct a situation so the one-to-one relationship *must* occur. Where is that? In the Teacher-Owned-Problem area, of course. In other words, many student misbehaviors are disguised attempts to get some kind of interaction with the teacher, even if it is a negative or troublesome interaction for the teacher.

Students also have needs for one-to-one relationships with other students. Once again, classroom environments that deny legitimate gratification of this need will cause students to seek ways to meet the need "illegitimately."

Teachers sometimes say, "I don't have time to meet with each student individually." Often this is a code for "I feel overwhelmed." Part of the overwhelming nature of the job of teaching is the tendency to think of students as nearly identical in needs, capacities, abilities, and nature. Obviously, no teacher could meet individually with each of 30 to 150 students each day. And fortunately that is not every student's need. A few students may need frequent meetings, the rest more infrequent. Also, the length of time for any one of these meetings can vary considerably. Most students, if they know they *will* have some one-to-one time with their teacher, are willing to postpone immediate gratification of the need, some-times for fairly long periods. The same is true with students' needs for optimum time with each other. If this were not true, most classes could not operate at all.

Many of the teachers who feel overwhelmed by their job readily admit that too much of their time is spent handling problems with individual students. In other words, rather than having a positive plan to relate occasionally with students, teachers find themselves spending as much or more time *coping with them* or *reacting to them* when they behave unacceptably. The best that can be hoped for at those times is that the relationship will not be severely damaged.

Relationships *can* be built. But to do it, teachers must create one-to-one time with students in the No-Problem area.

A fifth-grade teacher in La Mesa, California, faced with a large class (thirty-eight), many of whom were identified as "hyperkinetic" and on a waiting list for special-class place-ment, decided to use environmental modification to help these students meet their needs for individual and optimum time in the hope that they would then be better able to function in diffused time. He obtained refrigerator cartons and he and the students used these to construct rooms within the room. (The work itself not only provided lessons in mathematics and science, but the "rooms" turned out to be works of art when finished.) The rooms were used as "quiet places" where individual-time needs could be met and as one-to-one-relationship spaces where two or three students could meet to talk. The rules for use of this space were simple and agreed upon by the entire class: (1) no one could do anything that might harm anyone else; (2) no one could enter an occupied space without permission of the occupant; and (3) no smoking. (The last rule was inserted by the students as protection against having the teacher, the only smoker, ruin the room scheme by violating the state law prohibiting smoking in classrooms.)

To make room for the construction area, seldom-used and useless furniture was eliminated. The classroom was also expanded onto a patio and grassy area outside where many of the noisier activities were scheduled. (In Southern California outdoor areas are available almost the year round.)

This teacher also established a place, far removed from the classroom area, where students could go to "let off steam." They were encouraged to run to and from the place and to "yell their lungs out" while they were there—if that was their need.

The teacher also set up a schedule for one-to-one time with each student. This schedule was kept flexible, but generally allowed for a minimum of fifteen minutes with each student in any two-week period. Some students met with the teacher several times during that period; others only once.

Within a few weeks this potential "troublemaking" group functioned with less friction, fewer conflicts, more group caring than other classes containing fewer students with fewer learning problems. Their achievement, as measured by statewide achievement tests, put the group above the district average for fifth-grade students, which no one had expected. Most remarkably, this class was able after a few weeks to begin functioning efficiently in large-group situations.

By no means were all problems with this fifth-grade class eliminated. Youngsters with severe nervous dysfunctions continued to suffer from those problems. Those who were "slow learners" tended to remain behind their faster-learning peers. But the emotional "smog," the subtle game playing, the tensions, anger, and frustrations were dealt with, and for the most part handled in such a way that the climate became one of caring, concern, warmth, understanding. In such a climate a student can afford to be "different."

THE GREAT POTENTIAL OF THE TEACHING-LEARNING AREA

We need to say it again: One of the major frustrations of teachers, if not *the* major frustration, is that they so often feel a deep sense of failure because they cannot practice their profession—teaching. From coast to coast, teachers complain about lack of time to be a teacher, to facilitate learning.

Some blame today's youngsters because they may seem harder to teach, less interested, unmotivated, or lacking in discipline. One teacher admitted, "I feel I have to be an entertainer and compete with television to attract interest—and I don't have NBC's budget."

Today's kids *are* different in one respect: Compared to youngsters growing up in the Twenties when information about the world was relatively difficult to obtain, today's school-age children are walking encyclopedias. Therefore, when schools limit their function to the dissemination of knowledge and information, they find themselves being judged as boring and irrelevant by their more sophisticated audience. Television alone, for better or worse, has made obsolete the concept of the school as a dispenser of information.

Even in up-to-date schools that provide environments for learning skills of inquiry, methods of obtaining information, processes, and procedures, values clarification, problem-solving skills, and the like, teachers still face difficulties finding sufficient time for real teaching and learning.

We provide teachers with the necessary skills for enlarging the No-Problem area because *learning stops when students have problems, and teaching stops when students cause teachers problems.*

In the No-Problem area, too, relationships are improved and made stronger. As we explained in Chapters III and IV, active listening and the other counseling skills inevitably bring about mutual feelings of warmth, closeness, and intimacy in the teacher-student relationship. The same is true when teachers are teaching and students are learning in the No-Problem area of the rectangle.

Teachers feel good about themselves when they are permitted to teach and they feel warm toward students when the youngsters are motivated to learn; and students love to learn and feel good about teachers who can foster learning. On the other hand, teachers get to dislike kids who won't let them teach, and kids dislike teachers and schools when they feel, "I don't learn anything in school."

Within our theoretical concept of teacher effectiveness there exists a strange paradox having to do with the No-Problem area and the warm and close relationships that develop therein: Although the Twelve Roadblocks to communication are ineffective and harmful to students when they own a problem (Student-Owned-Problem area) or when the teacher owns a problem (Teacher-Owned-Problem area), students seldom feel the same roadblocks block their communication or lower their self-esteem while teaching and learning are in progress (No-Problem area).

When the teacher-student relationship is good because both are meeting their needs, it is usually safe (as well as quite appropriate) for teachers to direct, warn, moralize, give facts, advise, criticize, evaluate positively, analyze, question, reassure, and—yes, even use sarcasm, name-calling, or humor.

Study the following interaction between a high-school drama teacher and one of her rather talented students. Evaluate the quality of the relationship. Doesn't it seem warm and close? Notice the student's responses to the teacher's frequent use of roadblocks. They don't appear to be roadblocks, do they?

TEACHER: Sally, take the stage, and hurry. (*Ordering, directing*)

SALLY: Oh-oh. Now I'm next.

TEACHER: This time, Sally, I suggest you act much angrier. (*Advising*)

SALLY: Okay, I'll try.

TEACHER: If you don't seem really angry, no one is going to believe your deep hurt in the last scene. (*Warning*)

SALLY: Shall I pound the table?

TEACHER: That's ridiculous; don't be a ham out there! (*Negative evaluation, Name-calling*)

SALLY: I was only kidding, Teach.

TEACHER: You were only trying to get me all riled up, that's what. (*Analyzing*)

SALLY: *Touché.*

TEACHER: Come on now, if it's worth doing, it's worth doing right. I know you can do it. (*Moralizing, Reassuring*)

SALLY: I needed that.

TEACHER: Do you know your lines? (*Probing question*)

SALLY: Pretty well, I think.

TEACHER: Okay, Sarah Bernhardt, knock 'em dead! (*Humor*)

The lesson for teachers is: As long as the relationship is in the No-Problem area you can send all kinds and varieties of messages. You can be totally spontaneous, uninhibited, free. *You can be yourself,* whether that means being a clown, prodder, advisor, preacher, critic, taskmaster—or a mixture of all of these.

When teachers can teach and students can learn, and when each can be human, the classroom experience will be a joy for both.

VII. CONFLICT IN THE CLASSROOM

CONFLICTS are inevitable in human relationships, and the teacher-student relationship is no exception. Teachers trained in T.E.T. still encounter conflicts—some very minor, some very serious, and all shades in between. It is common for teachers to encounter situations when their I-messages are not effective in modifying unacceptable behaviors, or their efforts in modifying the classroom environment do not work. When these methods fail, they have conflicts on their hands.

When confrontation *and* environmental modification fail, it is usually because (1) the needs that motivate the unacceptable behavior of students are so strong that they cannot or will not change; or (2) the relationship with the teacher is so poor that students couldn't care less about helping to meet their teacher's needs. Consequently, in most classrooms, teachers and students find themselves at some time or other in a "conflict-of-needs" situation. As teachers put it:

I tell my classes how much I hate to spend my time cleaning up the room at the end of the day, but they still leave it a mess, day after day.

The other day I had to leave early to go to a meeting across town. I told my class about it and said that I needed them to get out of the room as soon as the bell rang, but they didn't. I finally had to get really mad and yell at them to make them move.

My fifth-graders are really great at taking playground equipment out, but they're terrible at bringing it back in. I've told them how much it costs to replace it when it's lost and how I get yelled at by the department head, but they don't seem to care. I even think they may be ripping the stuff off themselves.

Alva is a sweet little boy but he drives me crazy. I never know when he's going to do his disappearing act. He's been told that I get frantic when he takes off without telling me. I can't just take off and leave my class of kindergarteners to hunt for him! I don't know what to do.

Most teachers are all too familiar with such conflicts and spend a lot of valuable teaching-learning time trying to resolve them, usually without much lasting success.

We illustrate conflict-of-needs situations in our rectangular window in Figure 23. The bottom part shows how the teaching-learning area (the No-Problem area) is enlarged through modification of the environment and I-message confrontation. Note that an area at the very bottom of the rectangle remains. It represents unchanged unacceptable behavior that produces conflict-of-needs situations.

In this chapter, we deal with the conflict-of-needs area of the rectangle. What is conflict in the first place? What produces it? How do teachers typically try to resolve it? What

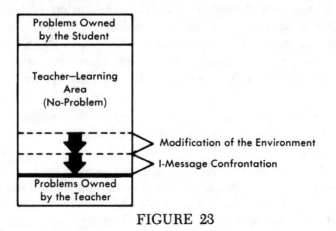

FIGURE 23

happens to both teachers and students as a result of the methods employed by most teachers when they try to eliminate it?

WHAT CONFLICT REALLY IS

Webster's Dictionary defines "conflict" as deriving from the Latin, *conflictus*—to strike together. Synonyms are: "disagreement," "war," "battle," "collision." As a verb, "conflict" means to show antagonism or to contend in battle.

In our human-relationship model, conflict means battles and collisions occurring between two (or more) people when (a) their *behaviors* interfere with one or the other's meeting his needs; or (b) when their *values* do not match. In this chapter we limit ourselves to conflicts that arise when *the behavior of students tangibly and concretely interferes* with teachers' satisfying their needs—when students prevent teachers getting their needs met, enjoying their rights, doing their thing. (In Chapter IX, we will deal with values collisions.)

Like rain and taxes, conflicts between the needs of teachers and the needs of students are inevitable. Not only are they bound to happen; they can happen rather frequently. This fact is in itself a problem to teachers who have been taught that there should be no conflict between "good" teachers and "good" students. It is difficult for these teachers to understand that conflicts are a part of all human interactions; they are neither "good" nor "bad."

There is even evidence that the frequency of conflicts in a relationship is unrelated to the health or satisfaction of that relationship. What *is* important is (a) the number of *unresolved conflicts*, and (b) the *methods used to try to resolve conflicts*.

WHAT REALLY PRODUCES CONFLICT?

Conflicts are not solely owned by the teacher *or* the students. Conflicts involve the needs of *both parties*; so we say: *Both own the problem*.

Let's look at the situation of the teacher who had to take time to clean up the room at the end of the day because the students left it a mess. What is the conflict? The teacher has a legitimate need to get out of the room without spending a lot of time cleaning up. The students are messing up the room and failing to clean up after themselves. The needs of both are involved.

Whether a conflict is a minor disagreement or a major battle, ruffled feathers or a knock-down-drag-out fight, the cause is always the same: One or both parties are saying, "What you're doing (or not doing) is making it difficult for me to live my life to meet my needs."

When needs are strong in a conflict-of-needs situation, I-messages, as we have said, may have little influence. A student who has a strong need to make a date with his "dream girl" continues his conversation with her in the hall instead of coming into the classroom on time. If the teacher sends an I-message, that student's attitude might be "Yes, I understand you're frustrated, but even though I don't want you to be frustrated, right now it's more important for me to talk to Alice."

HOW TEACHERS TYPICALLY RESOLVE CONFLICTS

Almost without exception, teachers think of resolving conflicts in terms of *winning* and *losing*. The win-lose orientation shows up in the way they talk about kids:

"I'll be damned if I'll let kids run all over me!"

"The trouble with today's schools is that the students are in the driver's seat."

"They're winning all the battles!"

"How can we teachers win? The administration is gutless and won't back us up, so we've had to give in over and over."

"Me? Why, I win a few and lose a few. I just always try to win the biggies."

"Kids today don't respect the authority of the teacher like they used to."

The following story is heard so often that it must represent a nationwide pedagogical philosophy about how teachers can assure themselves a top-dog position.

The first thing the principal did my first day on the job as a teacher was to herd all of us beginners together and give us his standard lecture, "How To Run the Classroom." It was simple. He said all we had to do was to start off with a tough, no-nonsense approach for the first few weeks. Then, when the students knew who was boss, we could ease up a bit.

For some teachers this philosophy is very difficult to live with because they have negative feelings about conflict in the classroom, much like those expressed by an elementary-school teacher in a T.E.T. class:

I guess I'm what you'd call a permissive teacher. I really hate all the yelling and screaming that other teachers do to keep the kids in line, so I just look the other way and try to pretend that things don't bother me.

This win-lose orientation seems to be at the core of the knotty issue of discipline in schools. Teachers feel that they have only two approaches to choose from: They can be strict or lenient, tough or soft, authoritarian or permissive. They see the teacher-student relationship as a power struggle, a contest, a fight. So it is not surprising that students, in turn, see their teachers as natural enemies—dictators to be resisted by whatever means they can muster, or softies they take advantage of.

When conflicts arise, as they always do, most teachers try to resolve them so that they win, or at least don't lose. This obviously means that students end up losing, or at least not winning. Other teachers, like the one who hated all the screaming and yelling, feel they must give in to students. This permissive attitude is also prevalent among advocates of the theory that "frustrating the natural drives of children is bad for them" and that it is a part of the teacher's job to put up with unacceptable behavior in order to reduce possible "psychic damage" (whatever that is) to the children.

Seldom is anything heard about psychic damage to teachers, even though this is often the outcome of permissiveness.

THE TWO WIN–LOSE APPROACHES: METHOD I AND METHOD II

The terms "authoritarian" and "permissive" have been so often used and misused in education that they have become emotionally loaded, bound to stir up heated arguments. To avoid confusion and heat in T.E.T. classes, we call the two contrasting win-lose methods Method I and Method II. In Method I, the teacher wins and the student loses the conflict. In Method II, the teacher loses and the student wins.

To illustrate, high-school teachers in most schools face the problem of tardy students, as in this situation:

Mr. Jones likes to start each of his science classes with a brief oral outline of the day's activities. Sylvia is frequently late to class. This requires him to repeat his earlier instructions or answer a lot of her questions about what is going on.

Here is how the Method I approach might go:

MR. JONES: When you're late to my class you miss the instructions I give at the beginning and I have to take my time to tell you personally what to do. I'm tired of doing that.

SYLVIA: Well, I'm on the Yearbook staff and we've really been busy lately trying to meet the deadlines set up by the printer. That's why I'm late.

MR. JONES: I know you're one of the editors and that it's a big job, but this science class is important, too. You can't graduate without completing it.

SYLVIA: I'm passing all the tests, aren't I? I don't see why I have to rush over here just so you won't have to tell me what to do when I get here. What's so hard about that?

MR. JONES: I didn't mind it for a while, but I'm tired of treating you like a prima donna because you've got a job in another department. From now on you get here on time or don't come at all!

SYLVIA: But—

MR. JONES: No buts! If you want to pass this course get here on time like everyone else! Now take your seat.

SYLVIA: (*Angrily*) All right! I'll try.

In this situation, as so often happens with Method I, the teacher had his own preconceived "winning" solution to the conflict: Sylvia was to get to the class on time. First he attempted to persuade her to accept it, but when she resisted he rolled out his big guns: She'd either get to class on time or risk failing a required course. In the face of this display of power Sylvia resentfully gave in. In Figure 24, Method I looks like this:

METHOD I

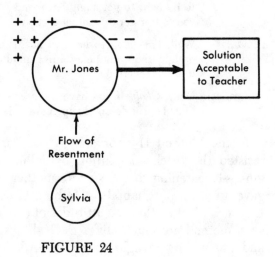

FIGURE 24

Here is how Method II might go in the same situation:

MR. JONES: When you're late to my class you miss the instructions I give at the beginning and I have to take my time to explain the assignment again every day. I'm tired of doing that.

SYLVIA: Well, I'm on the Yearbook staff and we've been really busy lately trying to meet the deadlines the printer set. That's why I'm late.

MR. JONES: I know you're an editor and that it's a big job, but this science class is important too. You can't graduate without completing it.

SYLVIA: I don't have to take your section. I can switch to Mrs. Magnuson's section.

MR. JONES: Her class is full. This is the small section. I don't think you can get into her class.

SYLVIA: Oh, she'll take me and she won't hassle me about being a few minutes late just because I'm working on something important. If you want to hassle people, why don't you yell at those guys that stand around in the bathroom smoking all the time?

MR. JONES: Look, Sylvia, I don't want to hassle anyone. I'm not trying to be hard to get along with, and I certainly don't want you to transfer to another section.

SYLVIA: Well, I'm going to have to do something if you get all uptight about my being a few minutes late—and I'm not even late every day.

MR. JONES: Okay, *Okay!* If you have to be late, you have to be late. I just hope it doesn't happen every day.

In the Method II approach to this conflict, the student resisted the teacher's solution by rolling out her own big guns—threatening to transfer to another section. Mr. Jones gave in, but not happily. Method II is diagrammed in Figure 25. Notice that the attitudes of teacher and student in each method are much alike: Each thinks, "I want *my* way and I'm willing to fight to get it!" Added to that fighting

METHOD II

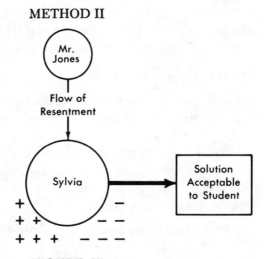

FIGURE 25

posture is another attitude: "If you don't like it, that's tough!" The postures for Methods I and II alike are competitiveness, stubbornness, discourtesy, inconsiderateness, disrespect for the needs of the other person. And each method usually makes the loser go away feeling resentful and angry.

T.E.T. instructors, who have worked with thousands of teachers in every kind of school, find that an amazingly high proportion of teachers either stay locked into one of these two win-lose methods or vacillate back and forth between the two, depending on the mood of the moment. Few teachers are aware of any alternative to the two win-lose conflict-resolution methods.

Even more distressing, few teachers are even aware that they are in fact employing "a method." Most teachers are "playing it by ear," or "flying blind." Usually they handle conflicts like their former teachers or their own parents.

It is also rare for a teacher to recognize any direct connection between his conflict-resolution methods and the behavior of his students. This is why our in-depth examination of the limitations and effects of Methods I and II comes as such a revelation to most teachers in T.E.T. classes. It also supplies new information to evaluate what they are doing in the classroom—to themselves and to their students.

What Is Known About Method I

Much good research exists on the effects of resolving conflicts by the authoritarian method—in families, in business and industry, and in many other organizations. While details of these studies are not of sufficient interest to most teachers, a list of the principal findings has helped many teachers in T.E.T. classes to understand exactly what happens when they use Method I:

1. It can be quick and efficient in situations requiring emergency action. ("Put down that sharp knife this instant!")

2. It may be the only method of choice when a large number of people are involved, making it extremely difficult to talk things over. ("The dance is over, doors must be locked in fifteen minutes, so everyone out quickly.")

3. It produces resentment and often strong hostility in the loser toward the winner. Nobody enjoys being told what to do and having his needs frustrated.

4. It produces little motivation in the loser to carry out the solution. Often the loser only goes through the motions of implementing the solution.

5. It often requires heavy enforcement on the part of the winner ("I spend over half of my time in the classroom being a policeman.") When the enforcer is not present, the losers don't comply.

6. It inhibits the growth of self-responsibility and self-direction, fosters dependence and the need to be told what to do.

7. It fosters compliance and submission mainly out of fear, and inhibits development of cooperation and consideration for the needs of others. Cooperation is never fostered by *making* a student do something.

8. It inhibits creativity, exploration, and innovation. Such qualities seldom flourish in a climate of fear and repression.

9. It fosters low producivity, low morale, low job satisfaction, and a high rate of turnover (dropouts).

10. It inhibits development of self-discipline and self-control. No chance exists to develop self-control when teachers control by power.

11. It is less likely to produce a unique or creative solution—what psychologists call "the elegant solution."

12. It often makes the winner feel guilty. ("This hurts me worse than it hurts you," or, "I'm only doing it for your own good.")

13. It usually requires the winner to resort to power and authority to get compliance. (We examine this significant characteristic of Method I in greater detail later in this chapter.)

What Is Known About Method II

Here are the findings of studies on the characteristics and effects of Method II—the permissive "Okay-you-win, I-give-up" method of resolving conflicts:

1. It can be quick—you just ignore the behavior, don't cause waves, get rid of the conflict by giving in.

2. It invariably produces resentment and hostility in the loser toward the winner. Teachers who give in frequently develop dislike and even hatred for students—and eventually for teaching.

3. It fosters in the winners (i.e., students) selfishness, lack of co-operation, lack of consideration for others. Students become unmanageable, uncontrolled, undisciplined, demanding. A class can become chaotic.

4. It tends to foster more student creativity and spontaneity than Method I. But the teacher pays a terrible price.

5. It does not foster high productivity and high morale. Youngsters usually hate classes of undisciplined and unmanageable students. It is a waste of their time because little work gets done.

6. It also makes the winners (again, in this case, the students) feel guilty about the teacher not getting his needs met.

7. It makes students lose respect for the teacher. They see the teacher as weak, incompetent—a "doormat," an "easy mark."

8. It usually requires the winner (the student) to resort to using his power and authority.

When Vacillation Is the Name of the Game

Teachers seldom use Method I or Method II exclusively; that is, they are rarely completely authoritarian or permissive. But when they use Method I some of the time, and Method II at other times, this vacillation is terribly confusing for students. It makes youngsters live in a rubber world where the limits are unknown. One day it's a crime to whisper to your neighbor; the next day the teacher just smiles. Obviously, this invites constant testing. When students have to deal with teachers who are now tough, now lenient, they must always be on guard. They also have to spend inordinate amounts of time pushing to get the answer to a crucial question: What are today's limits?

Teachers who have been influenced by advocates of permissiveness often allow students to do pretty much what they want until conditions become *so* chaotic, behaviors *so* unacceptable, that the teacher has to move in suddenly with a show of power to restore some semblance of order. This inconsistency is highly confusing to students and teacher.

In the end, the teacher may be even worse off than the students (who probably figured they had it coming). Permissive teachers tend to feel guilty about such blowups, especially if the event that triggered the eruption was minor, the straw that broke the camel's back. The guilt is likely to push the teacher back into the permissive, "anything goes" state, and the cycle begins all over again.

Students are further confused by the differences they find between teachers. Although they are remarkably sharp at "psyching out" teachers, it is difficult to adjust from a Method II, anything-goes class to another one run by a stern disciplinarian who demands instant obedience. This disparity is also why countless hours of valuable staff-meeting time have been wasted in endless debates about "uniform" discipline. The cry goes up, "We've all got to be alike [the spokesman always means like me] to end this confusion," and so the battle goes on—and on, and on.

How Methods I and II Rely on Power

We cannot stress enough that Method I and Method II are essentially *power methods* for resolving conflict. Using Method I, the *teacher* needs his power to win at the expense of the student losing. In Method II, the *student* uses whatever power he has to get his way at the expense of the teacher losing.

When teacher and student encounter a conflict, both invariably view it as a locking of horns, a battle to be won, a *power struggle.*

But what is this power? Where does it come from? Can you see it or feel it? Certainly it is not just physical strength, although it may be at times. Is it the words that are communicated? Or something more?

Power is intimately associated in people's minds with authority. If a teacher has authority over students, does she have power? Do you have to have authority to have power? Or vice versa? These are critical questions, and the terms "power" and "authority" are so frequently used in discussions of conflict in schools that we need to examine these concepts in depth.

AUTHORITY IN THE CLASSROOM

Ask a hundred teachers, "Do you need to use your authority to control students in your classroom?" Probably ninety-nine will answer strongly in the affirmative. Most will wonder why you are even asking the question when the answer is so obvious. "Of course, teachers need authority," they will reply. "How else can you have discipline, order, and quiet?"

The idea that teachers must use their authority is so deeply entrenched in our schools—in society for that matter—that anyone who challenges the idea is considered naïve, stupid, or anti-American. The idea is deeply rooted in the way parents raise children in our society. Few parents ever question the necessity for using authority to direct, control, discipline, and train children. It is not surprising, then, that parents have made sure to pass their authority on to the teachers of their children—even in the form of specific legislation granting teachers the right to act *in loco parentis* (in place of the parent). Such legislation formalizes the belief of parents that anyone who supervises their children needs authority, just as they need it. So society has granted teachers the authority of parents.

With parents and teachers holding such strong convictions about the need (and justification for) using authority with youngsters, it is a source of amazement to discover, as we have in thousands of P.E.T. courses and T.E.T. courses, that few parents and few teachers have any real understanding of this "thing" they feel they need so badly: authority. Most parents and teachers cannot even define the term accurately. Nor do they know what it does to youngsters or how it interferes with teaching and learning in the classroom. Finally, most parents and teachers have no conception of how authority erodes or destroys human relationships.

The first step necessary to understand authority is to recognize that in English the term is used to represent two entirely different ideas. Since one kind of authority enhances a teacher's ability to teach and the other decreases it, debates about the necessity for "authority" are futile.

Authority Type 1

One kind of authority is based on expertise, knowledge, and experience. ("He is an authority in his field," or "He speaks with authority.") To young children all adults appear to have this kind of authority. They seem to be wise, have superior judgment, great insight, unlimited information, and an eerie ability to predict the future. This kind of authority may be thought of as either *assigned* or *earned*, based on real or imagined wisdom and expertise which one person judges another to possess.

As a child grows up he gradually discovers that adult idols have feet of clay, that omnipotent adults are really quite fallible, do not possess unlimited wisdom, and frequently have faulty judgment. Many adults clearly recall the disillusionment they felt when they first discovered that their parents were capable of being wrong, really *wrong*—uninformed, inaccurate, or unable to control events in their own lives. Usually, the more fully the parents encouraged their children to assign unwarranted authority to them, the greater the disillusionment later on.

Although they don't use these terms, many teachers like to play a game with students that might be called "Let's Pretend I have Superhuman Powers." They encourage children to assign authority to teachers far beyond their real areas of expertise, to accept teachers' opinions as facts, and to allow themselves to be governed by this assumed adult wisdom. Students become very disillusioned with these teachers when they discover that wisdom is not always a function of age and that expertise in one area does not imply equal expertise in others.

It is important for teachers to understand how much influence they have with their students as a result of assigned or earned authority and how careful they must be not to extend this authority beyond the limits of actual expertness. Teachers *do* have expertise based on their training and backgrounds. Such authority granted them by students is legitimate, and the use of this authority to influence students is an obvious and valid part of the teaching function.

Unfortunately, younger children assign far too much of this kind of authority to teachers. They overestimate the authority. It is revealing to ask children in an elementary school to draw themselves and their teacher. Generally, teachers come out as huge monsters occupying most of the page, and the child's self is a tiny creature completely over-shadowed by the powerful adult. This "psychological size" difference gives added weight and import to the words and deeds of teachers.

In the normal course of events, the psychological size difference between teachers and students gradually decreases as students grow older, bigger, more mature, more knowl-edgeable. The unearned (or unrealistically assigned) author-ity decreases. Earned authority—the kind based on a teacher's real expertise—may not diminish. It might even increase.

Normally, the psychological size difference between stu-dents and teachers gradually decreases until parity or near parity is achieved in adulthood. This is not necessarily true of realistically assigned authority, because such authority is assigned by students as a result of recognition of real ex-pertise possessed by the teacher. In other words: *Real* ex-pertise does not diminish with time. And authority based on expertise almost never causes trouble in the classroom.

Authority Type 2

A totally different kind of authority derives from teachers' power to reward or punish students. This is *power-based authority*, resulting from (1) the teachers' possessing the power to dispense certain things students need or want (re-wards) and (2) the teachers' power to inflict discomfort or pain.

Teachers' rewarding power comes from students' de-pendence. When they first arrive at school as kindergarteners or "preschoolers," students have already mastered some ways of providing for themselves. But they must still depend on parents, teachers, and other adults for gratification of the majority of their needs; they are still very dependent on adults, so adults are very powerful.

Teachers, particularly of young students, possess the means

for meeting many of their students' needs. As students grow older and become more independent of their teachers, this power lessens, yet until students leave school, teachers retain many of the essential means for gratifying students' needs. This gives teachers real power, and it is this kind of power that teachers employ when they "use their authority." When teachers say, "I don't have enough authority in the classroom," they mean they need more power to reward and punish. When teachers complain, "Kids these days have no respect for authority," they mean that the rewards and punishments are too few or too ineffective.

And when we talk about an "authoritarian teacher," we mean one who relies heavily on the power of reward and punishment to control students in the classroom.

SERIOUS LIMITATIONS OF POWER IN THE CLASSROOM

No doubt power (authority) works as a method of controlling students—it has been used for literally centuries. Yet few teachers comprehend the very serious limitations of teacher power, or its dangers.

Teachers Inevitably Run Out of Power

A teacher has power in the classroom only as long as the students are in a condition of wanting, needing, deprivation, helplessness, dependency. Very young children, of course, are very dependent, and therefore will respond to many rewards. As youngsters grow older and less dependent on the teacher for what they need, the teacher inevitably *loses the power to reward*. This is why teachers in junior and senior high school often complain that rewards just don't work with older kids like they do with younger ones.

Teachers also gradually lose their power of punishment as children get older. With younger students most teachers rely heavily on punishment. They not only punish by withholding things students need but they can behave in ways that cause discomfort or pain to their students, either physically or psychologically. Slaps, spankings, tongue-lashings, extra work, failing grades, detention periods, ridiculing, shaming, embarrassing remarks, exclusion from class or school, standing students in the corner, forced exercises, reports to parents, and hundreds of other ploys have been used by teachers to create enough discomfort so students hopefully will comply with teacher demands—out of *fear*.

Punishing works pretty well (at least it gets some compliance) when teachers can make their physical and psychological size felt sufficiently so that students are afraid to stand up against them. But youngsters gradually lose their fear of teachers' ability to hurt them, and teacher power is correspondingly reduced. No fear, no compliance.

Paradoxically, most teachers genuinely reject dependence and fear as desired traits in the students in their classes. Here is their dilemma. Teachers say they want unafraid, independent, self-reliant, self-disciplined students, but when they have students with those qualities they find that power will not work well with such students. A junior high school math teacher told her principal:

I need help with George. I can't get him to do anything I want him to do. He does only what *he* wants to do. I told him I was going to give him a failing grade if he didn't start minding, but he doesn't care. He told me to go ahead, he'd had Fs before. Then I said I'd have to suspend him from class, and he shrugged his shoulders and smiled. I think he wants me to throw him out. What on earth am I going to do?

Obviously, George is not very much afraid of his teacher. He has reached a point where he is no longer dependent upon her—and now he is driving her up the wall!

The gradual loss of teacher power is illustrated in Figure 26; in which rewards are symbolized by pluses and punishments by minuses.

With first-graders, a teacher has countless ways to reward

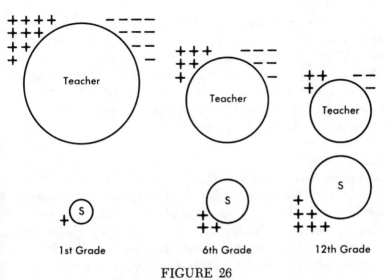

FIGURE 26

and punish, and the children can acquire only very few rewards from their own independent efforts. A twelfth-grader is able to acquire most of his rewards (meet most of his needs) from his own activities (sports, friends, girls [or boys], car, travel, etc.). This is why his teacher has very few effective rewards (grades, maybe) and almost no means for punishing (suspension from school, perhaps).

No wonder teachers of adolescents feel so impotent. They have so few effective rewards or punishments left. Older students simply will not be controlled by teachers' efforts to engineer their behavior with rewards and punishments. This is when teachers begin to blame students for their "rebellion," "lack of respect for authority," "resistance to adult authority," etc. We hear teachers say, "Must be something wrong with this generation of adolescents."

The point is, older students are difficult for teachers primarily because they have become more independent (able to meet their own needs). And since most teachers keep on trying to control with power, adolescents naturally react with resistant, independent, rebellious, and retaliative behavior.

The past ten years have brought a flood of books and articles whose authors examine and diagnose such phenomena as the generation gap, the rebelliousness of youth, the strain of growing up in America. Most of these theories seem to focus incorrectly on such factors as physical change, emerging sexuality, new social demands, the struggle to become an adult, etc. They create the impression that stress and strain and rebellion in the adolescent period are natural and normal.

We are now convinced that the rebelliousness of young people, the *Sturm und Drang* of adolescence, the difficulties of working with young people, and the so-called generation gap are not inevitable at all. Teacher-student relationships at the upper-elementary and secondary levels are much more strained and stressful because teachers relied so heavily upon power (backed up by rewards and punishment) when the children were younger. Then, when students are older, they begin to react to these techniques to an ever-increasing degree with anger, hostility, rebellion, resistance, and retaliation.

Teachers we have trained in T.E.T. see it happen all the time: Students do not naturally have to rebel against adults in the schools. But they will rebel against the adults' use of teacher power. Drop the use of teacher power, and much of the student rebellion in schools disappears.

Power Is Destructive to Students

The most damning argument against using Method I to resolve conflicts is that it has such destructive effects on students. Method I depends on power disguised as "authority," and power is terribly destructive in human relationships. To quote the poet Shelley, "Power, like a desolating pestilence, pollutes whate'er it touches."

The corruption and pollution of power, which poets and good statesmen have known for centuries, are nowhere more clearly observable than in the institution we call the school.

Schools are one of the last strongholds where power is sanctioned in human relationships.

Many people today are deceived into believing that only the present generation of students is rebelling and retaliating against the raw power of teachers and administrators in schools ("Something must be wrong with this generation"). They long for the old days when (so they think) students accepted authority and responded to it constructively.

This belief is dramatically refuted in each T.E.T. class. Teachers are asked in class to think back to when *they* were students and were at the receiving end of the power of their own teachers and administrators. "What did you experience?" "How did you feel?" "How did you react?" "How did you cope with efforts to reward and punish you for the purpose of making you behave in certain ways prescribed by adults in schools?"

Their memories are vivid. Occasionally, teachers recall an incident bringing such pain that in the T.E.T. class they again experience the same anger, even tears, provoked by an event fifteen or twenty years past.

As the teachers relate their feelings and coping mechanisms, the T.E.T. instructor writes them on the chalkboard— feelings on one side and corresponding coping mechanisms on the other. With very little variation, the lists appear as illustrated in Table 2.

After the class members have developed their two lists, they invariably express a common reaction: "Why, all of these feelings and coping mechanisms are so negative and 'bad'—there must be some positive or 'good' effects of power and authority." Even though they themselves have furnished the entries, a frequent reaction is "You must have tricked us in some way to get all negative effects." When the instructor then invites positive or "good" reactions to add onto the lists, few are ever submitted, though sometimes a class member will add one of these:

"I learned to obey—to do what they told me to do."

Feelings	Coping Mechanisms
Resentment, anger, hostility	Rebelling, resisting, defying
Frustration	Retaliating (striking back,
Hatred	fighting back)
Embarrassment	Lying, sneaking, hiding feelings
Unworthiness	Blaming others, tattling
Fear, anxiety, uneasiness	Cheating, plagiarizing
Unhappiness, sadness,	Bossing, bullying, pushing
depression	others around
Bitterness, vindictiveness	Needing to win, hating to lose
Impotence, immobility	Organizing, forming alliances
Stubbornness	Submitting, complying (buckling
Competitiveness	under, becoming the "good
Humiliation, apathy	dog" or teacher's pet)
	Apple polishing ("buttering up")
	Conforming, taking no risks,
	trying nothing new, needing
	prior assurance of success
	Withdrawing (dropping out,
	fantasizing, regressing,
	running away)

TABLE 2

"I worked harder to get top grades."

"I determined to show them I could do good work."

One teacher offered this: "Well, sometimes it was a comfort not to have to wonder where I stood in the pecking order. I knew I was the low man on the totem pole!"

If you, the reader, try to remember your own feelings and coping mechanisms, you will probably discover that your reactions to authority are also on the above lists. The purpose of this exercise obviously is to help teachers accept the idea that, if they as students reacted in these ways to power and authority, their own students will inevitably react similarly.

In the next pages we examine in more detail each coping mechanism that students employ in school, because we are convinced: When teachers fully comprehend the dynamics of these student coping mechanisms they will be more strongly deterred from using authority and power and, instead, learn the alternate method for resolving conflicts in the classroom.

THE COPING MECHANISMS STUDENTS USE

Rebelling, Resisting, Defying

These reactions to authority and power are almost universal. When people's freedoms are threatened, they resist and defy—or, as in rebellion, do exactly the opposite of what they are being pushed to do.

What happens when students are ordered to leave the pencil sharpener and get back to their seats immediately? You can watch them stall, poke, or defy the teacher by continuing to sharpen the pencil all the way down to a stub.

How many of you have demanded that a student go back out of the room and come in a second time, but more quietly —only to have him stomp into the room as noisily as before, with a smirk on his face?

A high-school youngster in one of his counseling sessions shared this with his counselor:

I won't even try to get good grades in school, 'cause my parents have pushed me so hard to be a good student. If I got good grades it'd make them feel pleased—like they were right or like they won. I'm not going to let them feel that way. So I don't study.

Students, young and old, are ingenious at finding ways to defy and resist their teachers' efforts to modify their behavior by power. A junior-high-school student related this story:

I have this Home Ec. teacher who hassles me about my short skirts. Just before I go into her class, I tuck up the waist of my skirt so it's even shorter. It blows her mind. When I leave I put it down to its normal length. She's not going to tell *me* how to wear my skirts.

Retaliating

It is a classic human response to retaliate against someone on whom you depend for gratification of basic needs, but, amazingly, people continue to be surprised by this behavior. The most cursory study of history reveals the age-old hostility that people have harbored for those in power, and their everreadiness to run terrible risks to get back at the "ins" in some hostile way. Teachers who dominate their students through "authority" run a high risk of this kind of aggression, retaliation, and revenge.

Often the most violent retaliation is directed against benevolent, paternalistic teachers who cover up their uses of power by saying, "I'm only doing what's best for you," or "Some day you'll thank me." Not only do these paternalistic teachers create feelings of anger and frustration that result from any situation where students lose; additionally, students are put in a "double-bind" because they feel guilty about biting the "benevolent" hand that feeds them. Bateson's research (on the pattern of behaviors sometimes labeled "schizophrenia") indicates that double-binds produce inner tensions to which some people respond by going "crazy." An out-and-out despot is probably easier to cope with than a benevolent one. At least the malevolent despot can be hated with impunity.

Indeed, fighting back may be one of the healthiest ways for a student to respond to a teacher's use of power. While we are certainly not advocating an atmosphere of antagonism and hostility as a model for classrooms, it is a fact that a student's own emotional health may be better served if he is a "fighter" and does not passively submit or withdraw.

Lying, Sneaking, Hiding Feelings

Lying is a very common way for students to cope with the power of teachers. They soon learn that it is unsafe to tell the truth to those who use power. The name of the game becomes "Tell Them Anything to Avoid Punishment" or "Make

Them *Prove* I'm Wrong." Many students learn never to say *anything* except under direct questioning, and then to tell only whatever might cause the teacher to shift responsibility and punishment elsewhere.

Students also cope with power-wielding teachers by playing the game of "Don't Get Caught." In this game the only crime is being *caught* doing something wrong. Power-oriented teachers and schools systematically teach students this form of amorality, a condition affecting our society even at the highest levels of government.

The game is simple. The teacher has the power, makes the rules, and must enforce them. The student's job: Break as many of the rules as possible, but in such a clever way that the teacher can't catch me. If caught, lie.

A school principal described this encounter with a player of the Don't Get Caught game:

A passing motorist came storming into my office one day, furious because one of the students in the school had thrown a rock, hit his car, and broken a side window. The playground supervisor, with the aid of a number of informants, quickly apprehended the boy who had thrown the rock. Upon questioning, the boy staunchly maintained that although he had thrown some rocks he could not have broken the window since none of the rocks he threw went into the street. However, he got a lecture from the irate car owner on the issue of personal responsibility and the evils of rock throwing. After he had said his piece, the motorist asked, "Well, son, have you learned a lesson from this?" The boy agreed that he had: "Yes, sir. Next time I throw rocks I'll hide behind the bushes where nobody can see me."

Blaming Others, Tattling

A natural way of coping with a teacher who uses punishment is to try to shift the blame onto other students. The formula is simple: "If I can make other students look bad, I may look better (or no worse) by comparison." Familiar to all teachers are such messages as these:

"He hit me first."

"She started it."
"Johnny pushed me."
"Teacher, those kids are throwing paint."

Teachers who try to engineer good behavior by frequent use of rewards also invite students to compete against each other or tattle to capture the rewards for themselves:

"I cleaned up my place faster than Sue."
"Frank and Karl are always writing notes."

It is only natural that each student wants to get the most rewards and have others get all of the punishment.

Cheating, Copying, Plagiarizing

The ubiquitous grading system of schools, an important source of teachers' power, fosters cheating, copying, and plagiarizing. A very large proportion of students admit to these forms of deceit. Even with the high risk of being caught, some students choose to cheat rather than suffer the punishment or disgrace of a poor grade or a rebuke from their teacher.

As most teachers know, even very bright children will cheat or copy; they are motivated by a strong need for the rewards that come with high grades.

Bossing, Bullying, Pushing Others Around

Teachers whose power takes the form of bossing and bullying students are providing youngsters with a model that some are bound to copy in their own relationships.

A four-panel illustration appeared on the cover of *The Saturday Evening Post* some years ago portraying the common chain reaction to bossing and bullying. The first panel depicted an angry boss behind his desk chewing out an employee, finger pointed menacingly in the abashed face of the helpless worker. The second panel showed the worker coming home and berating his frazzled wife. The third panel showed the wife yelling at her small son. In the final picture the child was giving what-for to the family dog.

This phenomenon occurs in power-oriented schools everywhere. Take a look at your school's playground or halls. Is there a lot of strife, bossing, bullying? If so, Method I (power) is undoubtedly the way teachers settle conflicts with students, and the method naturally carries over onto the playground.

Needing to Win, Hating to Lose

In a school climate full of rewards and punishments, youngsters early learn the value of winning and looking good. And they learn strong "avoidance responses" to losing and looking bad.

Teachers daily manipulate youngsters through commendations, grades recorded in teachers' notebooks, special privileges, gold stars, smiles, pats on the head. No wonder generations of "brownie point" children are so oriented toward winning, coming out on top, surpassing their peers. The trouble is that not every child can win; only a few come out on top.

What happens to youngsters with limited abilities, intellectually or physically? Or the just "average"? In most schools such children are forever reminded, directly or indirectly, that they are inadequate, incompetent, below average, underachievers, or losers. They are destined to go through life experiencing the pain of frequent failure and the frustration of watching enviously as others get the rewards. Such youngsters acquire low esteem, and build up attitudes of hopelessness and defeatism. Or they quit trying.

A classroom climate heavy with rewards is even more harmful to students who cannot earn them than to those who can.

Organizing, Forming Alliances

Students sometimes develop another coping mechanism to deal with the authority and power of teachers: They *organize*, mostly informally, but recently sometimes formally.

Students learn that "in unity there is strength," much as workers in business and industry have organized to cope with the power of management.

While most efforts of students to act in concert against teachers are ineffective, and self-destructive in the end, in recent years students have been more successfully organizing their resistance against school (and other adult) authorities by student demonstrations, petitions, student newspapers, and student demands for more voice in the governing structure of colleges, high schools, and even some junior high schools.

While it is regrettable that young people feel compelled to form alliances to combat the power of adults, thereby polarizing youth and schools into two warring groups, this coping mechanism appears to be one of the least destructive (to themselves and others) of all the ways young people devise to react to adult power and authority.

Submitting, Complying, Buckling Under

Most teachers who use Method I hope that students will accept their decisions and restrictions and not make a fuss. Such submission seldom occurs except when punishment is so severe that the student's overriding feeling is fear. While parents can (and do) use severe enough punishment over a long enough period of time to produce cowed, fearful, anxious, submissive children, teachers in most schools today lack the sanction and time to use severe punishments. In most states, teachers can be sued for applying the punishment that produces abject submission. The expectation that students will accept Method I decisions without a fuss is therefore grossly unrealistic.

Rather than surrender, students become "passive-aggressive": they overtly give in, but covertly resist. Among these ploys are the games students invent to curry favor with powerful teachers. Playing dumb, telling the teacher what he wants to hear, smiling, nodding, agreeing, complimenting, pretending admiration—all these are ways of coping that students learn, hoping the teacher will go easy or grant them privileges and rewards. Students become quite skillful at playing these games and clearly understand the underlying hypocrisy, even if teachers do not.

Even in the absence of severe punishment, some students, for reasons not well understood, choose to cope with power by obedience and submission. Teacher power is most likely to produce compliance in very young children in the lower grades, probably because rebelling or retaliating seems too risky to the youngsters. As these students approach adolescence submission can change very abruptly to fighting and rebelling coping mechanisms. These can be extremely serious, as in cases in the news where "good" kids suddenly go berserk and murder their parents or other adults.

Students who continue to be submissive and compliant are the ones who, as adults, retain a deep fear of people in authority positions. They really remain children throughout their lives, passively submitting to authority, denying their own needs, fearing to be themselves or to stand up for their rights, frightened of conflict. Such adults fill the offices of psychologists and psychiatrists.

Apple Polishing

One obvious coping mechanism in dealing with authority is to try to "get on the good side" of the person having the power to reward or punish. Students learn early that teachers do not mete out rewards or punishments equitably and consistently. Teachers can be "won over"; they can have favorites; they respond to apple polishing; they bestow rewards on the "teacher's pet."

Unfortunately for the apple polisher, this coping behavior is strongly resented by peers. Other children ridicule and reject the teacher's pet because they suspect his motives and/or envy his favored position in the class.

Conforming, Taking No Risks, Trying Nothing New

Teacher power and authority foster conformity rather than creativity, much as an authoritarian work climate in organizations stifles innovation.

Even the most able students in a Method I classroom quickly learn to conform, to stifle creative urges. Creativity flowers in a climate in which students feel free to experiment, a climate that values differences, not conformity to a single set of standards. Gifted students learn how to play the game, win the brownie points, fit in, keep their noses clean, keep the teacher happy. They withdraw behind a curtain of security and sameness. One senior-high-school student expressed it like this: "When I go to school I turn gray, do what they want, fill out their papers, and try not to be noticed. When school's out, then I turn on."

The coping formula adopted by a depressingly large number of students is simple: "In order to get rewards or avoid punishment I will keep my nose clean in class, conform to what's considered proper and do no more than I need to in order to get by. And I'll never do anything out of the ordinary."

Withdrawing, Dropping Out, Fantasizing, Regressing

If it becomes too difficult to tolerate the authority of teachers and administrators, students may withdraw or escape from the situation, psychologically or physically— a very natural protective device. Any person placed in an untenable or painful situation tends to try to escape, run away, remove himself from the cause of his pain.

The school situations that particularly produce withdrawal are those where rewards are great and punishment severe; where the dispensing of rewards and punishment is inconsistent; where tasks are so difficult that chances of reward are slim (and punishment therefore great); and where competition between students is fiercest.

Pity the slow learner, the immature child, the shy and

introverted student in a classroom where rewards and punishment are used as motivating influences, let alone to resolve conflicts. Since the less able students (or those with poorer self-concepts) are not as good at playing games to beat the system they tend to adopt more drastic withdrawal mechanisms. These range from only occasional to almost constant withdrawal from reality, and include:

Daydreaming, fantasizing

Turning off, passivity, apathy

Regressing to infantile behavior

Solitary habits, unwillingness to form peer relationships

School phobias

Running away from home, school

Psychosomatic illness (fevers, migraines, upset stomachs)

Truancy

Drug abuse

Compulsive eating

Depression, suicidal tendencies

WHY NOT USE METHOD II?

Knowing the destructive effects of Method I and its use of power, one could ask, "Why do teachers use Method I when the risks are so great, the effects on students so destructive, and the results so self-defeating for the teacher?"

The answer is the simple one that we have mentioned before: Teachers can see no alternative except Method II, which is an even less acceptable approach for most of them.

If teachers almost universally look at conflict resolution as a win-lose proposition, and if they discard Method I, where the teacher wins and the student loses, this leaves only Method II, where the teacher loses and the student wins. And most teachers for certain don't want to lose conflicts!

With Method II, teachers "get the short end of the stick." They don't get their needs met, they suffer, they can't do their jobs; teaching becomes a burden or even a nightmare.

When teachers give in (or buckle under) to the power of their students—when they are controlled, manipulated, pushed and bullied by students—they end up developing coping mechanisms of their own.

The same list of coping mechanisms that we used to categorize students' reactions to power applies to teachers in this context. These same coping mechanisms are the ones teachers choose whenever they lose and their students win conflicts. Regardless of who it is, the loser in conflicts must do something! When needs go unmet, you have to find a way to cope.

When teachers, for whatever reason, permissively use Method II and students therefore mobilize their power to make the teachers' lives miserable, we can predict that those teachers will develop any or all of the coping mechanisms previously described. Here are some examples:

Retaliating, by springing pop-tests on the class, lowering grades for misconduct or for petty errors in students' work, or by designing harder exams.

Organizing with other teachers to fight for more power or for more backing from the administration.

Rebelling, by going over the head of principals to superintendents or the state teachers union.

Resigning, escaping to another school.

Escaping, through heavy drinking, compulsive eating, daydreaming.

Developing ulcers or other psychosomatic illnesses.

Withdrawing, by not associating with peers.

Buttering up students, trying to be the most popular teacher, the "good guy" teacher, or the easiest grader.

Conforming, trying nothing new, doing only minimum work required to get by.

Not a very pretty picture, but it exists in many schools where teachers have slipped into permissiveness because they have been pressured into forsaking the authoritarian role, yet have not been taught alternative methods for resolving conflicts.

HOW POWER AFFECTS THE WINNER

When win-lose methods are used to resolve conflicts in the classroom, the winners pay a price, too. In a society that values power so highly, few understand the corruptive effects on people who wield power over others. Yet Lord Acton's principle applies: "Power corrupts, and absolute power corrupts absolutely."

First, teacher power gives power to its own victims (the students); it creates its own opposition, fosters its own destruction. Power provokes counterpower. "Uneasy rests the head that wears the crown," is a truth as applicable to teachers as to monarchs. We have shown how teacher power generates resistance, retaliation, rebellion, and often organizing efforts of the victims eager to "overthrow" the teacher. This invariably makes teachers think they have to acquire and use even more power to maintain control. They double their efforts to enforce their dictatorial rules and restrictions. And they must forever increase their vigilance. Result: less and less teaching-learning time in the classroom.

Second, using power reduces the teacher's *influence*. Teacher power does not genuinely influence students; it merely forces them to behave in prescribed ways. It does not persuade, convince, educate, or motivate students to behave in particular ways; rather, power *compels* or *prohibits* behavior—which is why students generally return to their former behavior as soon as the authority and power are removed (when the teacher leaves the room, for example).

It is paradoxical but true: *Teachers will have more influence on students by refusing to use their power and authority.* •

When teachers rely on power they suffer still a third consequence: They are deprived of warm, pleasant, friendly relationships with students. Youngsters dislike, and even grow to hate Method I teachers. How dreadful it must be for so very many teachers to go to work daily on a job where they must constantly associate with persons with whom they have unpleasant, hostile relationships. What deprivation!

Using power over others, especially when the recipients are smaller and more helpless than the person with the power, also produces *guilt*. Few people relish exercising power, especially when it requires punitive measures—as it so frequently does. Almost none of the teachers we have known enjoy bossing and punishing kids. "This hurts me worse than it hurts you" is more than just a rationalization for using power; it is an expression of a universal feeling of guilt.

Likewise, students who use power are just as liable to be corrupted by it as anyone else. They may become intolerable brats, insolent and abusive not only toward defeated teachers but toward all who stand in the way of gratifications. They tend to lack inner controls, and they are self-centered and unmanageable. Like Method I teachers, they are likely to become tyrants, and, in their tyranny, disrespecters of the feelings, needs, and property of others.

Power breeds resentment, and power-wielding students are very apt to be thoroughly resented by their teachers and by other students. It is terribly difficult to feel kindly toward these youngsters. As one would expect, they sense it and develop deep feelings of being unloved and for good reason. In reality, they are not lovable.

HOW POWER AND AUTHORITY ARE RATIONALIZED

Why has power and authority been so deeply entrenched and universally sanctioned in schools? What keeps it there, stunting students and making teachers miserable?

Working with teachers and school administrators in Effectiveness Training courses, our instructors are struck by the way school people cling to certain outmoded myths about authority, to rationalizations and justifications for the use of power to control students.

The Myth of "The Wisdom of Age and Experience"

Teachers—and for that matter, most leaders—who end up in positions of power and authority rationalize that they possess more wisdom than those they supervise. "After all," they maintain, "don't we have more experience? If we didn't, why were we placed in positions of leadership and authority?" Other versions:

"Father knows best."
"Teachers have more experience."
"The masses are ignorant."
"Students are immature."
"It's really for their own good."

Dwight Allen, dean of the School of Education at the University of Massachusetts, writes about the "original stupidity" of children—the myth that ". . . children are stupid until the teacher makes them smart. This myth is the twin of the myth of original sin. We seem to regard our young as miniature devils whose natures must be disciplined and controlled."

Probably all who have wielded power and authority over others have been able to rationalize their behavior because they have a low opinion of their "subjects." Blacks were thought to be racially too inferior to be allowed the vote. Women are said to be inherently "irrational and emotional." The masses are too "ignorant" to be trusted with a voice in governing our nation, and so on.

"Students Really Want Limits on Their Behavior"

Most adults cling to the belief that youngsters are insecure and unhappy without limits or restrictions. They are therefore thought to *want* adults to exercise authority through setting limits.

Some support exists for this notion. Children do have a

need to know how far they can go before their behavior is unacceptable. Only then can they choose not to engage in such behavior. They do want to know how far they can go before the roof caves in. Ambiguity about limits makes them feel insecure and anxious.

But it is one thing for a student *to want to know the limits of the teacher's acceptance,* and an entirely different thing to believe that he wants or needs *his teacher to set those limits unilaterally, arbitrarily, without the student's inputs and participation.*

Instead of saying that students want limits set on their behaviors, a sounder principle is:

Students want and need information from their teachers that will tell them the teachers' feelings about their behavior, so that they themselves can modify behavior that might be unacceptable to the teachers. Students do not want the teacher to try to limit or modify behavior by using or threatening to use authority. Students want to limit their behavior *themselves,* if it becomes apparent to them that their behavior must be limited or modified. *Students, like adults, prefer to be their own authority over their behavior.*

The Myth of "Responsibility To Transmit the Culture"

Another justification for using power over students is the commonly held notion that teachers (and other adults) have a moral obligation to transmit (even impose) community standards and values.

One of the most confusing dilemmas for teachers results from society's insistence upon casting them in the role of "transmitters of the culture." In an age of rapid change and indistinct guidelines to help teachers (or anyone else) know what the "culture" is, this role brings on severe problems. Most anthropologists agree that there is no American culture, only a multitude of subcultures constantly in flux. This makes the enforcement of "community-accepted standards" especially tough.

In addition, related issues immediately surface: *Who* is this "community"? What are the desirable behaviors? Who interprets them? What if the community is wrong?

Such issues aside, when power is used to enforce community-accepted standards of behavior it will generate the same coping mechanisms that it generates when it is used for any other purposes. The rule applies universally: *Power never influences.* Coercion by a powerful teacher never educates or persuades a student. He simply chooses whether to submit, fight, or withdraw until the power pressure is off and he can do as he pleases. So teachers who use power actually *lessen* their influence as transmitters of values. Again, the paradox prevails: *In order to have real influence, a person must not exercise power.*

Teachers may legitimately choose to assume the responsibility of trying to influence their students. But to do it effectively, they must disavow any forms of coercion and force!

"Isn't Power Necessary With Certain Kids?"

When teachers ask this question, they almost always think of students whose coping mechanisms toward teacher power are aggression, resistance, and fighting. To pour more power on power with a student who copes with power in these ways only reinforces the original problem. He will react with more of the same behavior; or he will be driven underground where the behavior is even more difficult to deal with.

Such "uncontrollable" students don't need more or better external controls. They need *internal* controls, and these come only from relationships in which their needs—as well as those of others with whom they relate—are respected.

The Myth of "Firm, but Fair"

Many teachers rationalize their authoritarianism by describing their method of discipline as being always "firm but fair." What they mean is, "It's okay to use power with students, because I'm always consistent and fair in administering rewards and punishments."

In T.E.T. our instructors assure teachers that consistency and fairness are essential—but only *if they choose to use power and authority.* Certainly, students much prefer their teachers to be fair and consistent *if they use power to control them.*

The "ifs" are critical. We say power and authority are harmful; inconsistently applied, they will be even more harmful. It is ridiculous to suppose that power is justified if benignly and consistently applied. Youngsters *never* want to be controlled by power and authority. But if they find they are being tyrannized by power (as is almost always the case), they certainly would prefer that it be "firm but fair." That gives them a fighting chance to learn which behaviors will be consistently rewarded and which will be consistently punished—so they gain some small measure of predictability and "security." When power is inconsistently administered, they can never win, and so they become frustrated, confused, bewildered, "neurotic."

VIII. THE NO-LOSE METHOD OF RESOLVING CONFLICTS

Few of the many critics of schools—and of the educational system in general—have offered constructive, viable alternatives and remedies. The critics are generally in agreement that classrooms are too often stultifying, oppressive, and dismal places where students are either apathetic—turned off and tuned out to learning—or hostile and rebellious. For both kinds of students, the critics say, learning is minimal, or what is being learned is far removed from the content being taught. They talk in discouraging terms about this "hidden curriculum," the *sub rosa* learning that students absorb when they learn how to beat the system instead of learning math, science, language, or whatever teachers are teaching.

The critics also deplore the dehumanizing atmosphere where this "education" takes place—environments that stifle creativity, promote conformity, destroy initiative, encourage mediocrity. Many describe schools in terms appropriate for prisons or concentration camps. Charles Silberman put it this way in his book *Crisis In the Classroom*:

We cannot afford to underestimate the psychological brutality, dehumanization and irrelevance of life in many of our nation's schools. The creative spirit of man is being destroyed within the schools many of our children are forced to attend.

These are strong words, a powerful condemnation by a responsible and articulate researcher. Are they true? Are there schools so bad that they destroy rather than build, stifle rather than encourage, mangle rather than make whole?

Yes, indeed—there are such schools, and there are such classrooms within otherwise decent schools. But we have also observed that schools are not uniformly oppressive, dull, inhumane places. Some are; others are not. Far too frequently, people have overgeneralized and concluded that, because there are schools that dehumanize and "destroy the creative spirit of man," all schools are bad or the entire public educational system is a loss. Better to conclude that some features of the system need changing, and that the need is more urgent in some places than in others.

While recent critics have served a very worthwhile purpose, raising levels of awareness and concern, we believe that criticism seldom if ever helps teachers in their efforts to change. Teachers are no different than other people. Being told that they are bad is not likely to make them "see the light" and swear off being "bad."

The critics have failed to promote change in the schools for two important reasons. First, they have focused for the most part on symptoms, rather than causes. When they talk about student apathy or anger, they are describing attitudes, feelings, or behaviors that are symptoms of the problem, not the problem itself. We agree that these symptoms must be relieved. But treating apathy, for example, in hope of effecting a cure for the illnesses of the school is much like treating a runny nose in hope of effecting a cure for pneumonia.

In Chapter VII we pointed out that many negative feelings and behaviors of students are coping mechanisms to offset teacher power. The *cause* of these behaviors and feelings lies in the methods used to resolve inevitable teacher-student and student-student conflicts. Unless the causal factor is changed, no amount of patching up or "Band-Aiding" is going to bring the relief so urgently and quickly needed.

In this chapter we offer an alternative method for resolving conflicts, a method teachers can use to make significant (even radical) changes in how they handle conflicts with students—changes that get at the root of the problem instead of treating symptoms.

The second reason why critics have failed to catalyze changes is that they have told us how bad things are but failed to do more than offer idealized models and conceptual schemes for "better schools," without providing practical guides to get such schools. They offer mostly slogans, platitudes, and the advice to "do better!" Some even advocate getting rid of schools—"deschooling" the society.

New ways for resolving conflicts are needed, so that no one has to "cope." New problem-solving processes can "evolutionize" the classroom and the school and evolve creative ways to improve the entire educational enterprise. Schools need a new philosophy and new methods for bringing about constructive change.

While many critics bemoan the oppression, the "systematized dehumanization," and lack of freedom they find in schools, others just as vocally protest that schools are too permissive. They say that the way to right the educational ship is to crack down on students, make them toe the mark, set higher standards, quit coddling them, let them know that education is a privilege. Once again, criticism (in this case directed against permissiveness) is of little help to teachers who want change.

Are the schools permissive? Are the critics correct who insist that modern schools are too "soft," too liberal, too permissive? From thousands of teachers and administrators who have taken our courses we have learned that school conflicts are resolved almost exclusively by Method I, the power approach, not Method II, the permissive approach. Those who claim that teachers are too permissive either use another definition of "permissiveness" (one unknown to us) or they do not know schools intimately. Teachers everywhere say that they may sometimes look the other way or ignore minor issues, but when the chips are down and serious conflicts develop over important issues, they use their power to try to win.

METHOD III: THE NO–LOSE METHOD
OF RESOLVING CONFLICTS

Method III approaches a conflict-of-needs situation so that the parties to the conflict join together in search of a solution acceptable to both—one that requires no one to lose. It comes as a surprise to most teachers, locked in for so long to the two win-lose methods, that such an alternative exists. Seldom do we encounter teachers in T.E.T. classes who employ the alternative method in the classroom. Most teachers have never been taught a thing about this third method in their own education for teacherhood; and even when teachers recognize it as a method commonly used in other relationships, few ever think to apply it to teacher-student relationships.

When teachers in T.E.T. classes are first told about Method III, the no-lose method of resolving conflicts, these are typical reactions:

"Is that all there is to it? It sounds so simple!"

"That's the way we hoped nations could resolve their conflicts in the United Nations."

"My wife and I use Method III to resolve most of our conflicts."

"I see children using that method all the time to resolve their fights."

"Sounds too good to be true!"

"It's a beautiful ideal, but will it work in schools?"

Yes, Method III is quite simple. And it is correct that Method III is used to resolve conflicts in other relationships— marriages, business partnerships, friendships, labor-management relationships, and many others. The method sometimes successfully settles property disputes in divorces, as well as other such out-of-court settlements in legal conflicts. Method III is often the *only* effective method for resolving conflicts between two persons or groups *having relatively equal power*. Where no power differential exists, power methods all too frequently end up in bitter stalemates; neither party is willing to give in to the other.

Most teachers and administrators (as well as parents) have never considered using Method III in their relationships with children and youth, *where there obviously is a power differential in favor of the adult*. In such relationships, win-lose power struggles have seemed necessary and inevitable.

HOW METHOD III WORKS IN THE CLASSROOM

Method III is a *process*. Several (perhaps many) interactions are necessary as the parties work through their conflict from beginning to end. In a teacher-student conflict, they put their heads together in a search for possible solutions that might work, then decide which solution would be best for the purpose of meeting both the needs of the teacher and those of the student.

In the following example Mrs. Walker and her student, Arthur, use Method III to resolve a classroom conflict centered around noise:

MRS. WALKER: Arthur, I cannot get my work done when you and your group talk that loudly, and I feel under pressure to finish with this group today.

ARTHUR: Well, you asked us to plan for the trip next week. I don't see how we can plan without talking.

MRS. WALKER: I see. You have a job to do, too, and talking is necessary.

ARTHUR: Yes. We have to finish up with the study questions today or they won't get duplicated by the time we have to have them Monday.

MRS. WALKER: It sounds to me like you're under pressure to finish today. I also feel like I have to finish hearing this group here before they can go ahead with their work. But the noise your group makes when you talk to each other really bothers my concentration. It's a real problem.

ARTHUR: Yeah?

MRS. WALKER: Do you have any ideas about how we could solve the problem so we'd both feel okay?

ARTHUR: Well . . . if it'd be okay with you, our group could work in the conference room at the end of the hall. It's always empty this period.

MRS. WALKER: That would sure solve my problem. Are you sure your group won't mind being crowded into that little room? It's kind of small for all of you.

ARTHUR: That's all right. We already talked about going there when you yelled at us before.

MRS. WALKER: That ought to solve the problem for us all then. Will your group finish your job today, or will you need to use the conference room again tomorrow?

ARTHUR: We'll finish today, I think.

Notice how the teacher needed to use the skills of effective confrontation and active listening, making sure by her I-messages that Arthur understood her plight, but also listening carefully to find out what *his* needs were. When the needs were known, it was not difficult to find a solution that allowed Arthur as well as his teacher to be satisfied. The conflict was ended. Both won. Neither had to resort to power.

In Chapter VII (page 179) we illustrated Methods I and II with a conflict situation between a high-school teacher, Mr. Jones, and his student, Sylvia, who was frequently late to class. Let's see how that same situation could be resolved with Method III.

LIBRARY ST. MARY'S COLLEGE

Mr. Jones likes to start his science classes with a brief oral outline of the day's activities. Sylvia is frequently late to class, requiring Mr. Jones to repeat his earlier instructions or answer a lot of her questions about what's going on.

JONES: When you're late to my class you miss the instructions and then I have to take my time to tell you personally what to do. I'm tired of doing that. (*I-message*)

SYLVIA: Well, I'm on the Yearbook staff and we've been really busy lately trying to meet the deadlines set up by the printer. That's why I'm late a lot of the time.

JONES: I see. You feel that your job with the Yearbook staff is so pressing that getting it done makes you late to this class sometimes. (*Active listening*)

SYLVIA: Yes . . . well, not exactly. That sounds like I don't think this science class is important. It's just that I go to your class all year and the Yearbook job just lasts a few weeks. You know what I mean?

JONES: You mean being late to my class is something temporary. You certainly have been on time until the last few weeks. Now it's different, but it'll only be temporary. Is that right? (*Active listening*)

SYLVIA: Uh-huh. By the end of next week we should have the proofs ready. Then I can be on time again.

JONES: The problem will soon take care of itself. (*Active listening*)

SYLVIA: Yes.

JONES: Now I understand why you've been late, but that's not what's bugging me. Let me say it again. What I object to is having to take time to tell you what to do after you get here. When you come in late, I have to stop whatever I'm doing and fill you in. I don't want to do that anymore, not even for just a couple of weeks. Do you have any ideas about how we could solve that problem?

SYLVIA: (*Thinks about it*) Well, how about Joyce taking my tape recorder on days when I'm going to be late and taping your instructions? When I come in I can listen to the tape very quietly and I'll know everything everybody else knows.

JONES: I don't see anything wrong with that idea. If you'll have Joyce bring the recorder up to my desk, I'll take responsibility for seeing that the instructions get recorded. Then when you come in, just come up to the desk and pick it up.

SYLVIA: Okay. I'll bring the recorder tomorrow.

JONES: See you then. Have a good day!

In this series of interactions, teacher *and* student were able to get their needs met through a solution suggested by Sylvia and accepted by Mr. Jones. Both could walk away from this encounter feeling good. Mr. Jones could say "Have a good day" and mean it! Compare this result with the results of Methods I and II in Chapter VII, when either Mr. Jones or Sylvia lost. Can you see how Method III generates positive feelings, how this "no-lose" process builds feelings of mutual respect?

The conflict between Mr. Jones and Sylvia illustrates some distinct advantages of Method III over the win-lose methods. For example, it does not make any difference *who* comes up with the final solution. In this case it was Sylvia. It could just as well have been Mr. Jones. The key question is not: Who can come up with the best solution? It is: *Can we find a solution that both will accept?* This is how Method III teaches that cooperation, not competition, solves problems best.

Another advantage of Method III is that the solutions do not have to please anyone except the participants. Sylvia's suggestion about taping class instructions might not be acceptable to some teachers, but it was to Mr. Jones. And since only he and Sylvia owned the problem, only they had to like the resolution.

Unlike "cookbook" approaches that offer standard solutions, Method III releases the creativity of the participants, frees them to find highly unique and creative solutions to their highly unique problems. Teachers need learn only this *one* process to resolve successfully their many conflicts with students, no matter how varied, complex, or difficult those conflicts may be.

Not only does Method III mobilize the talents, skills, and information unique to each set of participants but it has a uniqueness of its own: It is essentially a problem-solving process. In Method III, a conflict is defined as a problem to be solved, and solutions are then sought. If you compare Method III to other means of conflict resolution, its uniqueness is apparent. With Method III, conflicts are seen as healthy, nondestructive, natural events in the lives of teachers and students. Method III helps teachers view conflicts as *relationship-strengthening*, not relationship-damaging. They therefore become less reluctant to take on problems, less inclined to sweep them under the rug. So conflicts do get resolved, and in such a way that the former combatants are likely to end up with strong positive feelings about each other, not the negative feelings generated by Methods I and II.

We illustrate Method III like this:

As you look at Figure 27 you will notice some critical dif-

METHOD III

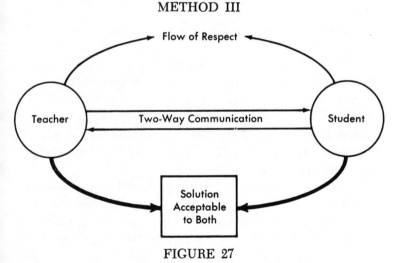

FIGURE 27

ferences between it and the diagrams of Methods I and II. Notice that in this diagram teacher and student are represented by circles of equal size to show no power differential. Also, they are drawn in a horizontal relationship, not vertical as in Methods I and II, where one party is in a superior power position. Now, as in our familiar two-way-communication diagram, no one is above the other, and each is communicating what is inside (needs or feelings).

Finally, in the Method III diagram, no pluses nor minuses are needed for teacher *or* student. Both still have power (and the teacher may possess even more), but *power has become invisible and irrelevant.* The teacher refuses to use power. The student knows it. The student therefore needs no counterpower. *Power has no place in Method III.*

The solution shown in Figure 27 results from a process of interaction as two people put their heads together to find an acceptable way to meet their individual needs. *The solution must be acceptable to teacher and student.* The needs of each must be met so that a two-way flow of mutual respect replaces the one-way flow of resentment shown in the diagrams for Methods I and II.

PREREQUISITES FOR METHOD III

Before teachers can accept the idea of using Method III to resolve conflicts, they must have acquired some competence in active listening. Only by using this skill will teachers be able to encourage students to talk about their needs of the moment. Students must feel that their needs will be understood and accepted before they will risk entering into a negotiating process.

Teachers also must state their own needs clearly and honestly, using good I-messages. Students will be fearful of Method III if they hear you-messages that blame, shame, or put them down. Their inevitable response to such messages will be a feeling that they have already lost the battle, so why enter into any problem solving?

Students also must be convinced that the teacher is trying out an entirely different method (not just the old Method I disguised as a new technique by which the teacher wins as usual). The teacher must somehow communicate this attitude:

I refuse to use my power to win at the expense of your losing, but I also refuse to let you win at the expense of *my* losing. I want to respect your needs, but I also must respect my own. Let's try a new approach that will help us find a solution that will meet both your needs and mine. The solution we're after is one that will allows us both to win.

In T.E.T. classes, teachers are advised to explain to their students, before using Method III, exactly what the method is and how it differs from Method I and Method II. Most students, even preschoolers, can understand such explanations, and when they do, they are less likely to suspect that the teacher is pushing some strange new manipulative method on them.

It is also helpful for teachers to explain Method III to students in terms of problem solving: "We have a problem here, and I wonder how, together, we might solve it."

Method III can also be presented to students as a kind of puzzle: "Let's put our heads together and work on this problem. I'll bet we can find some way to solve it so you'll be happy and I will be, too." Most kids love puzzles and are intrigued by the challenge that Method III poses to their creativity.

METHOD III: THE SIX–STEP PROBLEM–SOLVING PROCESS

Problem solving requires a step-by-step process that eventually leads to a resolution of the conflict, and Method III is a unique application of the six-step problem-solving process proposed by the famous educator John Dewey. While he was trying to apply "the scientific method" to the way an *individual* solves problems in his life, Method III is also a further application of the scientific method of problem solving for conflicts *between individuals or groups*. Its six separate steps are:

1. Defining the problem
2. Generating possible solutions
3. Evaluating the solutions
4. Deciding which solution is best
5. Determining how to implement the decision
6. Assessing how well the solution solved the problem

These six steps turn out to be invaluable guidelines for teachers when they use Method III in the classroom. Even though in some teacher-student conflicts one or more of the steps can be bypassed, teachers need to keep these six steps clearly in mind as they try to work through their conflicts with students. In the next few pages, we will examine each of the six steps and offer teachers some suggestions for handling each step and avoiding certain common pitfalls.

Step 1: Defining the Problem (Conflict)

Some wise person once said, "If you have defined your problem accurately and clearly, you are already halfway toward its solution." Step 1 is a critical step. Our experience shows that when Method III breaks down and fails, it is often because teachers have been ineffective right at the start—at Step 1. Here are some do's and don'ts for teachers trying to define the problem or identify what the real conflict is.

a. Do not even *try* problem solving until the students understand that Method III is not a gimmick to manipulate them. Explain it to them. Then use active listening. Many teachers tell their classes that they have taken a course or read a book from which they have learned a new way to solve problems.

b. Involve only those students in problem solving who are a part of the conflict—students who have information to contribute and will be directly affected by the final decision (e.g., they might have to follow new rules).

c. Students must enter into Method III *willingly*. Method III requires voluntary participation. Seldom can students be forced into being democratic.

d. Be sure there is enough time to finish at least one step in the process. While it is preferable to finish a problem in one sitting, this is often impossible, or it may create other problems. The process can be broken off at the end of any one of the steps and picked up there at the next session. In fact, with certain kinds of problems, a a time lapse may help, especially before Steps 2, 3, or 4.

e. Be sure to state your needs or feelings in the form of I-messages. Don't "undershoot" or try to minimize your feelings. Tell your students exactly how you feel. Follow the three-component formula for I-messages. By all means, avoid you-messages.

f. Do not overshoot your feelings either. On-target I-messages are essential. (Most overshooting of feelings is done to frighten students into entering the problem-solving process. It seldom works.)

g. State your *problem* (your unmet need), not the *solution you want*. Needs are very different from *solutions to meet those needs*. Most people have difficulty separating needs from wants. For example, the message "I want quiet in the room" is a statement of a want (a solution) that might solve your unmet need.

Here are statements of needs or unmet needs in such a situation:

"I have a headache."
"I don't like to repeat instructions."
"I cannot hear the group I'm working with."

Notice that these messages tell students what the teacher needs.
    "I want quiet in the room" tells them the solution you want, but leaves them in the dark about your needs.

h. Use active listening to help students express their needs, because they, too, are likely to have trouble separating their *needs* from *solutions they want. Do not go on to Step 2* until their needs and yours are both clearly understood. If the conflict is complex and involves several unmet needs, it helps to write these on a chalkboard or chart pad. Keep on refining the list until everyone is satisfied that their unmet needs are accurately described.

i. Remember that in Method III conflict resolution, John Dewey's "definition of the problem" must be expressed in terms of *conflict of needs*, not *competing solutions*.

j. Avoid introducting Method III for the first time in a class when the conflict is over a rule already decided by you (e.g., that students must clean out their desks on Fridays). In such cases it is far better to open up the whole issue of what class rules are necessary to regulate cleanups and forget all previous Method I decisions made by you without students participating.

k. Do not introduce Method III for the first time by bringing up only problems that bother *you*. It is far better to open the agenda by holding a *problem-airing session*, facing the class with something like, "What are the problems we are having? What could be changed to make our work easier? What rules do we need? What policies would improve the classroom?"

Step 2: Generating Possible Solutions

After a problem has been accurately defined, both teacher and student can offer solutions, although when students are inexperienced in Method III it may be best to get some of their ideas before offering yours. The following points will help.

a. *Do not evaluate* proposed solutions. This is crucial because students stop volunteering ideas when they feel they are being evaluated and judged at that stage. Evaluation comes with Step 3. It should never come with Step 2.

b. Encourage participation by injecting open-ended door openers, such as "What are some of the possible solutions to this problem?" "Let's see how many ideas we can come up with." Accept all ideas—quantity is desired in this step—and don't edit. Encourage even wild or unique solutions.

c. You may want to write down each solution (or ask a student to do it), especially if you are dealing with a problem that lends itself to many ideas. Record the ideas just as rapidly as you can—don't slow down the "brainstorming" process. A tape recorder comes in handy and kids love to be recorded.

d. Do not require students to justify or document their ideas.

e. Encourage everyone to get into the act, but do not push; do not call on particular students or "go around the room."

f. When the process lags, ask a refocusing question. For instance, "What are ways that no one has thought of yet?" Or "There must be more solutions we can think of."

Step 3: Evaluating the Solutions

a. Start the evaluation process with another open-ended question— e.g., "Now is the time to say which of these solutions you like or don't like. Do you have some preferences?" Or "What do you think about each of these ideas? Which are the best?"

b. Cross off the list any solution that produces a negative rating from *anyone* for *whatever* reason.

c. Use a lot of active listening to be sure that all participants accurately understand the opinions and feelings expressed. Your role as a facilitator is critical during Step 3.

d. Do not hesitate to state your own opinions and preferences. Do not permit a solution to stand if it is not really acceptable to you.

e. Use I-messages to state your own feelings—e.g., "I couldn't accept that idea because . . ." or "I don't feel comfortable with that solution because . . . "

f. Now is the time for documentation and analysis. Encourage participants to advocate their proposals, to tell the group why their ideas have merit. You can argue the case for your favorite solutions too!

g. Do not rush! Unless it is obvious that everyone agrees to one solution, take the time to let everyone have his say. If some of the participants have not spoken, encourage them with an I-message— e.g., "I haven't heard from everyone and I'm curious about *all* our feelings."

Step 4: Making the Decision

If Steps 1, 2, and 3 have been carefully followed, Step 4 will not be as difficult as it may seem. In some cases a clearly superior solution emerges. Everyone agrees, and Step 4 is over. Often, however, several high-quality solutions remain

LIBRARY ST. MARY'S COLLEGE

at the end of Step 3. If that happens, here are some hints that may help in arriving at a final choice:

a. DO NOT VOTE! Voting always produces winners and losers unless the vote is unanimous. Those who lose in a vote will be poorly motivated to carry out the decision. They might even be motivated to see that it fails. Consensus is what you are after.

b. You can take straw votes. They tell you where people are, but are not binding. Ask them to respond with an arm signal: Arm held over the head to signify "favoring a solution." Arm held parallel to the floor for "undecided or no strong feeling." Arm held down, pointed toward the floor for "disfavor or disapprove."

c. Test the proposed solutions. Ask students to imagine how each solution would work if it were chosen. "If we tried this idea what do you think would happen?" "Would everyone be satisfied?" "Do you think we would have solved our problem?" "Are there any flaws?" "Where would we possibly fail?"

d. Work toward consensus. Do not adopt a solution until *everyone* agrees to at least *try* it. Try to sense when agreement is close. The best way to test for consensus is to say, "It seems we all agree on number three. Does anyone *not* agree?" And *keep the decision tentative*. Ask the group if they would be willing to try out No. 3 to see if it works: "I'm willing to try this out, how about you?" This helps students understand that their decision will not be cast in bronze, that they can always reconsider and change it if it turns out that it is not the best.

e. Write down the agreed-upon solution. Some teachers ask all participants to sign a written statement, much like a contract, to indicate that they understand its conditions and terms and agree to them. If someone hesitates when it comes time to sign, you know that you have not yet achieved consensus. If this happens, tune in to the student's feelings. *Do not allow anyone to give in to group pressure, to capitulate, to become submissive.* Be sensitive to student messages that may indicate less than positive feelings about a solution. Get feedback. Check them out. Grudging submission is not consensus.

Step 5: Determining How To Implement the Decision

Potentially productive problem-solving efforts often end in frustration because decisions never get implemented. Generally this happens because the group failed to determine *who* does *what* by *when*. Without this step, *nothing* may be done.

a. Ask the group, "*What* do we need in order to get started?" Or "*Who* is going to be responsible for what? And by *when?*"

b. Take up the issue of "standards of performance," if it is pertinent. For example, a solution to keeping a room cleaned up may entail some discussion about standards of neatness acceptable to everyone: "What *is* a clean room?"

c. Write down (and even post) determinations of *who* does *what* by *when*. In some classes, a few students are designated official "timekeepers" to check up on whether commitments have been completed or to remind people of approaching deadlines.

Step 6: Assessing the Success of the Solution

Step 6 is important but need not always be formalized. The idea is just to check on the effectiveness of your efforts. Some questions to test the results later on are:

"Has the problem disappeared?"
"Did we make progress in correcting the problem?"
"Was it a good decision?"
"Are we happy with what we did?"
"How effective was our decision?"

One delightful (and obvious) criterion of effectiveness of a Method III solution is the disappearance of conflict—the absence of gripes and grievances and negative feelings.

More formally, a teacher may want to call the participants together again and ask, "Are you still satisfied with our solution?" Or "How did our decision work out?" Or "Did we solve our problem?" Here are some suggestions that may be helpful to teachers who later assess the effectiveness of Method III:

a. Be on the lookout for commitments that were made in the enthusiasm of problem solving but later turn out to be unrealistic or difficult to carry out. People sometimes find a commitment much more difficult to keep than they had originally thought. It's therefore a good idea to check with the participants from time to time to see how they are feeling about the decision.

b. When a solution fails to solve a problem, this probably indicates that there was some unexpected difficulty, either with the solution or with implementing it.

c. Nothing is sadder than to watch a class struggle to carry out a commitment to a poor decision because of a misguided notion that decisions are somehow sacred and unchangeable. *The whole point of Method III is to find creative solutions that allow everyone to get his needs met. When a solution fails to do this, it deserves to be discarded and another should be sought.*

d. Even if a solution seems to have solved the original problem, it is still wise to reexamine it from time to time. Situations change, needs change. *Do not chisel Method III decisions in granite.* Be ready at all times to reevaluate and search for a better solution.

We would like teachers to keep in mind the idea that *it is all right to fail;* that if things do not work out as expected, it most often means that the *decisions* were bad, not the *students.*

WORKING WITH METHOD III IN THE CLASSROOM

The following history was submitted by a teacher during a T.E.T. class* in New England. It particularly illustrates Steps 1, 2, 3, and 4 of the problem-solving process.

TEACHER: I have a problem that you can help me with. There's too much talking and I feel like I'm always having to quiet you down. I don't like that. There are times when I need to have quiet so I can teach, but when you're talking I have to repeat directions and go over material I've already talked about. Yet I know that you seem to have a need to talk. Let's think of all the things we can that might help meet my needs and your needs, too. I'll suggest some, and you suggest all you can think of. I'll list them on the board. Every suggestion will be listed without any comments.

* Taught by T.E.T. instructor Katherine Pigott Newman, Sharon, Massachusetts.

Later we'll discuss them and eliminate the ones you don't
want and I don't want.

(*The following alternative solutions were proposed and listed on the
board:*

1. *Rearrange the seating*
2. *Punishments*
3. *Talk whenever you want to*
4. *Have a certain time each day to talk*
5. *Talk only when others are not talking*
6. *No talking at all*
7. *Teach one-half the class at a time (other half can talk)*
8. *Whisper*
9. *Have only oral work*

TEACHER: Now let's cross out the suggestions we really don't like. I'll
cross out numbers two, three, and nine because I don't
like them.

(*Various students suggest crossing out numbers two, six, and seven.*)

TEACHER: Now let's look at the remaining suggestions. How about
number one, "Rearranging the seating"?

BETTY: You've tried that and it didn't work. (*After a brief discussion, class agrees to cross that one out.*)

TEACHER: "Have a certain time each day to talk"—what about that
one?

(*There are no objections to that solution.*)

TEACHER: What about "Don't talk when others are talking," number five?

(*There are no objections to that one.*)

TEACHER: "Whisper." What do you think of that idea?

(*There are no objections to that one.*)

TEACHER: That leaves us with numbers four, five, and eight. Does anyone want to add anything? No? Okay, then, I'll copy this on
paper and we'll all sign it. This is what we call a contract.
It's an agreement the teacher and the class have signed.
We both will try to live up to the contract. We'll try not
to break the contract.

In this brief problem-solving session, the teacher did some things rather well, but failed to do others:

1. She stated the problem in terms of her own needs, and used I-messages to convey her feelings. However, her I-messages seemed a little weak in specifying the "tangible and concrete effect" of students' talking.

2. She might have more vigorously encouraged the students to explore why they needed to talk. Perhaps a question would have helped, such as "I'd like to understand more your need to talk so often: Tell me what goes on in you at those times."

3. She might have given her reasons for crossing out those alternative solutions she didn't like.

4. The problem solving did not go beyond Step 4: Decision making. The teacher could have engaged the students in Step 5 by some such statement as "All right now, how are we going to put this into action? What has to be done? Who is going to do it? How can we make our decisions work?"

5. The teacher could have moved the class into Step 6, Assessment, by saying, "When shall we talk again and evaluate how well our decisions are working?"

A TAPE–RECORDED METHOD III MEETING

Here is a transcript of a tape-recorded session of a teacher* and her thirty third-grade students. The class had been holding regularly scheduled problem-solving meetings twice a week for five months.

This meeting is an excellent example of how a teacher can stimulate interaction *between the students* by using a lot of active listening. Reading this transcript, one gets the impression that many of the students are deeply involved in the problem; it is a *class* problem, not just a conflict between teacher and students, polarized against each other. The teacher almost seems to be just another member of the group.

* Marlene Anderson, Hinsdale, Illinois.

Obviously, she has been effective in reducing her "psychological size."

TEACHER: Who would share with us something you'd like to put on the agenda for our classroom meeting today?

BILL: Remember when you said the other day we could bring up that thing about the boys in our reading group?

TEACHER: That's right, but I can't quite remember all the details. Can you give me some facts about it to help me recall the conversation?

BILL: Oh, you know that problem about interruptions when we're having our reading period.

TEACHER: That's right. We have had quite a few interruptions from people who are not in our skill group.

STEVE: Yeah, and during our conferences, too.

TEACHER: Yes, this week during our conferences it seems to me we've had quite a few interruptions. I find it difficult to have a personal conference with a person when this happens, and I get very angry inside.

JULIE: You mean during study time when we're all doing something different and you're having conferences?

TEACHER: I seem to hear two concerns. We're having interruptions within the room in the morning during study time when everyone is working independently, and from outside the room in the afternoon when many people go to different rooms for reading class.

OTHERS: Yeah.

TEACHER: It seems unfair.

STEVE: It sure is.

TEACHER: Last week someone had a solution which we carried out and that was putting a sign on the door that said, "Do not enter."

JAY: That works sometimes, but people still come in and interrupt.

BILL: Some of the kids forget things and come back after them.

STEVE: Why don't they take them when they leave for their class?

TEACHER: You feel they need to take their materials when they go to class the first time.

KEN: You know what I think? I think they do it on purpose so they can come back and waste time.

JAY: Yeah, like they're wanting something besides their materials.

TEACHER: You're saying they want attention.

JAY: I'm not saying for sure that it is, but it could be.

JULIE: Another thing—it wastes our time.

BILL: It wastes their time, too.

STEVE: They get behind in work and then get in trouble with all their teachers.

TEACHER: Then they're not only interrupting us but they're hurting themselves as well.

STEVE: Yup.

TEACHER: It doesn't seem to be responsible.

BILL: Nope.

JULIE: Before I go to a friend's house, my mom always asks, "Do you have everything? Don't forget your things, and be sure to bring them home."

TEACHER: You're used to having someone remind you to take care of your things.

JAY: But that's not good because we don't always have someone around to remind us.

SHANNON: I usually remember my things.

TEACHER: You're pretty proud because you take the responsibility of caring for your things.

SHANNON: Yes.

BILL: I've got kind of a peachy idea what to do with people who interrupt.

TEACHER: You would like to share your idea.

BILL: Well, we could lock the door.

PATTI: If someone comes to the door, you could wave them away.

JOHN: What happens if a teacher comes to the door? They'd come in anyway.

TEACHER: You've found that adults haven't read the sign on our door and they interrupt.

JOHN: Yup, they think it doesn't mean them. They think they're special.

TEACHER: It seems unfair that adults don't pay any attention to the sign.

JOHN: Sure it's unfair. They should read our sign.

STEVE: I don't think locking the door is such a good idea because people would try to open it and would just rattle the door and that would bother us.

PATTI: What if we have a fire and had to get out in a hurry?

JULIE: That's kind of scary.

CAROL: We could put a sign up that says "Do not enter—that means *you*."

OTHERS: Hey, that sounds neat.

TEACHER: That sign out there seems pretty important.

CAROL: I'll go get it.

STEVE: I'll get a felt pen so we can add more words.

JOHN: Put an exclamation mark after the word "you."

OTHERS: Hey, yeah, that means with feeling.

(*Several people work together in rewriting the sign and hanging it up again.*)

TEACHER: Any other ideas?

BILL: How about those *inside* the room who interrupt?

JULIE: It's always the same ones.

JAY: They should miss out on their conference.

TEACHER: Planning conferences are pretty important to you, then.

STEVE: Sure they are. And if others chatter a lot and interrupt, they shouldn't get to be with you.

JOHN: Yes, I think so, too.

CAROL: I disagree. I just don't think that's right to punish them. They probably need more conferences.

BILL: I disagree, too.

SHANNON: I think free time should be taken away from them.

STEVE: I don't like that idea because we need our free time.

KEN: Those who interrupt conferences when we're all in the room are breaking our class rules, and it's up to us to be more careful.

CAROL: I think we've already made our class rules, and I agree with Ken. We have to be more responsible.

TEACHER: Several interesting solutions have been discussed. Perhaps I also need to be more responsible in working with people who break our rules.

CAROL: Yes, I think that would help.

KEN: You have to enforce the rules.

TEACHER: I wonder if someone could review for us the things we've talked about today.

BEVERLY: I will. Those people who leave the room will try to remember to take all their supplies when they go out. We fixed up the sign on the door. We're all going to try and use better self-control during study time so we can have conferences. And Miss Anderson will work with those who break our class rules and she'll help to enforce the rules.

TEACHER: Thank you, Beverly.

This transcript shows that these third-graders are well on their way to becoming self-responsible and self-disciplined. They speak their minds, yet listen to each other; they feel free to express their feelings, even when they are critical of each other; and they exhibit a degree of problem-solving effectiveness seldom seen even in adult groups. Can you also feel the warmth and intimacy in this teacher-student relationship?

Unlike the previous example of Method III problem solving (the talking-in-class conflict that progressed only through

Steps 1, 2, 3, and 4), this class dealt directly with problems of implementation (Step 5). They brought up the question of who is going to enforce the decisions, and even evaluated whether punishment should be used to handle infractors.

THE BENEFITS AND REWARDS OF METHOD III IN SCHOOLS

Although some of the benefits and rewards of the no-lose approach become readily apparent to teachers as they read our examples and case histories, others may not be so apparent. Most teachers want to be convinced that the benefits of Method III are worth the effort necessary for them to change and the extra time it may take.

No Resentment

When conflicts are resolved so no one loses, the resentment generated by Method I and Method II does not occur. Experience shows that a relationship gains strength when two people work through their differences and end up with a solution that meets the needs of both. Most people prefer an outcome where the other person's needs are met, as well as their own, rather than meeting their own needs at the expense of the other.

Why is this so? We think it is because winners in conflicts *feel guilty* if someone else has to lose. Even in sports and other kinds of competive games—"sanctioned conflict," if you will—a winner usually feels ambivalent about his victory. It is not pleasant to be a party to another's disappointment or downfall.

Motivation Increases To Implement the Solution

When teachers consistently report that students are highly motivated to carry out a Method III solution, it's because the "principle of participation" is at work:

People are more likely to accept a decision and are more motivated to carry it out when they have participated in making the decision—as opposed to one in which they have been denied a voice.

People want to keep a hand on the reins, maintain some control over their destiny. They resent and resist being co-erced and controlled by others, and develop hostility toward those who would deny them this opportunity. This is a uni-versal characteristic, but adults in our schools frequently for-get that *students are people, too.*

While Method III carries no guarantee that every decision will be eagerly carried out by all participants, teachers who use this creative way to resolve conflicts discover a sharp decrease in such responses as "Oh, I forgot!" "Is it time for that already?" "Who, me?" or "I thought somebody else was going to do that."

The only times they hear these phrases is when a student has really forgotten, not when he wants an alibi or excuse. Students who participate in making decisions have a stake in them, a commitment to them, a responsibility to see that they get implemented. Usually, students from Method I homes and accustomed to Method I teachers are absolutely overjoyed with Method III when they discover it is for real. Now they want to carry through with commitments zealously so they won't lose this opportunity to participate in making decisions about their own lives.

"Two Heads Are Better than One"

Method III enlists the creative thinking, the brainpower, and the experience of teacher *and* students. Consequently, unique and creative solutions often surface. The rationaliza-tion that teachers have more knowledge and experience and therefore "know what's best" for students may be valid for some kinds of problems; but even when it is true, a *teacher's knowledge and experience alone* cannot be better than the *knowledge and experience of both teacher and student* brought to bear on a problem.

Pitting the teacher's brain *against* the student's is only appropriate in Method I or Method II, because in these win-lose approaches one of the participants is always left out of problem solving. When both parties to a conflict bring their resources into the problem solving, their individual knowledge and experience are *combined*, not *in competition*. Method III is a "synergistic" process; two elements act to enhance each other, resulting in something better than each could produce alone (better even than the one *plus* the other).

This synergistic power of Method III problem solving is clearly apparent in the following experience reported by an elementary school teacher in Southern California who was enrolled in T.E.T.:

I used to try to control students by asking my class leading questions in such a way that the children were forced into ritual answers that the teacher wanted. For example, "Are we quiet when we walk to the library, class?" Then the students would answer like good little boys and girls, "Yes." "And do we run?" They would answer, "No, we don't run." I used to *rehearse* my classes before we would go on trips, or fire drills, or have visitors.

Well, the kids always agreed with me. "No, we never run." Then they always ran, pushed and yelled. When I got them back in the room, I asked a different question: "Do we keep our promises, class?" And the usual answer, "Yes, we keep our promises."

When you [the T.E.T instructor] played that tape in class and I heard how stupid that teacher on the tape sounded and how much I sounded like her, I decided to try something else. I decided to try Method III with a problem I'd been lecturing the class about for weeks—getting in on time after recess.

In the past I handled it in my usual way.

They were always late lining up and I'd have to go out and yell at them to line up. By the time they all got there and lined up and walked to the room, we'd wasted at least ten minutes. When we got in the room, I'd say, "When the bell rings do we continue to play, class?" And they'd say, "No." Then I'd say,

"What do we do when the bell rings, class?" And they'd chant, "Line up." Then I'd say, "From now on I won't have to yell at you to line up, right?" And they'd say, "Right!" And the next day there I'd be, yelling at them to line up.

Can you believe that? Well, this week I sent an I-message instead of asking my usual questions. I told them how tired I was of yelling at them to line up and how afraid I was that the principal was going to give me a poor rating because of all the time we wasted. Then I listened to them.

I couldn't believe my ears. They said they were sick of standing out there in the hot sun waiting for me and asked why they had to line up anyway. They couldn't understand why they couldn't come to the room when the bell rang.

I said that we'd always lined up, and they asked, "Why?" I thought about it for a while and then I said I couldn't think of any reason *why* students had to line up except that it was just the way things were done.

Well, they didn't buy that. We then decided to define our needs. Mine was to have them get from the playground to the classroom in an orderly, disciplined manner in as short a time as possible. Theirs was to avoid standing in a line for five or more minutes in the hot sun waiting for me to arrive to escort them to the classroom, and then having to march like soldiers.

We decided on a solution suggested by one of the kids— namely, when the bell rang, they were to walk to the room from the playground. I was to walk from the teacher's lounge, and we'd go in.

We've been trying it for three days now, and it's working beautifully. We save ten minutes a day in the roundup, a lot of time that I used to spend lecturing them on lining up and marching quietly. And I don't have to walk clear out to the playground anymore. But the biggest difference is how we feel about each other when we get to the room. Everybody used to be mad by the time we'd lined up and marched quietly to the room. Now we go into the room feeling good, or at least not mad at each other. That sometimes saves a whole afternoon.

The hardest part of this problem was for the kids to convince me that I didn't have a need for them to line up, that lining up was a *solution* to a need, and, in our case, a very bad one.

This teacher had discovered for herself that Method III sometimes evokes unpredictable and creative solutions that are stirred up when people together start looking at problems in different ways. This teacher (and the others in that T.E.T. group) then reviewed her other classroom rules to see if any more of them were like the lining-up rule—that is, solutions that might be poor ones for that class at that time.

No "Selling" Is Needed in Method III

As we pointed out previously, Method I usually requires the teacher, after determining a solution, to go through a second step of selling that solution, or persuading the student to "buy" it or accept it. The same is true for Method II, except that the student has to sell his or her solution to the teacher.

In Method III, the selling or persuasion is built into the problem-solving process (in Step 3). When a decision is made to adopt a final solution *acceptable to both,* the selling step is unnecessary because teacher *and* student are already sold on the solution. Hence, Method III often saves time.

No Power or Authority Is Required

Probably the most significant benefit of Method III is that it eliminates the terrible risks of using power, the necessity for its victims to develop coping mechanisms that are self-destructive or destructive to relationships.

Schools without power would be radically different from our present schools. They would be relatively free of the disruptive and destructive behaviors that students use to try out such coping mechanisms as aggression, retaliation, vandalism, clowning, flaunting rules, bullying others, scapegoating, lying, pushing, shoving, hitting, and the many other ways kids respond to adult authority.

Of paramount importance to teachers is this dramatic benefit of schools without power: *Teachers would not need to be afraid to go to work,* like countless teachers in public high schools and junior high schools.

Kids Like Teachers, and Teachers Like Kids

It is understandable why so many investigators and critics of schools have observed that most students dislike their teachers, and that an amazingly large proportion of teachers appear to dislike kids. These are the outcomes of both authoritarian *and* permissive approaches to conflict resolution.

Method III fosters relationships characterized by mutual respect, mutual caring, mutual trust. No-lose solutions bring people together and engender feelings of warmth. Teachers who eschew the use of their power and authority will find to their delight that students will be their friends and their friends will be their students.

Method III Helps Uncover Real Problems

Methods I and II tend to deal with surface problems. Earlier we referred to these problems as "presenting problems," issues that people use to test a situation—"safe" issues that are only used to start the problem-solving process. A teacher spots Sam clowning around, attracting the attention of students near him, and interrupting a quiet study period. The teacher may infer that Sam has a need to be the center of attention, so she moves in with a solution for that problem, so defined. She makes Sam stand in the front of the room where everyone can see him do whatever "clowning act" he cares to try out on the group. But Sam may not be seeking to be the center of attention at all. His behavior may be motivated by a need for one-to-one tutoring, a need to understand a lesson, or a need for individual help on the assignment. Without help, he is afraid his peers will think he's stupid, so he "clowns" as a cover-up of his real feelings.

Over and over again, teachers who begin to use Method III report that their preconceptions about problems in their classes were wrong. It is natural for all of us, when we see some behavior, to make assumptions about it. We then sometimes set world records in conclusion-jumping. Table 3 gives examples of wrong assumptions about student behavior.

Behavior	Assumption	Actual Problem
Late to class	Hates English	Has to walk too far from previous class to make it on time
Does not follow instructions	Is insubordinate	Has a hearing loss and sometimes does not hear the instructions
Clings to mother. Will not enter the kindergarten room	Is spoiled or immature	Is terrified of being abandoned
Never turns in his homework	Is lazy	Has a job until late at night and has no time for homework
Will not participate in physical-education activities	Is afraid of being laughed at—cannot take kidding	Is anemic and quickly fatigued by activity

TABLE 3

When teachers define conflicts with students *in terms of their own unmet needs* (and express their feelings as I-messages), instead of guessing at the motivation behind the students' behavior, the real problems begin surfacing. Until the real problems are known, solutions, no matter how elegant, are inappropriate and off target.

Students Become More Responsible, More Mature

Most school administrators and teachers say that one of the primary goals of schools should be to foster responsibility and maturity in students. These are essential qualities of the citizens society desires. "Education for responsible citizenry" has been proclaimed by educators for decades as an important, if not the most important, function of schools.

Embracing such an ideal in the abstract doesn't make it happen. As long as schools continue to rely heavily on adult power and authority, youngsters will not become responsible and mature. Controlling and directing children and youth by the use of power—by punishment or threats of punishment and by rewards or the removal of rewards—robs children of the opportunity to become responsible. It keeps them locked into dependency and immaturity.

We need to reiterate once again: Students, or for that matter adults, are denied the opportunity to act responsibly when they are coerced into a way of behaving. Doing something out of fear of punishment is as different from self-responsibility as is night from day, black from white. If a student is deterred from behavior that makes it impossible for his teacher to teach merely because of his fear of punishment, he certainly is not acting responsibly or out of consideration for the needs of another human being.

Each time a student is *made* to act in a certain way, *he is denied the chance to initiate that behavior* out of a desire to be a responsible member of a group. And when a teacher uses Method I, the student gets the message that he is not to be trusted; he is not considered responsible; he is not capable of acting out of consideration for the needs of others. In short, he is too irresponsible, too inconsiderate, too immature to initiate or carry out responsible, considerate, mature behavior. Receiving such messages, the student begins to believe them.

Method III signals to students that they *are* capable of mature behavior, that they can be trusted to understand the feelings of teachers, trusted to modify behavior when they learn it interferes with others, trusted to make decisions, trusted to carry them out, trusted to participate as full, responsible, mature members of a group.

Once teachers are helped to understand that a person in a position of authority and power retains power only by keeping his subjects weak, powerless, dependent, and immature, most of them take the first step toward replacing their power with nonpower methods in the classroom. We have been greatly encouraged to discover in T.E.T. classes in all parts of the country that most teachers do not want to foster irresponsibility and immaturity in the young people they teach. They just have known of no way to prevent this tragedy.

IX. PUTTING THE NO-LOSE METHOD TO WORK: OTHER USES OF METHOD III IN SCHOOLS

Applications of Method III are almost unlimited. Conflicts erupt in all classrooms, in all kinds of schools, with all kinds of students, over all kinds of problems. And conflicts surface in all school relationship—between one teacher and one student, between a teacher and the total class, between two students or two groups of students, between two teachers, between a teacher and a parent, between teachers and administrators.

It goes without saying: Conflict is inevitable whenever people find themselves in relationships with others—individually or in groups. But schools particularly generate frequent and continuing conflicts, because no other institution houses within its walls such an amazingly heterogeneous collection of people—all ages, all racial and ethnic backgrounds, all levels of intellectual endowment, all degrees of educational expertise, all levels of authority, all degrees of social and emotional maturity, all variations of talent. Is it any wonder that there is so much conflict in schools?

The hope for schools does not lie in reducing the volume of

conflict; the diversity of their populations makes this totally unrealistic. The effectiveness of schools—perhaps even their survival—depends on training people in skills and methods for resolving conflicts constructively. Schools require nothing short of a revolution in conflict management—constructively resolving the inevitable conflicts so that everyone can get his or her needs met and so develop to his or her fullest potential. This includes teachers, students, parents, custodians, secretaries, and administrators.

In this chapter we will demonstrate Method III in a variety of relationships, showing varying degrees of success. You will also become aware of some of the concerns and difficulties teachers experience with Method III, along with its many benefits.

HOW TO RESOLVE TEACHING–LEARNING
CONFLICTS WITH METHOD III

When teachers are first exposed to Method III it is easy for them to get the mistaken idea that this no-lose method is primarily a way of resolving conflicts brought about by student "misbehavior"—as if these are the only conflicts between teachers and students. In actuality, a large percentage of teacher-student conflicts spring out of the *relationship* between teacher and student in the Teaching-Learning area. Almost any adult can recall countless conflicts with former teachers over homework assignments, choice of subjects for term papers, a grade on an exam, the teacher's evaluation of an oral report, seating assignments, neatness of written work, and standards of performance, to name just a few.

It is in the Teaching-Learning area that teachers most often assume the strict authoritarian role. The rationale is that objectives are generally considered their prerogatives, seldom open to any negotiation with students.

In T.E.T. courses we encourage teachers to think beyond

mere "behavior problems" and become open-minded about applying Method III when conflicts arise within the academic sector of relationships with students. Some teachers immediately find many such situations where they can use Method III effectively.

This example comes from a shop teacher in a T.E.T. class*:

On the day of a quiz I was approached by one of my sophomore woodworking students who always has a gripe or a problem. He said, "Do I have to take this quiz today? I was out yesterday, so I missed the review and demonstration on the lathe machine. I forgot to do the homework, so I don't know anything about it."

I saw this as a place to try the problem-solving technique, so I suggested he do the homework while the others took the quiz and I would talk to him at the end of the class when I had a free period.

STUDENT: How 'bout if you give me that test you gave them, only let me do it as an open-book test?

TEACHER: Oh, you think you could do better if you could refer to your book.

STUDENT: Yeah, I could do good with my book. Remember once you let us have an open-book test?

TEACHER: The day everyone could use his book on the test, you feel you did well.

STUDENT: Yeah. I know *everyone* could use their books that day, but the other kids have a real advantage over me on this test. They had a lesson and demonstration that I didn't have, and besides I've never used the machine.

TEACHER: You feel slighted or cheated because the other kids had the advantage of review, et cetera, when you were out. You think that if I let you use your book you can balance the disadvantage.

STUDENT: Right! (*Pauses*). Why don't you just forget the test and give me a B? (*Laughs*)

TEACHER: We obviously have a problem. It needs a solution we can

* Submitted by T.E.T. instructor Katherine Pigott Newman, Sharon, Massachusetts.

both be satisfied with. I have some reservations about just giving you or any student a *machine* test and having you take it "open book." I'd like to be fairly sure by your test answers that you understand the material, including proper safety practices. I'm afraid that you could just make a list of things directly from the book without really understanding.

STUDENT: Yeah.

TEACHER: I'd like to try to write down what your problem really is.

STUDENT: What do you mean? Why do you want to do that?

TEACHER: Instead of me just telling you what to do, maybe we can solve the problem together.

STUDENT: Okay. I'll play your game.

TEACHER: Okay. You missed the lesson and demonstration on the lathe because you were out sick. Because of this and the fact that you've never used the machine before, you think you're at a disadvantage and should not take the test.

STUDENT: Right.

TEACHER: Okay. Let's think of some alternatives. Do you have any ideas?

STUDENT: Yeah, I could take an open-book test, but you won't let me.

TEACHER: Okay, but it's a suggestion we could discuss. Any others?

STUDENT: No.

TEACHER: How about what you said earlier? Just forget the test and give you a B.

STUDENT: Why even talk about it? You won't do it.

TEACHER: Well, let's think about it, along with the others, and then maybe come up with a solution we can both live with.

STUDENT: This is dumb! Why are we going through all this?

TEACHER: Let's just try listing all *our* ideas instead of me making a decision you may not like. Okay?

STUDENT: Okay.

TEACHER: Any other ideas?

STUDENT: No.

TEACHER: How about if I gave you an old test—similar to the one the other kids had. You can do it like homework and then come and try another test.

STUDENT: Would it count?

TEACHER: Not for a grade, but it would help you review key information.

STUDENT: Naa! (*Pauses*) Well, maybe that *would* help.

TEACHER: Or maybe you could reread the chapter and then try the test.

STUDENT: Yeah, that might work. Or maybe I could come in and see the film loops. That might help.

TEACHER: Maybe you could come in after school and have a demonstration.

STUDENT: Yeah, I guess so.

TEACHER: Any other ideas?

STUDENT: No. I like a couple of those.

TEACHER: Okay, let's review the list we made while talking.
> One—open-book test
> Two—give B, forget test
> Three—old test as practice with book; regular test without book
> Four—reread chapter
> Five—view film loops
> Six—after-school demonstration

STUDENT: I like either one, three, or five.

TEACHER: Let's take them one at a time, okay? Number one is unacceptable to me on machine tests, as I explained before, because of safety. How about number two?

STUDENT: No, I was just kidding about that. It wouldn't be fair anyway.

TEACHER: Number three is acceptable with me. How about you?

STUDENT: Yeah, that's not too bad.

TEACHER: Okay, we'll hold on to that one.

STUDENT: Number four wouldn't be too good. I don't think that would help. I like number five best, I guess. Number six looks good, but I can't come after school.

TEACHER: How about if we combined numbers five and six. You come in Friday during your study period and look at the film loops. Then I'll give you a demonstration while the others are working.

STUDENT: Can you do that?

TEACHER: Yes, if you think it would help. I'll be brief and cover only the high points while the others are working.

STUDENT: When should I take the test?

TEACHER: How about Monday during that same study period?

STUDENT: Yeah! That's good.

Later the teacher commented:

Much to my surprise, the solution worked. He came in the next day, watched the film, and I gave him a brief demonstration covering the key safety points. He told me that he reviewed the chapter before taking the quiz on Monday. He passed the quiz easily with a grade of B.

Apart from the successful resolution of the conflict, acceptable to both teacher and student, this experience in collaboration probably had a significant effect on improving their relationship. Very likely, that student's feelings toward his teacher were more positive after seeing him flexible and open to ideas, yet firm about his own convictions. The teacher's evaluation of the student as a chronic griper most certainly changed after observing him responsibly carrying out his end of the bargain.

Following is another problem-solving session. This nine-year-old boy's teacher* had been experimenting with the PPC

---

* Marlene Anderson, Hinsdale, Illinois.

procedure we teach in the T.E.T. course: the "Periodic Planning Conference," a method for achieving Method III agreements between teacher and student on educational objectives. The PPC capitalizes on the same principle underlying Method III conflict resolution: *Students will be more highly motivated to carry out decisions if they participated or had a voice in them.*

This transcript again illustrates how important it is for teachers to use active listening if they want to help students release and work through feelings, remove barriers along the way, and free students to engage in problem solving.

TEACHER: Hello, I see you've something you'd like to share with me today.

STUDENT: Yeah, I've read a lot this week.

TEACHER: You're really involved with this book.

STUDENT: I was wondering if all these books have the same thing in them.

TEACHER: You're wondering if all the *Boxcar Children* books are the same.

STUDENT: Do they all have the same stories?

TEACHER: The series of books all have the same characters but different plots.

STUDENT: Oh, that's what I've wondered about. They sure are good.

TEACHER: You'd like to read more of these kinds of books.

STUDENT: Yeah, I can hardly wait till I'm finished with this one. You know today in math class we had to do plus and minus and I wasn't so good 'cause we've been doing division lately and I forgot all about the others.

TEACHER: Wow, you just couldn't remember all that easy stuff.

STUDENT: Yeah, then I didn't even get the paper done. I wasn't used to it and the pluses and minuses were all mixed up.

TEACHER: Sometimes those math pages can really be tricky when they put all the different processes on one page.

STUDENT: It sure *can* be. I'm really getting good with my multiplication tables, though.

TEACHER: You're proud of the progress you're making in math.

STUDENT: I get all my work done, then I get to use the overhead or chalkboard or play math games.

TEACHER: Your math teacher makes math fun for you.

STUDENT: She sure does. Before, at the beginning of the year, I never liked school. Something's happened, though, and I don't know what, but now I just love school.

TEACHER: Wow, what an exciting feeling! I've noticed an improvement in your behavior in my classroom and none of the playground teachers has complained lately of the fighting that used to go on during recess.

STUDENT: You know why? Before I wasn't so used to playing with girls. Now I play with Julie and you know she has those stuffed animals and she lets me play with them. Then at recess we take them out and play outside.

TEACHER: It used to be hard for you to play with girls.

STUDENT: Yup.

TEACHER: You were afraid of them.

STUDENT: I sure was, but not anymore. I played with Ken, though, today, too. We played with some cars.

TEACHER: So you've discovered that you can play with both boys and girls.

STUDENT: Hmmm.

TEACHER: Jay, we have just a few minutes left. I wonder if you'd review what your plans are for next week.

STUDENT: Well, for sure I'm going to be reading *Boxcar Children*. You know since I've been reading this book I hardly have time to do my spelling.

TEACHER: You're so turned on with reading that it's been difficult to balance your time to include spelling work.

STUDENT: I'm really ahead, though, in my spelling.

TEACHER: You're not concerned at this time about your spelling work.

STUDENT: No, not really. I have a little bit of ditto work to do for my reading-skills teacher.

TEACHER: I have an English paper on the use of capital letters, question marks, and periods to return to you.

STUDENT: Oh, I see something on that I need to correct.

TEACHER: Okay, you can take it along with you and correct it next week.

STUDENT: I think I'll do some kind of art project to go along with my book.

TEACHER: Thank you, Jay, for sharing your plans.

STUDENT: You're welcome.

In her evaluation of this session, the teacher added a post-script that says a great deal about the therapeutic effects of individualized instruction and mutual goal setting *in a relationship with a teacher who knows how to active-listen and problem-solve*:

The most interesting part of this situation is the change in this child's behavior. He was one of the largest boys among a group of thirty children. He was a continual whiner, always blamed others, and was frequently in fights on the playground. After six months of being in an environment where individualized instruction took place and emphasis was on mutual goal setting through Periodic Planning Conferences, this student had shown a tremendous change in his attitude and behavior in school.

HOW TO RESOLVE CONFLICTS BETWEEN STUDENTS WITH METHOD III

Conflicts between students have harmful effects in classrooms, not only in reducing the teaching-learning time of the participants but also in disrupting the entire group of students. Wishing away such conflicts will never work because youngsters of every age inevitably get into disagreements, verbal spats, quarrels, fights, even knock-down, drag-out battles.

Typically, teachers try to handle such conflicts by power methods—using force, threatening punishment, or actually punishing. Most teachers admit to feeling very ineffective or impotent when it comes to dealing with student conflicts.

The Method III no-lose approach is as effective in resolving student-student conflicts as in teacher-student conflicts. The principal difference is the teacher's role, because in student-student conflicts the teacher is a facilitator for getting the six-step Method III process going between students. The teacher is more like one of those labor-management mediators whose stock-in-trade has been described as "keep 'em talking."

This role is well illustrated in the following conflict-resolution session* with two fourth-graders, Laura and Ann. Ann is described by the teacher as "disliked by other children because she is a pest, and so no one wants to be seated with Ann as a partner."

ANN: Mrs. T., Laura won't sit with me and help me with the map project.

LAURA: It's because Ann doesn't want to work. She just wants to talk and fool around and she writes on my papers.

ANN: I'm just pretending to write on your papers.

MRS. T.:   Girls, it seems to me that you both have a problem. I think that I could listen to both sides of the situation and perhaps we could come to some conclusions and even find a solution.

GIRLS: All right. What do we do?

MRS. T.:   Just tell me how you feel and I'll listen very carefully.

ANN: Laura said she wanted to sit beside me and now she doesn't. She doesn't really want to anyway. She just did it so you'll

* Submitted by a New England teacher, Mrs. T., in a T.E.T. class of Katherine Pigott Newman, Sharon, Massachusetts.

like her and think she's nice. I really want her to work with me.

LAURA: I did want to work with you, but you're spoiling my work and I want to get it passed in on time. You don't care about your own work and you want me to be the same as you.

MRS. T.:   Ann, I hear you saying that you'd like Laura to be your partner on this project, but you two aren't getting along together. Laura, I hear you saying that you'd like to work with Ann but getting along together is difficult because she's not working seriously. Let's list all the possible solutions to this problem.

ANN: Laura could be more patient and help me.

LAURA: I could leave Ann and we could work separately.

ANN: You could move our desks far apart.

LAURA: (*Not really serious*) You could send a note home to Ann's mother saying she's a big pest.

ANN: (*Serious retaliation*) Tell Laura's mother that she thinks she's perfect.

LAURA: Ann could settle down and do her work and stop fooling around.

ANN: Laura could wait till I catch up to the part she's working on.

LAURA: We could try again together.

MRS. T.:   I'll read these possible solutions as I've jotted them down. Which of all these do you think is the best solution? (*Reads solutions*).

ANN: We could try again . . . and if it doesn't work we could separate our desks.

MRS. T.:   May I suggest something? Now that you know what bothers each of you about the other, why not try again for a day and try hard not to do the things that bother each other. Come and tell me at the end of the day how it worked. We can all talk again then, but really try to make this work. I know that desks can be moved far apart, but I think that's the easy way out and I also think you girls are grown-up enough to handle this map project and this problem together.

Here's Mrs. T.'s subsequent write-up of the outcome of this brief no-lose session:

The girls are now working together; and so far two days have passed without a request for separation. Although Ann's pattern has been to "test" her friends to the extreme to insure their true friendship (maybe because her friendships so often terminate and she wants to get the hurt over with), for now, Ann has a friend and a working partner.

We cannot resist drawing an exciting suggestion from this real-life situation: In but a few minutes, Mrs. T. offered Ann *a new model for all her interpersonal relationships*. With several repetitions this might radically change Ann's ineffective methods of relating to her peers and encourage her growth. Should that happen, Mrs. T. will have been an educator in the truest sense of that word—not just a teacher of subject matter but a developer of the total child. This is what educational administrators theorize about but is seldom practiced in schools.

A different conflict between students was resolved by another teacher trained in T.E.T. methods. This teacher[*] reported the following Method III problem-solving session with a group of her third-grade boys:

TEACHER: The third-graders seem to be having a problem at recess time. I hear complaints about not letting some people play in the games and about cheating.

DICK: Yeah. When Tom and Curt come out they take over and make their own rules.

VIC: Everybody is afraid of them. Evan and Jay gang up with them.

DON: We tell them the rules, but they cheat anyway.

FRED: Tom runs away with the ball when he's out.

[*] Submitted by a New England teacher, Mrs. J., in a T.E.T. class of Katherine Pigott Newman, Sharon, Massachusetts.

DICK: We pick teams, and then Tom just goes on any team he wants to. The others go with him.

MIKE: But you always yell, "No newcomers."

DICK: Well, it's pretty hard after you've started a game to have more people show up and want to play.

MIKE: I don't show up late; you don't think I play good. I never get my ups or you'd know I can play.

DICK: Well . . .

TEACHER: Mike, you feel Dick hasn't had a chance to see you play so he can't really know how you play.

MIKE: I can't improve if I don't get to play.

DICK: Well, yeah, I guess that's right. You can play.

TEACHER: Many of you are afraid of Tom and Curt. You feel they cheat.

DICK: Maybe we could make up some rules and make a copy for each third grade. Then everyone would read them and they might not cheat.

VIC: If there was no cheating we'd get more time to play.

DON: Maybe Tom and Curt cheat because they don't really know the rules. They might like to have them written down.

PAUL: Can we make up some rules?

TEACHER: You'd like to make up a list of rules for each third grade. Sounds like a good idea to me. Why don't those who'd like to work on the rules get together. When the list is ready let me know and the class can discuss them.

Here's what the teacher reported happened next:

About six of the boys worked diligently on the rules. The class was shown the completed list and objected only to number six ("No newcomers"). It was decided that once the game began it was okay to call no newcomers. Copies were made of the rules for the other classes with an explanation of number six. The rules were then posted in each room, and the teachers were all delighted with the results. It was interesting to note that no one in the other classes objected to the rules in any way.

I commended the boys for the way they had organized themselves initially and expressed my pleasure about the manner in
which they dealt with their problem. Mike is happier and no
longer does little things to irritate his classmates. The boys do
not complain about Tom and Curt anymore.

Serious conflict between students can lead to violence, and
in some cases to mobilization of gangs in support of a member
involved in the conflict. From one of our T.E.T. instructors comes this story, told to the class by Mr. C., the principal of a school in the predominantly black and low-income
Watts area of Los Angeles, scene of the violent riots several
years ago.

Two sixth-grade girls were fighting with each other, not only in
the classroom but wherever they met. Each had enlisted the backing of older brothers and sisters and friends, so that the quarrel
was becoming a gang war, threatening to break out into violence
since some of the older gang members had weapons and were
threatening to use them.
  Mr. C., the principal, and the classroom teacher for the two
girls had discussed strategies, but nothing had worked. They
were about ready to separate the girls by transferring one to another class. Before moving one of the girls, however, Mr. C. had
decided to confront the class, to "read them the riot act," as he
put it, and had asked his T.E.T. class members to help him construct a high-potency I-message that he could use to do the job.
The class objected to this. They tried to convince Mr. C. that it
was only the two girls who were fighting and therefore he should
confront *them*, not the whole class. After a while Mr. C. bought
that idea and agreed to call the two girls into his office for a
problem-solving session. The class then helped him construct a
good clear message about his fear of the girls' quarrel erupting
into gang warfare and his feelings of helplessness in preventing
that from happening.
  The following week Mr. C. came back to the T.E.T. class with
a request to talk about what had happened. He was bubbling
over with excitement. He told the class that he'd pay anyone of

them a hundred dollars if they could guess the outcome of his meeting with the two girls. None could, and it was obvious that he was astounded himself.

He had sent the prepared I-message to the girls when they got to his office, and then sat back to see how they would react. He said that they just sat there for a few moments and then both started to talk at once, each blaming the other for all the trouble. "Before I took this course," said Mr. C., "I'd never have been able to handle what happened."

This is the report of what happened, as told by Mr. C. in the T.E.T. class:

"They screamed obscenities at each other and threatened each other with the vilest consequences. A few weeks ago I'd never have allowed them to behave like that, not in *my* office. But it's a good thing I was able to active-listen, because after a while they began to calm down. Their voices got down to a normal conversational level and they quit swearing. It was almost as if they *needed* to have that chance to really scream at each other before they could do anything else. What all the screaming was about was that one of the girls, in front of a whole group of friends, had called the other girl a street whore. Actually, the girl said that she only told the other girl she *looked like* a street whore, that she never said she *was* one. As I heard their feelings and helped them understand each other, it became clearer and clearer that the real differences between them, believe it or not, were over makeup and grooming.

"This is the part that is so unbelievable. Out of that near-war came a solution that nobody would believe. Those two girls decided that what they needed was a class in grooming for girls!

"I've helped them get started. One of the women on the staff is sponsoring the grooming class, but mostly the two girls have worked together to round up community resources from department stores, salons, and cosmetic companies. They have a group of thirty-eight sixth-grade girls that will meet two days a week after school to learn how to dress and put on makeup.

"I'm convinced that Method III really works! *My* solution was going to be calling the cops!"

While such a dramatic and unpredictably constructive solution cannot always be expected from Method III in serious student-student conflicts, T.E.T. instructors are accustomed to hearing accounts of some rather amazing outcomes, turn-arounds in relationships thought to be "impossible," "pathological," "irreparable." Those of us working to help teachers learn how to use Method III are no longer surprised by such incidents. Method III does work—sometimes it works miracles. And to those of us trained in the psychological or psychiatric tradition, which taught us that significant change in relationships occurs only after intensive and prolonged psychotherapy, the positive effects of Method III have not been easy to believe.

The lesson may be profound: that professionals have grossly exaggerated the effects of early social and psychological deprivation; greatly underestimated the capacity of children and young people to make constructive changes in behavior when given a climate of acceptance and trust, *plus* exposure to *methods* that give them the feeling they have a real chance to get their basic needs met.

The repair of psychologically deprived children and youth may be easier than most of us ever dreamed.

HOW TO USE METHOD III TO SET CLASSROOM RULES AND POLICIES

No one can successfully argue that rules and regulations are unnecessary in human relationships. In the family, rules and policies are needed for its survival and for the security of its members. Hospitals, universities, agencies, businesses and industrial organizations all need rules and policies. So do municipal, state, and federal governments. People in groups, large or small, establish laws to define, regulate, and limit the behavior of all members of those groups. Without rules, regulations, agreements, policies, contracts, laws, people could not function in human relationships.

The alternative to various kinds of rules, regulations, and laws is anarchy.

Nowhere is this more true than in schools and classrooms. As we said earlier, students have a great deal of difficulty trying to function in a setting where they don't know the limits, where the difference between acceptable and unacceptable behaviors is not understood. When there are no rules (or where rules are ambiguous) conflicts are rampant and must be resolved over and over. Ambiguous situations are terribly threatening to students and teachers alike, which cause undue amounts of energy to be spent trying to figure out how to behave or how to cope, rather than using this energy more constructively.

Yet, while some classrooms may make it difficult for students to function because there are no clearly understood rules and policies, it's far more common for students to face the opposite situation—classrooms overloaded with rules, many making absolutely no sense at all, or existing exclusively for the teacher's benefit.

Most schools work with two sets of rules for students: "formal" rules and policies (often distributed to students and faculty in booklets) and "informal" rules and policies that become part of the school's tradition. Sometimes the informal rules and regulations are retained long after their original purpose has been served, unquestioned in most cases even though obviously no longer appropriate, as in the following case:

An elementary-school principal, new to the building, discovered that students were required to exit from the cafeteria after lunch and take an indirect route to the playground, passing by many classes still in session, instead of going directly across a blacktopped area far removed from classrooms. When he asked staff members about the rule, they told him that it had "always been that way," that going to the playground by the roundabout route was "the way it's done here."

The implication was clear to the principal—the staff seemed to feel that rules were rules and there didn't necessarily have to be a reason for them. However, one teacher who had taught at the school since its construction recalled the rule's genesis.

It seems that during the first weeks of the school's operation a crew of men arrived to install the blacktop outside the cafeteria. To avoid possible injury and many sticky shoes, students were asked to go to the playground by the indirect route—which was still being used, eighteen years later.

Such situations would be hilarious if they were not so aggravating and demoralizing. Students everywhere are forced to try to function in schools where rules are made by and for adults, in some cases by adults long departed and for reasons no one can remember. This applies to both formal and informal rules.

Also, in most schools, student "participation" in setting rules and policies has been minimal, for the most part limited to trivialities—maybe setting the date for the homecoming dance or deciding the color of the bulletin board in the cafeteria.

We say with some assurance that three conditions are almost certain to create conflicts between teachers and students: (1) when there are no clear-cut rules or policies; (2) when rules and policies are not formally spelled out and are therefore difficult to understand or interpret (or know about); and (3) when rules and policies are imposed on students by adult authorities without student participation, especially if such rules appear unfair or unreasonable.

To avoid conflicts, schools and classrooms must institute procedures that involve students (and teachers) in the process of making the rules and policies they will be expected to follow. In Chapter XI we will suggest ways of getting an entire faculty involved in setting (and changing) rules of the school. Now we deal only with student participation in setting *classroom* rules and policies.

HOW RULE–SETTING CLASS MEETINGS WORK

Traditionally, the rules students are required to follow in classrooms are determined solely by teachers. Just as traditionally, many students break those rules or engage in "testing" behavior. Teachers therefore spend a great amount of their time (estimated at fifty to sixty percent) policing their classes, trying to enforce rules, punishing students who break them.

An alternative to this unhappy state is using Method III to involve both teacher and students in a joint effort to determine what rules are needed in the classroom. In T.E.T. we call this "The Rule-Setting Class Meeting." Ideally, the meeting should take place on the first day of school, although some teachers have instituted it successfully after taking the T.E.T. course and after classes had been functioning for several weeks.

Overcoming the Threat

Some teachers are afraid to hold rule-setting meetings with their classes even after they have been trained in Method III because they are sure that students will not make adequate rules, or may make rules too lenient or too stringent, or silly.

Teachers who have these fears have forgotten some of the principles of Method III. First, the class cannot make rules about situations outside the teacher's authority. They simply cannot decide, for example, to let classes out two hours early, or to change the law regarding smoking in the room. *The group can only make determinations within the teacher's "area of freedom."* Even within that area, students cannot make rules unacceptable to the teacher, because in Method III all decisions must be by *consensus* of the group, and the teacher is a member of the group. (In win-lose methods it *would* be risky to try the group process; after all, the teacher could be outvoted.)

Preparations

We suggest you tell the class about your objectives for such a meeting. Here is one statement you might use: "This meeting is for the purpose of our setting rules and adopting policies that we can all agree upon about all important and predictable behavior of both the students and teacher." Make it simpler for younger students. You might say, "Let's talk about the rules we need so we can all learn a lot and get along together. I need your help in deciding what these rules should be."

It is very important that students understand you will not use power to insure your getting only the rules *you* want. It is equally important that they understand you will not let them use *their* power either! They must understand the philosophy of Method III—that everyone must be satisfied with all decisions made; no one is to feel he has "lost."

The physical setting is important. Students should be seated in some arrangement that allows them to see each other, face-to-face.

Conducting the Meeting

First, you and the students should come up with a list of situations that need rules the most. Keep this list limited to activities *most likely to cause problems*. Your combined experience will probably suggest such perennial headaches as:

Getting into seats at start of class

Getting out of seats at end of class

Storage of materials

Problems when teacher is working with a small group

Noise or talking when teacher is presenting or giving instructions

Working with complicated equipment

Caution: Don't try to come up with rules for *everything*. Remember that if problems arise during the year (or semester), you can stop to make rules then. The principal purpose of this meeting is to demonstrate that students *can participate* in rule setting; that rules are needed for a group to function; that the class belongs to all its members; that each person's rights must be honored (including the teacher's).

Use butcher paper or the chalkboard. When enough problem areas have been identified, ask for suggested rules for the first item. Remember, you can suggest rules, too.

Try to follow the six steps of the problem-solving process (see p. 227). *Keep evaluation out of Step 2.* If you think you hear considerable agreement on a rule, test it out: "Anyone object to that rule?"

It is extremely important not to drag out the process so students get bored. *Keep up the pace. Work rapidly.*

Write down each rule as it is adopted. Reproduce the list later so each student has a copy. Put a copy on the bulletin board. Or make a large poster. Or put each rule on a piece of cardboard and thumbtack all of them around the room.

Above all, let the class know that any rule can later be changed if it proves to be unworkable.

The Teacher's Role

Obviously, the effectiveness of the rule-setting meeting will depend greatly on your leadership in this meeting. You'll need to:

a. Use active listening frequently.

b. Put aside digressions by such comments as "That's another issue—let's stick to this problem for now."

c. Use I-messages to get your needs across or to express your unwillingness to accept certain suggested rules (e.g., "Teacher punishes those who talk").

d. Avoid positive *or* negative evaluation (e.g., "That's a good idea" or "That's a silly suggestion").

The Benefits of the Rule-Setting Meeting

There are so many tangible and intangible benefits from class participation in rule setting that it is difficult to list them all. Here are only some:

a. Students will be more motivated *to follow the rules*.

b. Creative thinking will be encouraged.

c. Students will learn that teachers are human and have needs.

d. The rules will be more relevant and usually of a higher quality than those that teachers set unilaterally, without consideration for the students' needs. "Dumb" rules will be avoided.

e. Less enforcement by the teacher will be needed; responsibility for enforcement will rest with the entire group.

f. Predetermined rules will prevent many unacceptable behaviors and conflicts.

g. You will be giving students a lesson in democracy, demonstrating how *difficult* it is to make laws as well as how *rewarding* it is to be allowed to do so.

The model for students which the teacher provides in the rule-setting meeting is probably more valuable than all the pamphlets, lectures, films, or books about democracy that students will be exposed to during their school career. Method III rule setting is democracy in action, *experiential* democracy, not just words about an abstract concept.

What About the Time Involved?

Teachers sometimes resist the idea of the Method III rule-setting meeting because they fear it will take a lot of time. It *will* take time. In fact, we advise counting on no less than a half a day. It might even take one or two days with some classes. We also recommend that the rule-setting meetings be held *prior to almost any other class activity,* rather than waiting for trouble to occur.

Is this time worth it? Remember how much time teachers ordinarily spend, day after day, enforcing Method I rules. And how much time is ordinarily spent confronting students or modifying the environment.

Mutually agreed-upon rules will make much of this continuing expenditure of time entirely unnecessary. Our opinion, based on inputs from hundreds of teachers (as well as business leaders, administrators, shop foremen, and others) who have used Method III to set rules with their groups, is:

Participative rule setting ultimately saves countless hours of dealing with unacceptable behaviors, handling conflicts, and enforcing rules made by "the boss."

Here is the appraisal of one teacher with several years' experience in using Method III for setting classroom rules:

Of all the courses I have taken in classroom management, T.E.T. has to be rated the most valuable. Of all the things I learned in T.E.T., the most beneficial is Method III. When I took the course, I was about ready to quit teaching because of the constant need to be a disciplinarian. T.E.T. showed me that the real problem was my Method I rules. I made them and I had to enforce them. That's all I accomplished most of the time. When I let the class set the rules, this changed. I have time to teach now, and the students like me more because I am a teacher instead of a disciplinarian. I don't know if they learn any more, but we have a lot more fun learning it.

HOW TO DEAL WITH TYPICAL PROBLEMS TEACHERS ENCOUNTER USING METHOD III

Method III is simple in concept but not so simple in execution. Invariably teachers encounter problems, especially during the early transition period from using Method I or Method II.

Competing "Solutions" versus Competing "Needs"

Some teachers report that they repeatedly made the mistake of defining their conflicts with students in terms of "competing solutions." Classic hassles of this type go on in most schools. One goes something like this:

TEACHER: We waste a lot of time each day before going out to recess. How are we going to solve the problem of getting everyone to sit in his seat quietly so we can be dismissed?

CLASS: (*Shrugged shoulders, puzzled looks*)

TEACHER: Well, every day I have to yell at you to sit down and be quiet. Especially you, Julio, and Victor.

JULIO: Well, you could stop yelling at us.

TEACHER: If I didn't yell, you'd never sit down and be quiet.

JULIO: That's true, but it would sure be a lot quieter in here if you weren't yelling. . . .

Situations like this convince teachers that students like Julio and Victor are obstructionists and difficult to "manage." Students see the teacher as an old grouch, out to make their lives as miserable as possible. Both are wrong.

In the above situation the teacher must face up to an undeniable question: Does she *need* to have thirty bottoms firmly seated on thirty chairs? Getting everyone seated is a *solution* to the teacher's need for some form of transition from one activity to another. Julio and Victor do not *need* to stand in the back of the room talking. That, too, is a *solution*— perhaps to their need to organize activities in the upcoming recess period. When the teacher sends her solution, they end up pushing their own solutions, playing a game of "My Solution Is Better Than Yours."

Such an argument cannot be resolved short of someone having to give in, be permissive, not get his way. Conflicts defined in terms of competing solutions turn into Method I power struggles. Somebody wins and somebody loses.

Teachers tell us that even after they have learned to differentiate between needs and solutions, it may still be hard to get students to give up their tendency to define problems in terms of *their* own pet solutions or wants. Teachers find that it takes a lot of listening for students to clarify and separate their ideas and desires from what they truly need.

Teachers also must find the courage to send honest I-messages to let students know whenever one of their "wants" or "solutions" is not acceptable to the teacher:

"I couldn't accept that solution, Mary, because [give reason], but tell me what your needs are."

"That would make you happy, but I would still have my problem."

"I can understand your wanting to do that, but maybe there is some other solution that would enable you to get your needs met."

When Students Don't Stick to the Agreement

Teachers find that occasionally a student does not carry out his end of the bargain even after a mutually acceptable solution has been reached through Method III. When this happens some teachers are tempted to revert to Method I and use their power. This reaction is disastrous and invariably wipes out the progress the teacher has been trying to make in convincing students that she has stopped resolving conflicts with power. Furthermore, resorting to power to enforce agreements or rules or decisions gradually shifts the responsibility from the student right back to the teacher.

We encourage teachers, first, to send a strong I-message that accurately communicates their disappointment and the negative consequences (to them) of a student's failure to act as agreed. More than likely, the I-message will bring forth a message from the student telling why he did not (or could not) stick to the agreement. With this additional data, the teacher is in a position to decide what to do next. Among the alternatives are:

1. Give the student another chance.

2. Find some way he can be helped to remember or keep his commitment.

3. Go back to the problem-solving process and try to generate a better solution—one that is easier for the student to carry out responsibly.

What About Problems Outside the Teacher's Area of Freedom?

Solving problems with Method III can be such an exhilarating experience that some teachers and their classes get carried away and try to make decisions that they have no authority to make; they try to solve problems outside the teacher's "area of freedom." For example, if a school district has a district-wide rule prohibiting smoking in school buildings, a teacher who asks his class to come up with a decision about smoking would be operating outside his area of freedom. He has no authority to change the smoking rule because it was made at a "higher level of authority."

Within a teacher's area of freedom are such problems as noise in his class, neatness, assignments, division of labor, handling and storage of materials, seating arrangements, lesson planning, and so on.

Figure 28 shows how a teacher's area of freedom is narrowed down by laws, rules, and policies already made by per-

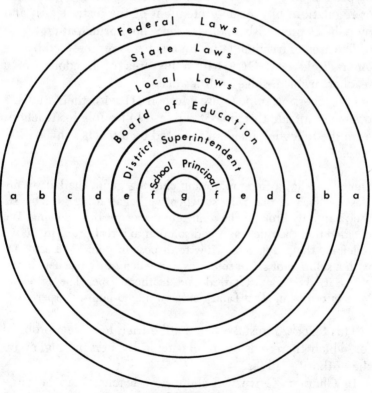

FIGURE 28

sons at higher levels of authority, beginning with federal laws and extending down to rules for the teacher's school building.

Area (a) represents the reduction of the teacher's freedom imposed by federal laws—e.g., "compulsory education." Obviously, a teacher has no authority to ask his students to make a decision about whether they should attend school.

Area (b) shows the reduction of the teacher's freedom imposed by state laws—e.g., "Textbooks must be approved by the state superintendent of instruction." So no teacher has authority to problem-solve with students what textbook they would like to use.

A teacher's freedom is further cut down by local laws (c), by policies laid down by the Board of Education (d), by rules or regulations of the superintendent of the district (e), and by policies previously made by the school principal (f).

The area of freedom left for a teacher is represented by the inner circle (g). Only within his area of freedom can a teacher problem-solve with his class.

If teachers attempt to use Method III with their students on issues outside this area, it can lead to trouble for teachers, as in the following incident reported by a teacher in a T.E.T. class:

Our school has a rule prohibiting chewing gum. The kids in my class really hate that rule, so when we began using Method III they naturally brought the gum rule up for problem solving. We decided that the rule was a bad solution to a real problem. So we redefined the problem as "How to dispose of gum." We came up with a solution or set of solutions, but when other teachers heard about it, they almost tarred and feathered me. The principal later informed me that I must enforce the no-gum rule, period.

This teacher's mistake was that he tried to solve a problem for which there existed a rule made by persons higher up the authority ladder.

In Chapter XI we will show how teachers can be more influential in bringing about changes in rules that have been made by their principals, by their superintendents, or by the Board of Education.

"What If We Can't Agree on a Solution?"

Most teachers have had so little experience as members of any decision-making group that they are skeptical about a group's ability to find solutions acceptable to all its members. They naturally wonder what to do if they are problem solving with a single student or a group of students and can't decide on a mutually acceptable solution.

The fact is, surprisingly few no-lose sessions fail to produce an acceptable solution if the six steps are followed carefully throughout the problem-solving process. Occasionally stalemates do occur because students are still distrustful and Method III is still new to them, or because they are still in a win-lose (power struggle) frame of mind.

When an acceptable solution is slow in coming, teachers need to try everything they can think of—such as:

1. Keep talking and thinking creatively.

2. Go back to Step 2 and generate some more solutions.

3. Try another session tomorrow.

4. Make strong appeals, such as "There must be a way to solve this. Let's try harder to find an acceptable solution," or "I'm sure there is a solution somewhere."

5. Bring the difficulty out in the open and see if there might be some underlying problem that has not been dealt with—some "hidden agenda" that blocks progress. Say, "I wonder why we're having trouble finding a solution. Is something else hanging us up?"

When Youngsters Build Punishment Into a Solution

Teachers often encounter students who, after a decision is reached, want to build into the agreement some penalties or punishments to be administered if anyone fails to live up to his end of the bargain. Youngsters are so accustomed to being punished for infractions of rules that they mistakenly assume this is the only way to handle broken commitments. Surprisingly the punishments they suggest are often rather severe.

You need to remind such youngsters that the new method of resolving conflicts is a *substitute* for punishment, that you don't want to resort to punishment anymore. Remind them that this new method depends on trust, that you *assume* everyone who participated in making the decision will carry it out. Talking about punishment or penalties communicates distrust, doubt, and pessimism. Kids often remark, "When teachers trust me, I feel like being trustworthy. But when teachers distrust me, I feel I might as well go ahead and do what they already think I'll do."

The basic principle is: With Method III, teachers should adopt an attitude of "innocent until proven guilty," or, more to the point, "responsible until proven irresponsible."

How to Enforce Rules Outside the
Teacher's Area of Freedom

Teachers will be confronted with student behavior prohibited by rules of higher authority, outside the teacher's area of freedom. How can they handle such rule-breaking behavior effectively and with the least chance of damaging their relationships with students?

Here are some suggested procedures consistent with our philosophy.

First, determine where the student's rule-breaking behavior fits into your rectangle for him. If it is in the No-Problem area, you may choose to make no attempt at enforcement. This condition usually exists when a rule seems to the teacher petty, useless, unfair, or unenforceable, and where nonenforcement is unlikely to result in criticism of the teacher. Examples: rules about gum chewing; the proper form for addressing adults; holding hands in the hall, etc. Nonenforcement of such minor rules is common. Few teachers enforce all school rules. Those who do look cranky and mean to students. At the same time, when some teachers do not enforce rules and others do, such differences may undermine attitudes toward rules in general.

If the student's rule-breaking behavior is "below your line" (in the Teacher-Owned-Problem area), the following step-by-step procedure is recommended:

1. Determine if the student knows the rule and the prescribed consequence for its infraction. If he does not, inform him.

2. If, after you are certain he knows, he still asks to be free from the restrictions of that rule, tell him, "I don't have the authority to give you that freedom—it's outside my sphere of influence."

3. If, after you are certain he knows the rule, you believe he will go ahead and break it, send a clear I-message. Example: "When you break the rule about not climbing up and sitting on that high fence, I'm afraid I'll be held responsible or bawled out for not enforcing the rule or for not protecting your safety if you fall and hurt yourself."

4. Be sure to shift gears and active listen after sending your I-message.

5. If he does not change his attitude, move into Method III. Then you will probably learn what needs are motivating him to break the rule.

6. If Method III does not produce a solution acceptable to you, then you can (a) tell him what the consequences will be the next time; or (b) administer the consequences this time; or (c) make an effort to have the rule changed if you feel it is an unreasonable rule—e.g., in your faculty meeting or with the principal.

ARE THERE TIMES WHEN METHOD I IS NECESSARY?

Teachers in T.E.T. classes almost always ask this question. Its answer depends on a deeper understanding of certain concepts.

First, teachers must clear up a possible confusion between Method I and strong attempts to influence a student—e.g., giving orders, directions, commands. Keep in mind that Methods I, II, and III are alternatives for *resolving* a conflict *after it arises.* A tough-sounding order ("Keep in line") is not Method I; it is a strong "influence attempt." If a student is happy to comply, there is no conflict and it is unnecessary to use any of the three methods—nothing needs resolving. If the student *resists,* a conflict exists. If the teacher uses his *power* to overcome the resistance (resolve the conflict so that he wins and the student loses), only then has he used Method I.

Secondly, teachers need to understand more about strong influence attempts and the conditions that make them effective or ineffective. Certainly it is okay to attempt to influence your students; we all attempt to influence others as we go about meeting our needs. A human-relations problem arises only when the recipient is resistant to influence attempts. Influence attempts can be either I-messages or you-messages; neither is Method I or Method III. Such messages are influence attempts, not methods of resolving conflicts. An interesting advantage of the I-message is that if the recipient resists it (and conflict results), the sender's posture has set the stage for Method III conflict resolution much better than a you-message could have.

We all use a wide range of influence attempts, from weak to strong. Their relative strength is determined by the content of the message (from a single request to a direct order); the tone or loudness of voice; facial expression; use of physical force (pulling a child from the path of a speeding truck). Yet, unless conflict arises, none of these influence attempts can be called Method I or II or III.

Weaker influence attempts run less danger of being perceived by students as power plays. But they may not be influential enough under certain circumstances. If they don't work, the teacher must be prepared either to accept a "no" answer or to switch to a stronger attempt.

Under normal conditions, very strong influence attempts are usually perceived by students as threats; failure to obey may bring punishment. Usually the student's feeling will be strong resentment. The teacher will ordinarily pay one of two prices: Either the student will resist and fight back, or he will be afraid to bring the conflict into the open, leaving the resentment hidden, smoldering, and cumulative.

In two situations very strong influence attempts may be perfectly acceptable to students: (1) unusual circumstances and (2) where there are game-type rules. "Unusual circumstances" are those where speed of response is critical ("Don't jump now," "Duck your head"); where danger is clear and present ("Don't strike that match, the gas is on"); or where noisy or chaotic conditions demand a loud message from the teacher.

Students may accept strong influence attempts in games or other structured, task-oriented groups, as when a P.E. teacher yells, "Count off by fours!" or an orchestra teacher yells, "Louder on the brass!" Under these conditions, strong or loud influence attempts are not likely to provoke resistance. The real problems arise when teachers act like martinets and use strong influence attempts when these are not justified.

When conflict *does* arise from influence attempts, under certain circumstances the use of Method I by a teacher may be worth the price when (1) there is clear and present danger; (2) the child cannot understand the logic of your position; and (3) there is time pressure ("Get down the stairs or you'll miss your bus.").

When teachers use Method I in such situations because they feel it is necessary and justified, they can take steps afterward to prevent damage to their relationship. They can (1) explain to the student why they used Method I; (2) say they're sorry; (3) actively listen to the student's feelings; (4) offer to make up for it in some way acceptable to the student; and (5) initiate planning with the student to avoid his getting into a similar bind in the future.

The experience of teachers who try to use Method III is, in general, that infrequent use of Method I will not seriously damage relationships with students. Yet Method I does cause resentment in students. In some cases a teacher's use of Method I may result in the loss of the relationship, especially if the student's frustrated need is strong enough. That is always the major risk of using power.

X. WHEN VALUES COLLIDE
IN SCHOOL

SOME conflicts between teachers and students cannot be successfully resolved by Method III.

We ask teachers to face this limitation because, once having acquired the skills to make Method III work, they generally feel that they have finally looked over the crest of the hill. They feel relief and satisfaction in having achieved a major objective. They think, "Now, at last, I can take care of whatever may befall me as a teacher. I have quit taking responsibility for problems that rightly belong to students; I have learned how to communicate so that students will be more motivated to help me when I have a problem; I have learned how to prevent or eliminate many problems and conflicts simply by changing the environment and by structuring time; and I know how to resolve conflicts to get my needs and my students' needs met without having to use power."

But, to their dismay, teachers come up against certain conflicts that often are not resolvable, even with their newly learned nonpower methods and skills. These conflicts occur in schools over issues involving cherished beliefs, values, preferences, personal tastes, life-styles, ideals, and convictions. A very small sample of such issues includes:

Boys' hair length

Girls' skirt length

Other dress codes or standards

Drug use

Neatness, cleanliness, personal grooming

Proper language

Politeness, manners

Ethical or moral behavior

Justice

Honesty

Choice of friends

Patriotism

Religion

Sexual behavior

Beards and moustaches

People often are not willing to place these issues on the bargaining table; their values and beliefs are not amenable to any modification attempt nor to problem solving to find a mutually acceptable solution.

Many teachers claim they prefer not to enter the values arena of their students, unless these values relate directly to the content of instruction. They say they prefer to leave these teachings to families, churches, and other agencies. A commonly expressed attitude is "Just teaching my subject is tough enough without having to take on issues like how to dress or which drugs are okay and which aren't."

Unfortunately, conflicts over values cannot be avoided or wished away. When teachers try to avoid them they often get worse, not better—more irritating, not less. When value differences crop up between teachers and students, *something* has to be done. The first step is to recognize these conflicts as value conflicts or "value collisions," the term we prefer. Teachers need to be able to separate them from the conflict-of-needs situations discussed in Chapters VII, VIII and IX.

HOW TO IDENTIFY A VALUE COLLISION

The problems and conflicts that involve values are the ones remaining in the bottom of the rectangle when all others have been taken care of. It is not hard to tell which ones they are. They are the ones that leave you scratching your head when you try to think of a "tangible and concrete effect" to put in your I-message to convince the student that his behavior has a *real* consequence for you—interferes with your needs, your rights, your life. You know you are in a value collision when you confront a student about his behavior and he looks at you as surprised and shocked as if you had just fallen out of a tree or stepped out of a space ship.

You may also be able to tell that you have hit the "values area" when a student drops some hint (possibly unspoken) that tells you to lay off, to get off his back, or to stop hassling him. Or he may begin to counter your value judgments by making value judgments about *you!* You know you are getting into a value conflict when you have a powerful impulse to say, "To hell with I-messages! You're a dirty, smelly, unwashed, hippy-looking *bum!*" or some other inflammatory (but sometimes satisfying) judgmental statement.

We need to refer again to the rectangle and identify the value-collision area. Figure 29 shows how the acceptance line may be pushed down by the use of I-messages, modification of the environment, and Method III. These skills have increased the size of the Teaching-Learning area and decreased the size of the area of Unacceptable Behavior. What is left are conflicts involving values.

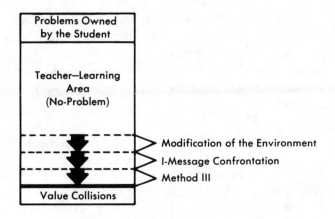

FIGURE 29

WHY I-MESSAGES SELDOM WORK
IN RESOLVING VALUE COLLISIONS

I-messages are not very effective in influencing a student to modify behavior based on a strong value or belief. Why should he change? He is not convinced that his behavior tangibly and concretely affects you. It is almost impossible to construct a three-component I-message when someone's

Description of Behavior	Tangible and Concrete Effect	Feeling
1) When you come to school in that dirty old sweatshirt . . .		I am disgusted.
2) When you do a half-hearted job on an assignment . . .		I am disappointed.
3) When you swear like that . . .		I am shocked.
4) When I see you, an athlete, smoking . . .		I am surprised.
5) When I see you hanging around with that crowd . . .		I am worried.

TABLE 4

values are different from yours; you will have trouble with the second component, the *tangible and concrete effect* on you. Try it in the situations outlined in Table 4. Watch how difficult it is to come up with a tangible and concrete effect that the student would buy.

Now, for comparison, try filling in the "tangible and concrete" component of the I-messages in Table 5, where the student behaviors are more likely to produce a tangible and concrete effect on you.

Description of Behavior	Tangible and Concrete Effect	Feeling
1) When you take books of mine off my desk without letting me know about it . . .		I feel frustrated and upset.
2) When you interrupt my conference with these students . . .		I'm upset and anxious.
3) When you take all the red tempera paint . . .		I feel "unfaired against."
4) When I find my films left out where they can get all scratched up . . .		I am anxious.
5) When you leave the science materials scattered all over the table . . .		I am frustrated.

TABLE 5

Wasn't it much easier to come up with tangible effects on you? If someone confronted *you* with a message like "When you take books of mine off my desk without letting me know about it, I have to spend a lot of time hunting for them and that makes me frustrated and upset," wouldn't you be motivated to help out in the future by changing your behavior in some way? Contrast that with your motivation to change if you had received the messages in Table 4. Do you see the difference? People are seldom motivated to modify behavior unless they are quite convinced that they are interfering with another in some very real way.

While I-messages have a low probability of getting a student to modify a value or a value-based behavior, we are not suggesting that teachers shouldn't try I-messages. They might work. They may also have some positive effects on the teacher-student relationship.

A "self-disclosure message" (an I-message without tangible-and-concrete component) at least lets a student know where you stand.

Suppose a student is wasting time he could use to finish an assignment that is due. You might share your feelings about his behavior, disclosing yourself so your feelings will not come as a surprise later. You might say, "I get concerned about your getting behind in your work when you just sit there staring out the window." Obviously, no tangible effect on you exists that the student would buy. But this message lets him know (1) that you are aware of what seems to you to be a problem; (2) that you care enough to say something about it; (3) that you are not "coming down on" the student or reprimanding him—merely sharing a feeling; and (4) that the door is open for the student to discuss what is going on.

As with any other I-message, you *must* then shift to active listening to help the student handle his reaction to your confrontation ("I'm too upset to work" or, "I was really trying to think about my assignment—where to start").

Self-disclosure messages occasionally cause students to change behavior, but don't count on it. Don't be surprised if they continue to behave in the same unacceptable way. And whatever you do, *do not send another I-message!* You must assume that the first one was heard. Once you have disclosed yourself, further disclosure is unnecessary and is usually heard by the student as an attempt to nag or hassle him.

WHY METHOD III SELDOM WORKS
IN RESOLVING VALUE COLLISIONS

In a conflict involving values, students rarely agree to enter into problem solving with you, and for the same reason that they do not buy your I-messages: They do not believe you are going to suffer any *real* deprivation or hurt as a result of their behavior. They do not want to enter into problem solving because *they do not see there is a problem.* Students simply refuse to move into a negotiating process—what is there to negotiate?

For this reason, Method III is almost always ineffective: students resist solving problems which they feel exist only in your imagination or which they feel are none of your business.

Adults are no different. Would *you* be willing to sit down with someone and negotiate your right to choose your own friends? Are you willing to use Method III with a good friend to problem-solve your style of dress, your taste in music, whether you should wear a beard, how you decorate your house? If a friend tells you he doesn't approve of the church you attend, are you willing to enter into negotiation with him about changing your affiliation? The answer is undoubtedly the same that students give to teachers who want *them* to negotiate their values: "Not on your life!"

When teachers begin to understand and accept this particular ineffectiveness of I-messages and Method III, they are puzzled and confused. One teacher expressed it this way:

Well, what am I to do? You say I can't count on I-messages or Method III to try to resolve one of these value collisions, but darn it, the behavior is still "below my line," so here I am, still feeling unaccepting of Johnny's slouching around in his chair and I wish he'd sit up straight. Why, he is going to ruin his spine! I can't just ignore it, or ignore my unaccepting feelings.

WHY METHOD I IS INEFFECTIVE IN
RESOLVING VALUE COLLISIONS

When people in positions of authority encounter value conflicts with youth, the traditional and almost universal reaction is to use their power. Politicians, especially around election time, decry "permissiveness" and beat the drums for strong "law and order" measures against rebellious youth. Most of the behaviors they find objectionable fall neatly into our value-collision area.

Teachers, too, are tempted to resort to "law and order"—punitive, strong-arm, Method I power techniques—to try to resolve serious value conflicts with students. The more serious they consider the behavior, the more tempted they are to "lay down the law," to take a hard-line approach.

How does it work? Unfortunately, very ineffectively. No matter how desperately teachers think they need power, or how they cloak it, it usually brings disastrous results.

Some evidence exists that the *most dangerous* use of Method I is in the values area. Values deal with civil rights, personal rights, rights of individual choice, personal ideals, and independent action. This is why coercion in values collisions is so strongly resisted. Throughout history men and women have sacrificed their lives for their rights and ideals. Our own American Revolution was essentially a war over ideals and values. After winning this war the American patriots spelled out many of these rights in the Constitution, especially in the Bill of Rights.

Students, too, can become revolutionaries—fighting teachers and other adults who deny them their rights or who try to impose restrictions on their freedom to think and believe independently. Students have even died in the cause of defending their beliefs—remember Kent State?

While Method I seems so natural to teachers trying to resolve problems of values, we strongly recommend that power *never* be used to impose a teacher's values on students. Legal or ethical questions aside for the moment, the use of power is the most ineffective of all possible ways to handle value conflicts, principally because of the intensity of students' resistance (passive and active).

After so many prolonged and intense power struggles with young people, educators and parents should have discovered that Method I is not the way to win value conflicts with kids. Even when power does force a change in behavior (they cut their long hair, for example), their values remain unchanged. A youngster does not adopt the adult's value (short hair) because he was made to cut it. In fact, the loser in these power struggles usually intensifies his belief in his own values, and vows to retaliate or determines that he will resist change even more strongly in the future. More significantly the loser hates the winner, and the relationship deteriorates or is perhaps destroyed.

Using Method I in value collisions with students has recently become a legal problem. Much to their surprise and chagrin, educators have found themselves hauled into court over such issues as hair, dress codes, freedom of the student press. After all, fighting back is one of the more successful ways to cope with another's use of power, and going to the courts is a legitimate and often effective counterattack. What's more, to the embarrassment of schools, courts have generally ruled in favor of students in cases where the issue involved the civil rights of students. The embarrassment is usually not so much due to losing the case as it is to having been caught violating the democratic principles they so often claim to be teaching.

WHY METHOD II IS INEFFECTIVE IN RESOLVING VALUE COLLISIONS

Another choice available to teachers is Method II— ignoring the behavior, giving in, doing nothing, permitting students to continue whatever is unacceptable, and then trying to act as if it were acceptable.

While this method does leave students free to "do their own thing," teachers pay a terrible price for being untrue to *their* values and to themselves as persons. The price they pay is that they feel they are losers. Permissive teachers find themselves resenting students, organizing against them, withdrawing, escaping by "playing sick," transferring to another school where, hopefully, students will know the "proper" way to dress, or speak, or wear their hair. Some teachers react by leaving the teaching profession entirely, dreaming of some new job where value collisions won't ever occur.

Pretending to accept behavior that you do not like or turning your head and looking the other way are not likely to resolve value collisions. In the first place, teachers cannot hide their feelings from students. If a teacher tries to pretend, for example, that swearing is acceptable to her but it really churns her up, her facial expressions or body movements will inevitably give her away.

Have you ever said or done something to which someone responded by wincing and smiling at the same time? Which of these came across as the *real* message? Didn't the wince tip you off that the smile was only a cover-up, a mask to hide real feelings?

Students pick up these clues with unerring accuracy, so when adults try to hide their real feelings about young people, they come across as phony, manipulative, unreliable. More reason for teachers to send self-disclosure messages, even though these carry no guarantee of getting students to change behavior. Students would rather have honest teachers, even if the openness does shake them up now and then.

Rather than smiling and pretending that it doesn't bother you when a student uses an obscene word in your presence, try sending a self-disclosure I-message: "When you say that word it jars me and I get resentful. It's just the way I've been conditioned, and I can't help it." You are making no claim to have been damaged in any real sense, but the student at least can decide whether he wishes to continue to behave in a way that he knows offends you. He certainly will not even face that decision if your message is a smile or some other pretense of acceptance.

HOW TO DEAL WITH VALUE COLLISIONS

Now that we know what *won't* work when teachers and students collide over values, is there anything that *will* work? Must teachers resign themselves to living daily with ideological strangers whose words and actions offend their sensibilities and clash with what they consider right and proper? Do teachers have to accept the reality of working in an environment where one generation constantly clashes with another over values and beliefs? Are there effective ways of reducing value collisions so that teachers can get on with the business of teaching and students can learn from teachers' knowledge and experience?

In the remainder of this chapter we offer principles and methods that can significantly reduce the frequency of distracting and destructive value collisions.

Become An Effective Consultant

At the outset let it be clear that we believe teachers have not only the *right* but even the *obligation* to operate in the arena of values, beliefs, and personal convictions. We have already pointed out the futility of ignoring value differences and the collisions over them. We have cautioned against false acceptance and the martyr posture. And we have tried to discredit the strategy of giving in or giving up—letting the student win at the expense of the teacher's needs going unmet (Method II).

We also made the strongest of arguments against teachers using power and authority to try to impose their values and beliefs on students—a dangerous approach to say the least.

Now we offer a positive and constructive suggestion for

teachers: *You may become an effective consultant* to your students on matters of values. But being an *effective* consultant may be more difficult and require more skills than you think.

First, a consultant must get hired by a person (or group, or organization) because that person is dissatisfied with the way he is and is willing to explore the possibility of changing. So a consultant is really a hired "change agent." He is generally regarded as an authority (Type 1 authority: having experience and expertise) by the one who hires him. So a consultant starts out his relationship with the client with considerable "money in the bank." Even with this head start, many consultants fail to change their clients. But effective consultants seldom fail. Here is why.

The effective consultant works by four basic rules:

1. He does not start out trying to change the client until he is certain *he has been hired.*

2. He comes *adequately prepared* with facts, information, data.

3. He *shares his expertise* succinctly, briefly, and only once—he doesn't hassle.

4. He *leaves responsibility with the client* for accepting his efforts to effect change.

Teachers can increase their effectiveness as consultants (or change agents) by applying the above four principles in the classroom.

How to Get Hired by Students. Unless they have already destroyed their relationship with their students, most teachers are perceived by students as having more expertise, wisdom, experience, knowledge, and skills than they really possess. In other words, teachers invariably have greater "psychological size" in the eyes of their students. Because of this, they usually can get hired—but not always.

How can a teacher sell his services as a consultant? By doing what effective consultants do: Make a presentation of what you have to offer and how it might benefit the students with whatever problems you think they might have. An effective sales presentation does not depart too far from the following pattern (highly condensed here):

I've been hearing messages that make me think you are experiencing some problems (or concerns, puzzlements, difficulties) with adults who hassle you about how you dress (or about hair styles, drugs, swearing, sex). . . .

I've been doing a lot of reading and thinking about just that problem (or have some ideas, some thoughts, some solutions) and I think you might find them useful. . . .

I'd like to have the chance to share my ideas with you and get your reactions. . . .

Would you be willing to set up a time, convenient to you and me, say an hour or so as a starter, just to see if my ideas interest you in any way?

This initial "request for a brief hearing" (or some variation of it) usually works, because it conveys *no negative evaluation* of the students (prospective clients); it *does not oversell your services*; it only asks a *small commitment* from the students. Remember, until you are hired, no consulting can take place.

How to Be Adequately Prepared. Students often "fire" teachers immediately because the adults failed to do their homework. They tried to consult on issues and problems without doing what is invariably required of an effective consultant—painstaking research and careful analysis.

Depending on the type of problem for which you are offering your consulting services, this may mean doing some of the following: reading the literature; gathering data through interviews; preparing charts; selecting an appropriate film; organizing your own experience systematically; preparing a tape; outlining your ideas; writing a brief position paper; acquainting yourself with both sides of the issue; developing a vivid demonstration or group-participation exercise; and so on. The opportunities are unlimited for becoming adequately prepared, but adequately prepared you must be to establish yourself as a potential helping agent or expert consultant.

Share Your Ideas Only Once, Don't Hassle the Client. This critical rule is violated by many teachers who, in their zeal to change students (or, more accurately, to reform them), send a barrage of messages which students regard as preaching, lecturing, brainwashing, pushing, hassling, persuading, or the infamous Oriental water torture. Nothing will turn students off more quickly than being hassled and harangued. Instead, an effective consultant *shares* his expertise (and we have chosen that term deliberately). Another term that goes well with effective consulting is "offer."

To apply this principle, teachers will need to use their active-listening skills frequently. Attempts to change others (even *offering* them new ideas, new facts, new solutions), almost without exception, provoke resistance and defensiveness. Seldom do clients buy something new without defending their old set of beliefs or habitual patterns of behavior. Students are no different. They will fight your ideas, defend their own, and do both vigorously. Your most valuable tool at that point is to *shift gears* immediately to active listening:

"You think that idea is unsound."

"It doesn't fit your experience."

"You find that hard to believe."

"It doesn't make sense to you."

"You have some strong reservations about my suggestion."

An effective consultant must *hear resistance and defensiveness* as soon as it emerges, and then must *demonstrate acceptance* of his client's feelings.

Leave Responsibility With the Students. An effective teacher-consultant needs to remember the principle we presented earlier—that of *problem ownership*. Who owns the problem? When acting as a consultant, it is your client (the student) who owns the problem: You have presented him with some new way of behaving or thinking, and a consultant's advice—his new input—causes a problem for the student. He has been challenged, he's shaken up, his equilibrium has been disturbed, his cherished values have been threatened.

Teachers who feel they simply *must* get students to buy ideas or values or behavior patterns, or else they feel they have failed as teachers, violate this important principle and eventually get fired by their clients. The youngsters express their feelings more or less like this:

"Boy, this guy just won't quit."

"He's really got a hang-up about clothes."

"Wonder what's bugging him to make him such a missionary."

"Here we go again—more hassling!"

"Damn it, it's my life not hers!"

"Get off my back—I already know what you think."

Some teachers see at once that these principles of effective consulting can be applied to their regular teaching duties. Indeed, *the rules for expert consulting are also excellent guidelines for good teaching*. The best teachers first "get hired" by their students to teach them something. Then they prepare rigorously, making sure they bring something interesting and exciting, not what students already know. They never reteach unless somebody says, "Hey, I didn't understand that! Show me again."

Finally, outstanding teachers understand that learning has to be the responsibility of the student himself, so they put into practice what has been so beautifully stated by Kahlil Gibran in his book *The Prophet*:

Then said a teacher, Speak to us of Teaching.
And he said:

No man can reveal to you aught but that which already lies half asleep in the dawning of your knowledge.

The teacher who walks in the shadow of the temple, among his followers, gives not of his wisdom but rather of his faith and his lovingness.

If he is indeed wise he does not bid you enter the house of his wisdom, but rather leads you to the threshold of your own mind.

The astronomer may speak to you of his understanding of space, but he cannot give you his understanding.

The musician may sing to you of the rhythm which is in all space, but he cannot give you the ear which arrests the rhythm nor the voice that echoes it.

And he who is versed in the science of numbers can tell of the regions of weight and measure, but he cannot conduct you thither.

For the vision of one man lends not its wings to another man. . . .

Model What You Value

A second way to handle value problems is to model the behavior you would like to establish. To check on how efficient this method is, take a look at your value system. See how many of your values were adopted (sometimes intact) from people you admired. Who modeled for you? Have you adopted values from important people in your life? Were any of them teachers?

The greatest obstacle to teachers becoming models is the "double standard" prevailing in most schools. "Do as I say, not as I do" is not a very effective way to teach values. It does teach students a value, but not the one usually thought of. It teaches students that if you are strong enough you can make others obey rules you don't have to obey; that rank does indeed have its privileges; that the double standard is okay.

Check out not only your own modeling but also the "official" modeling that your school does. Does the school where you work discriminate against any groups—teachers, students, the young, the old, males, females? Do your school's rules allow adults to behave in ways denied to non-adults? Can adults hit students (corporal punishment), while students are not allowed to strike even other students, let alone "punish" adults by striking them?

Does your school provide separate and very unequal toilets and lounges for faculty and students? For faculty and administrators? Can adults smoke on campus, but not students? Do faculty members have a menu in the cafeteria different from that of students?

If so, what values are being modeled? Are they consistent with the stated goals and objectives of your district or school? Usually these statements contain important value objectives. Are the practices in keeping with the stated objectives? If not, why not? Nothing so infuriates students as the hypocrisy of adults—who publicly propound one set of values, but practice another, especially when the *real* values put students in a caste system at the lowest level.

And how about your own behavior? Do you have a double standard, too? If so, you are modeling that standard as the approved one. If you value honesty, then be honest with students. If you value neatness, then be neat in dress and manner. If you value promptness, be on time. If you value democratic principles, then don't be autocratic. But if you value fascism or the law of survival of the strongest, then don't try to preach democracy or humanitarianism.

Consider for a moment how well the modeling of parents and teachers has worked. For the most part, American students are more alike than different in their values—much more. Many teachers who worked in foreign schools in the AID or Peace Corps programs can attest to the culture shock of encountering a *really* different value system. One way of viewing the students in your classroom is to see them as, on the whole, in pretty good shape. The value differences between them and you are really minor, a small percentage of the total number contained in your respective value systems. You and your students are probably about ninety-five percent in agreement. The five-percent (or less) difference is hardly worth ruining relationships over, is it? Far better to try to gently influence students in that area of difference.

The key to getting students to adopt your values through modeling is to maintain good relationships with them. One of the chief benefits of the T.E.T program is that teachers learn how to build effective relationships. In doing so, they model the methods of T.E.T. Modeling Method III is infinitely more effective than a lecture on the democratic process. Sending I-messages daily works infinitely better than telling students to be open and honest in their communication.

Also, lecturing tends to model lecturing, which is why kids know how to lecture. By the time they are ten years old they can give impeccable lectures on all kinds of value subjects. Try them out! Ask them to talk about the "evils of tobacco," booze, playground safety, or cleanliness. See if they don't do as well as the adults they have heard for so long. As an aside, one of the reasons peer-modeling is so powerfully influential is that it is almost never done by lecture, almost always by action. Teachers wishing to compete with peer pressures in shaping values must keep this in mind. Do it, don't talk about it! Practice, don't preach!

One note of caution about modeling as a way of influencing young people: *It may not work*. Values constantly change. Old ways disappear, new ones replace them. Modeling an outdated value, no matter how well done, will probably not gain many converts. But even when students don't buy a teacher's values, they admire and respect the teacher's modeling of his own belief. So even when the value the teacher wants to transmit is rejected, another equally important value is modeled and bought—non-hypocrisy, standing up for what one believes, even if the belief is unpopular or rejected.

A terrifying thing about teaching is that there is no way to avoid modeling. Students are superaware of what teachers do, say, and wear. They tune in far more than many teachers think they do. Teachers are on display before their students every day, day in, day out. Their actions, the modeling, probably have far greater impact on students than all the things they *ever* say. Which is why "Do as I say and not as I do" is not an effective method for teaching values —or for that matter anything else.

Modify Yourself To Become More Accepting

It's easier for most teachers to accept new methods for modifying students or the classroom environment than to make efforts to *make changes in themselves*. Yet self-modification is the *only method over which the teacher has sole control*.

The idea that teachers modify themselves to improve the teacher-student relationship is not nearly as popular as trying to modify students so they may better adjust to teachers and the school environment. Teaching is generally considered a profession for fostering the growth and development of children and youth. Seldom is teaching considered an activity that might he enhanced by the growth and development of the *teacher as a person.*

Yet every teacher accepts the notion that in relationships with others—a spouse, a friend, a colleague, a principal, a relative—there are times when he or she must become more accepting in order to prevent serious conflicts. A change in one's attitude, developing a little more acceptance of another or understanding a bit better what goes on inside another— these self-modifications (often minor changes) can markedly alter one's relationship with another.

For teachers who bask in their role of authority figure, modifying the self is not the approach of choice, so their efforts go into making students change. If that fails, the conflict is too often perceived as "irreconcilable" and the student labeled "incorrigible."

Modifying the self is really not as difficult or threatening as most teachers seem to think. Teachers make significant changes in themselves during our T.E.T course. When we ask them to evaluate, among other things, changes they see in themselves that are attributable to the course, they list such reactions as:

More flexible, accepting, realistic, accommodating, effective, patient, intimate, loving, relaxed, involved, fun-loving.
Less rigid, demanding, uptight, strict, disappointed, impersonal, angry, afraid, perfectionistic, mechanical, grouchy.

One of the most frequent comments we get on teachers' evaluation forms is "I like myself a lot more now." Our guess is that their students like them better, too. We can infer from research that in all probability a teacher who feels accepting of himself will like his students. And greater self-acceptance will reduce value collisions because teachers will feel greater acceptance of students who hold different values.

So we know teachers can modify themselves in the direction of becoming far more accepting of their students. Taking the T.E.T. course is only one of many ways for teachers to do it. Here are some other avenues open to teachers who want to feel better about themselves and their students:

Getting to Know Kids. Read anything you can get your hands on about children, adolescents, the youth culture, the rights of children. Research studies support the notion that people are hostile toward those they do not understand. Contrary to the saying "Familiarity breeds contempt," understanding a different culture or a different age group will increase one's acceptance of their behavior and characteristics. Invite your students to talk about their values and beliefs—how they got them, what they mean to them. Active listening will encourage them to share their feelings with you. Choose one student with whom you have major value collisions and active-listen to him in a private conference. You will find yourself feeling more accepting of the student when you better understand the basis for his beliefs and values.

Achieving Growth Through Groups. For teachers who want to increase their understanding and acceptance of themselves, there is no better way than to participate in some of the currently available group growth experiences— encounter groups, T-groups, sensitivity groups, human potential groups, human-relations training groups, effectiveness-training courses, and many more. A word of caution: Don't hesitate to leave a group if it is not what you want or if it is somehow disturbing you.

Individual or Group Psychotherapy. For thousands of people, working with a licensed professional therapist has been the most rewarding experience in their lives. Yet, unfortunately, to many people, especially teachers, going into therapy still carries the stigma of being mentally ill, or "sick." In actuality, psychotherapy has been far less successful for seriously disturbed people than for those who are relatively healthy. Most therapists agree with us that psychotherapy is far more effective with people who function quite well but want to function even better, for those who are not incapacitated but want to understand themselves more deeply, for those who have a lot of potential and want to actualize it.

Choosing a good therapist is not without its problems. As in every profession there are therapists with all degrees of competence. So get as much information as you can before you select a therapist. Recommendations from friends, ministers, or doctors are to be valued. If you prefer a psychologist, he or she is more likely to be qualified holding a Ph.D.; being licensed or certified by the State Examining Board; possessing a diploma in professional psychology; being a member of the state and/or county psychological association. Competent psychiatrists are usually well known to their medical colleagues in the community, so ask several physicians for their recommendations. Again, don't accept a professional therapist with whom you do not feel comfortable. An effective "helping agent," no matter what his or her professional affiliation, is one who comes across as warm, accepting, and understanding—above all a *good listener*.

Understand Your Own Values. In recent years, many people have benefited greatly by participating in a relatively new group activity, most frequently called "values-clarification workshops." Their purpose is to help people better understand what they truly value and then organize their lives more purposefully to do what they value doing, achieve whatever goals they cherish the most, and act more consistently with what they believe and value most strongly.

These workshops use specific techniques and methods for people to assess their values. Write a list of ten things you most like to do. Then make a list of your strongest beliefs, the things you are most willing to stand up for. List the items in rank order from the most to the least important. Don't hesitate to rewrite or reorder your lists. Would you be willing to stand up before an audience and affirm your values by reading them aloud?

Ask yourself how you came to value these activities and beliefs. Are they *really* what you value and believe, or what someone (perhaps a parent) talked you into (or forced you into) believing? Discovering that some of your values are not based on your own real experiences but borrowed from authority figures may free you to discard them as not belonging to the "real you." If a teacher realizes that her strong compulsion for neatness and orderliness (or proper language, or manners, or conservative clothing) was pushed on her by her mother, chances are she may modify that value, which then would make her much more accepting of students' lack of neatness and orderliness in the classroom.

It comes as a revelation to some people to learn how many of the values they hold are not their own, especially when they have been so unaccepting of others who do not share those values.

In T.E.T. classes, the following questions help teachers clarify their true values:

"Do I have the right to choose my own values, independent of what my parents (or other important people) believe?"

"Must I simply comply with what my parents said I should believe?"

"What is preventing me from dropping any of the values I thought I embraced and keeping those I want to keep?"

Holding Your Own Values versus Pushing Them On Others. It is one thing for a teacher to maintain his own values, but quite another to try to impose them on others. Ask yourself, "Do I have exclusive access to the truth about what is good or bad, proper or improper, moral or immoral?"

Teachers involved in constant hassles with students over values often are persons with very strong and very rigid concepts of what is right and wrong for *everybody*. The more certain teachers are that their own values and beliefs are universal truths, the greater seems to be their need to impose them on their students (and on others, too). Seldom are such efforts successful. They just generate more value collisions.

Learning from Students. Teachers willing to listen to kids or "get into their shoes" have found themselves being influenced by their values and beliefs. Notice how many male teachers now wear their hair long, sport bushy beards, and wear faded jeans. It is also difficult to deny the recent influence of young people on adults when it comes to tastes in music, attitudes toward civil rights for minority groups, conservation, environmental pollution, alternate life-styles, compulsive and competitive striving for money, alternatives to getting married immediately, and many other choices. Adults *can* learn from the innovative values of youth. *Try them out.* You may find they fit you more comfortably than your old ones.

Do You Like Kids? All teachers might profitably ask themselves this question. Do you like kids, or just certain types of kids? Do you like girls but not boys (or vice versa), white kids but not black or brown ones, passive students but not assertive ones, athletes but not artists, kids from well-to-do families but not those from poor homes?

And do ask yourself this most fundamental and penetrating question: *"Why do I find it so difficult to accept someone who chooses to be different from me?"*

Find the "Serenity To Accept"

If in your relationship with a student you have tried but failed to resolve a value collision by being an effective consultant, or by modeling, or by modifying yourself, a fourth method is at hand. Not entirely with tongue in cheek, T.E.T. instructors tell teachers, "You may pray." And they add, "Here is a prayer by Reinhold Niebuhr which we think is most appropriate." This well-known prayer, though it has become almost a cliché, asks for the very qualities we feel teachers need.

> God, grant me the serenity to accept the things
> I cannot change, the courage to change the things
> I can, and the wisdom to know the difference.

From whatever source, from inside themselves or outside, teachers particularly need to find the serenity to accept what they cannot change—their students' values, beliefs, and convictions. Niebuhr's prayer could well be "The Teacher's Prayer."

XI. MAKING THE SCHOOL A
BETTER PLACE FOR TEACHING

Parents can freely choose their parenting style, and independently decide what kind of teachers they will be with their own children. Not so with teachers. Their freedom of choice is significantly limited by institutional or organizational factors; teachers are members of an organization whose norms, rules, policies, prohibitions, and job definitions strongly influence how they respond to students and how they teach them.

When teachers are ineffective in relationships with students, it would be folly to ignore the influence of the organization. When teachers are ineffective in facilitating learning, to a great extent their failures must be attributed to organizational factors that define and limit the role of the teacher.

An educational philosopher once said that if we are to free students in the classroom we must first free teachers. He obviously recognized that teachers are not free; like students, they are controlled and directed by power and authority; their own rights are often not honored; they are not given the chance to participate in decisions they are expected to carry out or enforce; their administrators often do not listen to them with empathy and understanding; and they constantly work in an atmosphere of evaluation, judgment, and fear.

Teachers are expected to meet the needs of students even though their own needs are not being met. Our theory of effective human relationships, based firmly on the principle of mutual need satisfaction, requires that teachers must meet their needs, by and large; else they will not be in any kind of mood to try to meet the needs of students.

In this chapter we offer teachers ideas and guidelines for influencing their schools to become better places for teaching.

What can teachers do to help change the organization so their needs more likely will be satisfied? How can teachers be more effective change agents in their schools?

First, teachers need a deeper understanding of the nature of the institution we call "school" and the characteristics of that institution that make it difficult for teachers to function effectively.

CHARACTERISTICS OF SCHOOLS
THAT CAUSE PROBLEMS FOR TEACHERS

All schools are not alike, obviously, and so the following characteristics will not be found in every school to the same degree, nor will all of them be found in every school.

Teachers Are Subordinates

Almost all schools are organized along hierarchial lines, with teachers as subordinates to principals or assistant principals. In turn, principals are subordinate to superintendents or assistant superintendents. For whatever unfortunate reason, most schools have been organized very much like the ancient model of military organization. Inherent in the military model are such principles as unity of command, span of control, a hierarchy of power and authority, directives coming from the top, the necessity for respect for authority (obedience), punishment for infractions of rules, and so on.

Despite all the claims that schools are democratic institutions designed for a democratic society, most schools are anything but democratic, and nobody is more aware of this than teachers. The real world of most schools is one where conflicts are resolved by power and authority.

Teachers Do Not Participate in Decision Making

In most schools, teachers are expected to *implement* decisions but are seldom given opportunity to participate in *making* those decisions. School administrators generally reserve the right to make decisions on the most important issues. Faculty meetings in many schools are not permitted by administrators to become decision-making meetings but are restricted to information sharing, discussions, and socializing. Rules and policies in schools, laid down unilaterally by administrators, often do not reflect the wishes (or meet the needs) of teachers.

Rigidity and Resistance to Change

Critics of education are in almost complete agreement that schools are exasperatingly resistant to change. Although most educators have known for some time what is wrong with schools, they cannot seem to bring about needed reforms. Particularly when it comes to what goes on in classrooms, most schools are run amazingly like the schools of a hundred years ago.

Imposition of Uniform Values

For complex reasons, most schools impose on teachers and students a rigid code of values or uniform standards of conduct to regulate the clothes they wear, the speech they use, the morals they must uphold, the issues they cannot discuss. Schools dictate what is proper behavior and acceptable beliefs. Most schools make few allowances for different learning styles, teaching styles, or life-styles. The tyranny of the majority is imposed on those who do not fit the mold.

Putting the Blame on Others

Schools are notorious for everyone putting the blame on others for what is wrong. Students blame teachers, teachers blame principals, principals blame superintendents, and superintendents blame school boards. Shifting responsibility also goes the other way—downward. School boards search for new superintendents, superintendents are on the lookout for new training programs for principals, and principals feel their lives are made miserable by the inadequacies of teachers. Teachers can always blame each new generation of students.

Parents, too, are not excluded from this network of blaming the other guy. They blame teachers and administrators. In return they get blamed by everyone—for having damaged their children even before they are sent off to school, where they are supposed to be fixed up.

WHAT TEACHERS CAN DO TO INCREASE THEIR EFFECTIVENESS IN THE ORGANIZATION

Teachers can take many positive actions to make the school a better place for teaching, rather than assume the typical defeatist posture of assigning blame and shifting responsibility for their problems onto others.

Accept the Importance of Your Role

No other person in the school organization has as much potentiality for influencing students—for good or bad—than the teacher. Teachers are "the first line" (a term borrowed from industrial organizations—i.e., the "first-line supervisor"). The student's primary relationship is with his teacher. It is from the teacher-student relationship that he will experience growth and fulfillment or be stifled and damaged.

As a teacher, you're not really on the bottom rung of the school hierarchy at all. You are at the top. It all starts and ends with you and what you do with your students. Education is your classroom and your relationships with students. Education is not buildings, programs, equipment, administrators, systems, curricula, books and materials, budgets, etc. All those appurtenances are supposed to exist only to help you do a better job as a teacher and helping agent for your students.

If teachers would only accept the importance of their role, value it strongly, protect its integrity, defend it against erosion, more of them would walk proudly through the corridors of their schools as *professionals.*

Always Look Through Your "Window"

Teachers have relationships with many kinds of people, and each is capable of behaving in ways that may harm the teacher's relationship with his students or cause problems that interfere with the teaching-learning process. We refer to supervisors, deans, custodians, principals, office secretaries, coaches, school psychologists, school counselors, nurses, attendance officers, assistant superintendents, personnel officers, business managers, other teachers, school-board members, PTA officers, and parents.

When we urge you to look through your "window" at all times, we mean that it is crucial to see each person with whom you have an interaction *through the rectangular window.* In Figure 30, think of each of the different kinds of people in schools as "the other." Every time you have an interaction with another, it is critical that you first locate the behavior of that person in the proper part of the rectangle, using your own honest feelings as your sole criterion.

Suppose the custodian tells you not to let students place their chairs or desks in a circle, because it causes him too much extra work. Look at his behavior through your window and ask yourself, "Is his behavior (telling me what not to do) acceptable or unacceptable to me?" If you locate his behavior

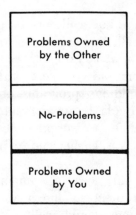

FIGURE 30

in the top third of the rectangle, which by this stage of your effectiveness training we certainly hope you would, then say to yourself, "The *custodian* owns the problem—*he* is troubled, *his* needs are being threatened." Now, you should know better than to send him any of the roadblock messages, so you use active listening to show your understanding and acceptance of his feelings: "Jim, you don't like the extra work of rearranging the chairs after we have had them in a circle." By that one simple response you have strengthened your relationship with Jim. The thought in his head is likely to be, "Here is a teacher who really understands my problems, really cares about me."

Here are the possible outcomes of your active listening:

1. Jim might very well solve his problem by himself ("I guess teaching is different these days and desks are just going to get moved").

2. Or Jim might say, "That's right," and push you even harder to restrict the kids, in which case you will want to send an I-message telling him *your* needs ("Jim, it helps me so much to have the students in a circle when we have group discussions, I really would find it unacceptable to give it up; it would make me much less effective as a teacher.").

3. Jim might then accept your needs and drop the subject, or he might remain adamant about not wanting the chairs moved. If the

latter happens, then Jim and you have a conflict of needs (*both own the problem*). Recognizing this, you can invite him to join you in Method III problem solving. ("Jim, I guess we have a problem here. Let's put our heads together and try to come up with a solution that would meet your needs as well as mine. Got any ideas?")

We have just tried to show that teachers need to use T.E.T. skills in all their relationships in the organization—not just those with students. And the key to their effectiveness is the rectangular window through which they can view the behavior of the other person. Only after deciding "who owns the problem" can you select the relevant skill.

If teachers learn to apply T.E.T. skills to all their relationships, many of their common conflicts will be avoided. In addition, they will find that they are more frequently getting their own needs met, and at the same time building better relationships in the organization.

"CAN I USE THE CONFRONTING SKILLS WITH MY BOSS?"

Teachers are known for their timidity in dealing with authority figures. One very good reason is that they hesitate to stand up to those who hold the club of evaluation in their hands. Principals and superintendents not only have power, they traditionally use it. They can grant or withhold future employment, decide on salary increases, recommend or deny tenure, and so on. Too many teachers feel that the risk of displeasing their bosses by standing up for their own needs is simply too great.

So they give in or give up, and quite predictably they feel resentful, build up hostilities, gripe, feel miserable, withdraw or resign. They predictably respond with one or more of the same coping mechanisms that students use when they lose and teachers win.

In T.E.T. classes it is sometimes difficult to convince teachers that they have legitimate needs and the right (even the duty) to try to satisfy those needs; if their needs are ignored or remain unsatisfied, it will be impossible for them to foster and maintain effective relationships with students. Teachers have a right to do their thing, to be professional teachers, and to have a satisfying job with decent working conditions. To get all this, teachers must confront their bosses, even if it seems scary.

Teachers' fears about standing up for their rights can be markedly reduced if they follow these six steps whenever their bosses are standing in the way of their getting their needs met:

1. *Send a Good I-Message.* You may want to prepare by writing out several I-messages before you go to your principal, polishing and re-fining until the message feels right and expresses accurately the situation as you see it.

2. *Shift gears and Active Listen.* Principals are human, too. They will have feelings about what you have said. Even the best I-message will invoke some defensiveness. If you want help from the principal, you must be willing to help him handle your confrontation.

3. *Send Another I-Message.* You may need a stronger one if your first I-message produced no results. Do not hesitate to voice your disappointment (if you really *are* disappointed) at having to bring up the problem again.

4. If the problem continues unresolved even after this, ask the principal if he would join you in a meeting with *his* boss to get help in resolving the conflict between the two of you. Ask the principal to call the boss for an appointment for both of you.

5. If your principal refuses to accept your invitation, tell him that you plan to go to his boss alone but you would still prefer that he accompany you because he can better present his position in person. (The odds are your principal will go with you.)

6. Go see the principal's boss without him and first explain how you tried Steps 1 through 5. Then tell him what your needs are and the tangible effect on you when they are not met. Ask for his or her help in getting your needs met.

Some teachers break out in a cold sweat just thinking about "going over the boss's head." They see it as insubordination, or fear that the principal will see it that way. In typical Method I power struggles this may well be the case. Principals who rely heavily upon power are apt to see any behavior by teachers (other than abject submission) as insubordination. True, if you have not tried Steps 1 through 5 before going to the "big boss"—if you make no attempt to settle the problem face-to-face with the principal *before* going over his head—most principals will judge this as unprofessional, if not insubordinate conduct. But if you follow the six steps, you will find you are not without recourse when your needs are not met and that going over the boss's head is preferable to— and more ethical than—being a sacrificing, submissive, unhappy subordinate, unable to teach at full capacity because of your unmet needs.

Many principals enrolled in our L.E.T. classes (Leader Effectiveness Training) tell us that they do not want "sacrificing" teachers when the price paid is poorer-quality performance in the classroom. They *want* teachers to speak up, to inform them when things are not going well. Principals are dependent for their success mainly on the success of their teachers. So they cannot afford to have teachers in their school who perform poorly. They feel they must do everything in their power to help them improve.

It may also be reassuring to teachers that even "unreasonable" principals rarely stand by and watch one of their teachers "go over their head." When they see that a teacher is serious about getting "topside" help in meeting his needs, problems have a way of getting resolved before that actually happens.

Strength in Numbers

Teachers often ask if they might be more successful confronting the principal if they went as a group, or whether this might be construed as "ganging up" on him.

Certainly, there can be strength in numbers; it lets a principal know that a number of teachers are unhappy or unsatisfied, not just one. Going as a group also gives teachers more courage because a group does provide its members considerable safety—it is far less likely that the principal will get angry in front of a group, and highly improbable that he would retaliate against the entire group.

Taking the point of view of principals for a moment, it is understandable that some might feel somewhat overwhelmed by a group of confronting teachers. So teachers might want to try sending only one spokesman or representative to try to work out a solution to the group's problem. Or the spokesman might be sent just to get the principal to agree to a subsequent meeting with the entire group under conditions satisfactory to the principal.

One word of caution: Be sure that the group is relatively homogeneous—that the unmet needs are much the same for each member of the group. Otherwise the principal may feel "jumped on" by a number of people, each for a different reason. If a lot of differing needs are up for discussion, it is far better to let each person handle his or her own confrontation with the principal. This is a good place to point again to the power paradox: You cannot use power and still be influential. If the principal thinks a group is confronting in order to exert pressure or to overpower him with numbers, the group will lose its influence.

HOW TO BECOME MORE EFFECTIVE IN GROUP MEETINGS

Teachers can become more influential in making schools a better place for teaching by learning how to be more effective in group meetings—meetings of the total faculty, committee meetings, or meetings of task groups. By and large, teachers have rather negative feelings about groups and committees. This is because many teachers have learned from experience that groups are often set up to study a problem and make recommendations, but then nothing happens. Ask teachers and most will say that in their schools committees are formed to *avoid* decision making. "Appoint a committee and that will take care of it" is a running joke in many schools. Not only do teachers complain about group meetings being a waste of time and energy, but many believe the old wheeze that defines a camel as a horse designed by a committee.

In many schools faculty meetings are painfully boring, and serving on faculty committees is something to be avoided like the plague. Most schools have standing "faculty committees," for the usual reasons ("We've always done it this way"; "The principal wants it"). The titles alone convey a quality of depressiveness—e.g., "The Woodrow Wilson High School Faculty Committee To Study Language Arts Curriculum Coordination: Meetings at 3:00 P.M., the third Wednesday of alternate months, in the school library."

It is usually such groups that teachers remember when they put down the group process as a whole. Their experience has proven to them that these groups do not function very well, and seldom produce decisions or get results. Actually, the group decision-making process can be very creative, and groups can learn to produce high-quality solutions and solve problems that individuals acting alone can seldom solve. When groups don't function well, it's because members are not trained in group process; do not understand Method III; do not listen to each other; and stifle two-way communication by using the communication roadblocks. Group members have rarely had training in how to be responsible members of a problem-solving group. Since most teachers and principals spend so much of their professional lives working in groups, it is astounding that they have had, at best, only minimal training in this crucial skill.

While teachers usually understand that effective *leadership* can be learned, they are often surprised to hear that effective group *membership* also requires learning specific functions and special skills. These functions and skills fall into three categories: (a) those required before the meeting;

(b) those required during the meeting; and (c) those required after the meeting.

Before the Meeting

1. Read the minutes of the previous meeting before going to each meeting.

2. Come to the meeting having clearly in mind what problems or items you want to put on the agenda.

3. Get to each meeting on time.

4. Bring all materials needed.

5. Set aside the time necessary for the meeting so there will be no interruptions (phone calls, messages, visitors, etc.).

During the Meeting

1. Submit your items for the agenda. State them as briefly as possible—do not elaborate.

2. When you have an opinion or feeling, state it honestly and clearly. *Do not sit on feelings!*

3. Stay on the agenda item being dealt with, and help others stay on it.

4. Ask for clarification when you do not understand what someone is saying or what an agenda item means.

5. Participate actively. When you have something to say, say it. Do not wait to be asked for your opinion.

6. Insist on following procedures that will help your group function effectively:

    a. starting on time

    b. getting the agenda set

    c. staying on the subject

    d. keeping order

    e. listening to others

    f. keeping records

    g. getting important issues, problems, concerns, or agenda items on the chart pad or board

    h. arriving at decisions

    i. quitting on time

7. Protect the rights of others to have their opinions or feelings heard. Encourage silent members to speak.

8. Listen attentively to others. Use active listening to clarify what others are saying.

9. Try to think creatively about solutions that might resolve conflicts. Try out these ideas on the group.

10. Avoid communications that disrupt a group—humor, sarcasm, diversions, asides, jokes, digs, etc.

11. Keep notes on what you agree to do after the meeting.

12. Constantly ask yourself these questions: "What at this moment would help this group move ahead and get this problem solved?" "What contribution can I make to help this group function more effectively?" "What does the group need?" "How can I help?"

After the Meeting

1. Carry out assignments and commitments.

2. Pass on to others those decisions or solutions they should know about.

3. Keep confidential anything said or done in the meeting that might put a member in a bad light.

4. Refrain from complaining about a decision that you agreed to. If you have second thoughts, bring them up at the next group meeting.

5. Refrain from out-of-meeting appeals to your boss. Your feelings about the group's activities should be expressed *in* the group or not at all.

You can be helpful to the groups you are working in by providing each member with a copy of these Rules for Responsible Group Membership.

HOW TO BE AN EFFECTIVE CONSULTANT

Teachers can have a profound effect on their schools by becoming consultants to their principals and colleagues. They can share their new ideas and insights; demonstrate their newly learned skills; offer their successful experiences to others. But to bring about change and improvement in their schools, teachers need to learn how to be *effective* consultants.

In Chapter X we described the four principles of the effective consultant. You may wish to review them, so we list them again here as a reminder:

1. He does not start out trying to change the client until he is certain *he has been hired.*

2. He comes *adequately prepared* with facts, information, data.

3. He *shares his expertise* succinctly, briefly, and only once.

4. He *leaves responsibility with the client* for accepting his change efforts.

Acquiring the status of an expert consultant in your school—even throughout the schools in your district—may not be as difficult as you think, provided you follow the four principles.

How you go about the task of becoming a change agent will vary from school to school; and, of course, your particular area of expertise will determine what is appropriate for you to do. To illustrate how much you can do, we outline below some possible activities for you, if you decide you would like to earn the role of consultant in your school district in the field of Effectiveness Training, the subject of this book:

1. Talk to fellow teachers about T.E.T. at coffee breaks or whenever you get a chance.

2. Model the skills. Be a good active listener. Send I-messages. Put Method III to work in your own classroom. Invite other teachers in to see how you and your students operate with the no-lose method.

3. Offer to demonstrate the skills for faculty groups, using your own class. Your students will be turned on about the process and in all probability will really enjoy helping to spread the word by these demonstrations.

4. Offer to conduct human relations study groups using the T.E.T. book as a study guide.

5. Offer to give your time and information to the principal individually, especially about how to use the skills to conduct more effective faculty meetings and how to use Method III to set rules and policies.

6. Demonstrate the skills with role-playing scenes at P.T.A. meetings. Conduct a typical student-centered discussion group or a content-centered discussion.

7. Ask the librarian to order several copies of this book for the professional library in the school.

8. Contact an authorized T.E.T. instructor to set up a meeting with interested faculty members to explain T.E.T., to answer questions, and to explore setting up a training class. T.E.T. instructors are also available to conduct mini-workshops or "lecturettes" for larger groups.

9. Offer to act as a facilitator, using Method III and lots of active listening, to help your faculty group resolve a chronic problem plaguing the staff. Probably nothing is so impressive as seeing Method III bring about the resolution of a problem that may have had a group hung up for months.

10. Offer to share with the staff the Rules for Responsible Group Membership (pp. 318 to 319). Mimeograph them and hand them out. Lead a discussion about them and their implications for how the staff could function better.

11. Offer to demonstrate classroom discussions in other teachers' classes. Offer to act as a facilitator or process observer for other teachers when they use Method III to establish classroom rules and policies.

These ideas represent only some of the possible ways you can become known as an expert and as a person who can help bring about changes. You have every right to try to "sell" your ideas to others. Just remember to leave the decision about "buying" to them. Don't hassle your clients.

BECOME AN ADVOCATE FOR YOUR STUDENTS

Schools are one of the very few institutions where the recipients of services have almost no voice in evaluating their quality or the way they are delivered. Businesses and industrial organizations make an effort to respond to preferences and complaints of customers. Retail stores permit customers to return purchases if they are not satisfied. Church members have a strong voice in determining the type of minister they want or the church activities that will best meet their needs.

But who listens to the ultimate "customer" of the school? How much voice are students given in determining the quality of education? Who deals with student complaints about the quality of the teaching, or their working conditions?

Is it any wonder that schools have changed so little for centuries? They get very little feedback from the real consumer, nor do they ask for it. The consumers of education do not even have the option of shopping around for better services, unless their parents are affluent enough to afford a private school.

Schools need consumer advocates, and no person in the organization is in closer touch with the needs, dissatisfactions, and complaints of students than the teacher. Yet how many teachers make an effort to go to bat for their students, to be their advocate with the administration or the school board?

Most teachers define their role as enforcers of school rules and practices, defenders of administrators' policies. Supposedly their job is to engineer conformity and compliance; never to encourage complaints or criticisms; always to protect the principal from exposure to discontent.

We are suggesting, even urging, that teachers become strong advocates for their students. Using the skills learned in T.E.T., teachers can have much more influence on the organization if they make a vigorous effort to change conditions and practices in schools that dehumanize students, deny their civil rights, erode their self-esteem, repress their spontaneity, and kill their natural desire to learn.

Teachers could have more influence than they think—and most of them are well aware of what schools do to mutilate the spirit of the young people they teach. They can change this.

Special Section HOW TO HANDLE
LEARNING PROBLEMS IN THE HOME:
The Parent-Teacher-Student Relationship

IN THE eyes of parents, teachers become the "other parents" of their children. So parents have (or should have) a legitimate concern about what teachers do to their children. Will the teachers be an influence for good or bad? Will they help the children learn? Will the kids like their teachers? Will the teachers make the youngsters behave? Will they teach them what they ought to know?

In the eyes of teachers, parents are the "other teachers" of the students. So teachers have a concern, also legitimate, about what parents do to students when they go home from school. What kind of home environment does the student have? Will parents see to it that students do their homework? Will parents be critical of the teachers' teaching methods or their methods of discipline? Will parents expect too much of teachers, especially when it comes to correcting problems students develop at home?

Parents suffer if the teacher-student relationship is bad; teachers suffer if the parent-child relationship is bad. Each has a stake in the relationship that the youngster has with the other adult. Despite this mutual interest in each other's behavior, a parent and a teacher seldom have a very close or significant relationship with each other. They don't see each other very often, and when they do, their time together is extremely limited.

It is no wonder that parents have traditionally been very ineffective in influencing teachers to change, and that teachers have been quite impotent when they try to modify parents' behavior. Parents and teachers are actually rather independent and separate agents; each has an important relationship with a youngster, but they do not enjoy a close or significant relationship with each other, even though each may be affected by the behavior of the other.

In this chapter we focus on this unique triangular relationship between teacher, parent, and student; and we offer constructive suggestions for resolving the most common problems between the three.

Parents are the first teachers that children have and, for the first four or five years, usually the only ones of any importance. When you consider that during the first five years of his life a child will learn about ninety percent of all he will *ever* learn, the importance of the quality of parental teaching becomes startlingly plain. Parents are not merely the first teachers; they are by far the most important ones. The parent-as-teacher role often lasts until the child becomes an adult and sometimes beyond. So while this book has been principally about the teacher-student relationship in the school, and most often in the setting of a typical 960-square-foot classroom, the communication and problem- solving skills of T.E.T. are just as applicable to the teaching relationship that a parent has with his child in the home. In fact, considering the importance of the teaching and learning that take place before a child ever sets foot inside a school, *these skills may be even more important for parents than for teachers.*

THE PARENT AS TEACHER TO THE CHILD

A child's education begins at birth (or even before birth, according to some experts), and only ends when death intervenes in the process. Parents are continually teaching their children about the world in which they grow up.

Many parents are extremely effective teachers when their children are infants. Their "area of acceptance" is very large, and they seldom have unrealistic or severe expectations; much of the behavior of the learner is acceptable to parents. If he cannot yet grasp a rattle, they do not condemn him or punish him or label him a "psychomotor underachiever." Most parents will simply try again the next day. Their attitude is "He's not yet able to learn to grasp his rattle, but he'll get there one of these days."

Most parents also extend a great deal of freedom to an infant so he can learn on his own whenever he is ready. Most parents also leave complete responsibility with the child for *what* he learns, and *when* he will learn it. The capacity for the infant to learn is accepted and trusted. Seldom are there serious questions in parents' minds about their infants' innate learning *potentiality*. To the surprise of no one, the trust and acceptance of parents are usually vindicated, and they see evidence every day of how much their child has learned almost completely on his own—how to roll over, how to recognize mother, how to pick up an object, how to kick his legs, how to communicate when he's hungry or thirsty.

There is something very beautiful about parents as teachers when their children are mere babies. It is as if parents are inherently equipped to be effective teachers of very young children. Professional teachers could learn a lot from such parents.

As the infant grows and begins to toddle and talk (both learned with no formal teaching), something comes over parents. They begin to lose their teacher effectiveness. They start to "train" their children. They begin to "teach lessons." They push too hard. They use rewards and punishments. They lecture and evaluate. They compare their children with other children. They worry and fret. They use all the Twelve Roadblocks. They send blaming you-messages. They use their power and authority.

The alternatives to these ineffective teaching methods—

the new methods that have been presented throughout this book—are equally valid for parents who want to be more effective as teachers of their children. Parents, too, can learn how to bring out the best in the young people they teach.

WHO OWNS YOUR CHILD'S LEARNING?

People don't often look at it this way, but learning is a natural function like breathing, eating, sleeping, and drinking. All organisms do it, and essentially must do it themselves. Since your child will be an incurable learner, your job as a parent should be to permit his doing it. The very best teachers are almost like silent partners in the learning enterprise; they offer opportunities for learning, provide "stuff" and materials for learning, but keep their own counsel, stay out of the learner's way, and respond only when asked. It may be difficult to do this at first, but when a child is happily engaged in learning, think of his behavior as being in the No-Problem area of your rectangular window (see Fig. 31), and leave him alone.

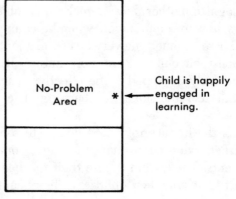

FIGURE 31

If your child encounters some problems in the learning process, which *frequently* happens, think of his behavior as located in the top part of Fig. 32—"Problems Owned by the Child."

Suppose he is trying to learn how to stack his blocks to make a tall tower. He gets upset and begins to cry when they fall because he is not stacking them straight. *He* owns this problem, not you:

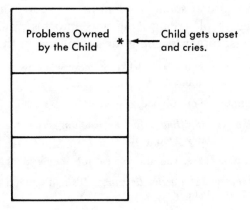

FIGURE 32

Having properly located your child's frustration and crying in the top part of the rectangle, you can do one of two things: (1) stay completely out of the situation and let him try to find a solution (or learn on his own how to make the tower), or (2) use active listening by reflecting his feelings:

"You get upset when the blocks fall down."

"You're finding it hard to stack the blocks so they won't fall."

Most of the time the child will then just continue his learning process, feeling that mom or dad really understands what he is going through in this difficult endeavor of building a tower. More than likely, he'll learn how to make that darned tower—if not today, then tomorrow or the next day.

Certainly you as a parent can encourage your child to learn something you might want him to know, but always remember: You cannot learn it for him, nor can you *make* him learn it. Suppose you'd like your child to learn how to play Ping-Pong. You could let your wishes be known with an I-message. ("I sure would enjoy showing you how to play

Ping-Pong. How about it?") If he accepts your invitation, about all you can do as his teacher is demonstrate, explain, and encourage. The actual learning is up to the child. Not only that; the youngster very well may choose not to learn because of some problem he is experiencing. Now his learning to play Ping-Pong gets into his problem area and you must forget teaching for a while, as in this illustration:

PARENT: I sure would like to show you how to play Ping-Pong. How about it?

CHILD: I'm no good at games.

PARENT: (*Shifting to active listening*) You're afraid you wouldn't be any good at it.

CHILD: Yes. You always beat me at everything. I'm too little.

PARENT: (*Still active listening*) It's really tough to be little and not be able to win.

CHILD: (*Nods*) Why don't we play Old Maid? You don't have to be big to win at that.

PARENT: (*Active listening*) That seems like a fairer game to you.

CHILD: Yeah. Then when I'm bigger I'll learn how to play Ping-Pong.

PARENT: Okay.

Teaching a skill like Ping-Pong is like teaching anything else. *Teaching and learning will occur only in the No-Problem area.* Parents sometimes forget this, especially if what they want to teach is very important to them. Dialogues similar to the following between a father and his son take place in many homes each Spring:

DAD: Well, here it is Little League time again! I see in the paper where they're having the sign-ups at the recreation center tomorrow. You going?

SON: I don't know. Maybe.

DAD: What do you mean maybe? Why, this is the chance we've been waiting for all winter! Of course you're going to sign up!

SON: (*Turns away*) I don't want to.

DAD: (*Puts arm around son's shoulders*) Come on now! You're going to be the best pitcher in this town. Boy, do I wish I could've had the chance you've got! I'd probably have made the majors if I could've played in a real league like this as a kid. You just don't realize how lucky you are and how important this early training is. Go get your glove and I'll show you how to throw the old fork ball.

SON: I'm tired. Besides, I have to do my homework. Anyway, it's too cold outside.

DAD: (*Shakes head*) I'll never understand you. You get every advantage, I break my back to help you learn all I know, and you say, "It's too cold outside." Well, don't come crying to me when those tough hitters beat your brains out, kid.

SON: Okay.

DAD: Huh?

SON: (*Leaving*) Got to do my homework, dad. See you later.

DAD: You get down there and sign up tomorrow, hear?

Who knows what might happen in these father-son interchanges if dads would quit pushing and take time to listen to the feelings of their sons? Obviously something was bothering the boy in this example, some feelings that caused him to have doubts about playing baseball even though he realized how important it was to his father. And he was in no mood to learn much of anything right then, especially not about the old fork ball.

HOW TO MAKE YOUR HOME A LEARNING ENVIRONMENT

Teaching at home can be made a great deal easier—and you will help your child learn much more—if you can think of your home as a learning environment.

Good learning environments for children have plenty of "stuff" for kids to touch, smell, hear, manipulate, and look at. And it need not be expensive stuff either. Thrift stores are full of old children's books, gadgets, dolls, and other used toys. Pieces of lumber for stacking and building can be found almost anywhere. Old tires make great swings. Crayons and a roll of butcher paper; old pots and pans; a corner of your yard for a child's garden; a white rat or hamster for a pet—there is no end to what parents can do to enrich a child's environment at very little cost (See Chapter VI). It's trite but true: Whenever young children are busy, they are learning.

Most home environments can be modified to make it easier for a child to learn the many "how-to" things—such as how to hang up clothes, how to brush teeth, how to put away playthings. The section in Chapter VI on simplifying the environment in the school contains many suggestions that can be applied in the home—hooks installed so that small children can reach them to hang up clothes; stools for reaching storage drawers or for standing tall to brush their own teeth; old boxes for keeping toys and junk. The principle is simple: *Instead of nagging, hassling, and overteaching, arrange the home environment so the child can learn on his own.*

Parents will be far better teachers if they remember that children would much prefer to learn from their activities rather than "be taught" by an adult.

YES, PARENTS MUST BE HIRED AS TEACHERS

Too many parents try to teach before they are hired for the job. It is simply not true that youngsters are always eager to learn from those who are obviously wiser or more competent. In fact, someone once observed that expertness is often a real handicap in teaching, because learners do not like to be made to feel inadequate or inferior.

The following incident occurred in the family of one of our P.E.T. instructors who set out to teach his seven-year-old daughter, Michele, how to play pool, shortly after the family had purchased a new pool table. Michele had been getting quite a lot of pleasure out of hitting the balls with her cue, but she handled it clumsily and ineptly. Dad was an experienced pool shooter and naturally eager to pass on his skills to his offspring.

DAD: Here, honey, let me show you how to hold your cue.

MICHELE: I know how to hold it.

DAD: No, you're not holding it right. Watch me, this is the way I do it, see?

MICHELE: I do it *this* way. (*Demonstrates her "inept" style*)

DAD: But, if you do it that way you won't hit the ball in the middle.

MICHELE: Yes, I will.

DAD: Honey, you want to learn how to play pool, don't you?

MICHELE: I know how to play.

DAD: But I mean learn how to play really well. Now, give me your left hand and I'll show you how to make a bridge for your cue. (*He demonstrates, but Michele's hand strongly resists his efforts to mold it to the right shape.*)

MICHELE: Ow! That hurts when you press my hand down!

DAD: I'm sorry. I was just trying to give you a solid bridge so your cue would slide easily.

MICHELE: I like my way better. Let's play a game now.

DAD: You're not ready to play a game, 'cause you don't know how to make a good bridge.

MICHELE: Watch me hit this one. (*Uses her incorrect bridge*)

DAD: See, you hit the ball underneath rather than in the middle.

MICHELE: I don't want to play anymore. It's no fun.

DAD: Well, you'll never learn if you feel that way.

By his insistence on being his child's pool teacher, this father lost his chance to teach because he failed to get hired for the job. Initially, he made no attempt to ask Michele if she wanted instruction. Then he repeatedly refused to back off when he encountered Michele's obvious resistance—an almost inevitable reaction of kids when they are pressured to try something new. This incident illustrates several important principles which parents so often forget:

1. Get yourself invited as a teacher before you start teaching.

2. Kids learn more easily from experience than from formal instruction.

3. When resistance to your teaching occurs, back off and stop teaching. (Active-listen to the child's feelings.)

4. Don't let your teaching take all the fun out of the activity.

"YOU CAN LEAD A HORSE TO WATER, BUT..."

When you use parental authority and power to teach your youngsters, you are bound to create problems—anger, resentment, fights, tantrums, and tears. You may want to review the effects of power detailed in Chapter VII. Your children will respond to power-based and authoritarian teaching with the same coping mechanisms that they adopt when you use power to discipline them.

Parents usually do not realize it, but they actually lose influence when they resort to power in an attempt to make kids learn something. When teachers in school use power, students can at least try to get a transfer to another teacher or wait out the year or the semester in resignation. Or they can play hooky. When parents resort to power at home, their children cannot get a transfer to another home or wait for a new parent next year. But they can play hooky by staying away from home as much as possible or by running away from home. Interviews with parents of runaways almost universally reveal that these parents are dedicated users of power in trying to teach their kids "what's good for them."

Parents and children in a no-lose environment where power is unnecessary find that they are continually influencing each other. And they can learn from each other all of their lives.

HOW PARENTS CAN TEACH THEIR VALUES

Parents generally assume major responsibility for teaching children values, beliefs, standards—what's right and what's wrong according to the parents. This is where most parents fail so miserably. All we have said about teaching values in school (see Chapter X) applies to parents with their own children.

Because values are learned more from how parents behave than from what they preach or teach, parents must rely heavily on *modeling what they value*. As we stressed earlier, "Do as I say, not as I do" is a most ineffective precept for teaching children.

Our four principles for being an *effective consultant* are as crucial for parents as for teachers. Parents *can* be influential "change agents" for their children's value-based behavior, but only if they learn what successful consultants practice:

1. Get hired first.

2. Be adequately prepared with facts.

3. Offer your values once; don't hassle.

4. Leave responsibility with the "client" for buying or rejecting your values.

We want to underscore that the skills for teaching effectively are not the exclusive property of people who hold teaching credentials or certificates—they may be used by parents as well. In fact, these skills are in many ways more important to parents than they are to professional educators because the parents' teaching job covers a much wider and more comprehensive "curriculum" and certainly involves a much more intimate and long-lasting relationship. We feel strongly that a child from a family that adopts these skills as part of the normal daily living pattern will be far better able to handle formal schooling, in whatever form, no matter how good, bad, humane, or inhumane it may be. Probably one of the most valuable and nurturing functions of the family is to provide a safe haven for its children, a climate of acceptance, a place to seek refuge when the outside world is hurtful. It is the knowledge and use of these skills that can enable parents to offer such a place of comfort and safety to their children as they go through life.

WHEN YOUR CHILDREN HAVE PROBLEMS AT SCHOOL

Many otherwise reasonable and accepting parents "get their button pushed" when their kids get into predicaments at school and bring their problems home.

When children enter school they are bound to have many more relationships than they had before, and parents are going to hear about it. What they hear will sometimes be pleasing messages of joy and success ("Mommy, I found a new friend today. Her name is Cindy and I like her"). But all parents are going to hear distressing messages—fears, disappointments, setbacks, failures, dilemmas, such as:

"I hate school and I hate my teachers."

"The kids at this school aren't very friendly."

"Mrs. Rasmussen is the worst teacher in the world."

"I'm going to quit school when I'm old enough."

"The principal at our school is mean. He hates kids."

"The vice-principal is stupid. He had better not hit *me* again."

"Two kids beat up on me and the teacher didn't do a thing about it."

"I think I'll change to industrial arts. They make you take three years of English in college prep."

"Everybody at my school is a doper."

"What's the use of studying? Going to school doesn't get you anywhere."

"They told me they were going to bus me to another school if I didn't be good."

"I'm the dumbest one in my room. Everybody knows it."

Somewhat less likely to be "button pushers," but still disturbing to parents are the nonverbal messages that children sometimes send after a school experience: slamming doors, sulking, crying, cursing, refusing to talk, running away, glaring, daydreaming, throwing things, sobbing.

Parents need to remember that these, and hundreds of other messages, are the children's ways to initiate an interaction or to announce, "Hey, listen! I have a problem." *All these messages are codes that mean something is going on inside the child;* all are cues and clues that the child owns a problem, and the parent must locate these verbal and nonverbal behaviors in the top part of the rectangular window (see Figure 33).

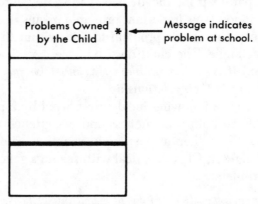

FIGURE 33

The key to being effective in helping a child with a problem at school is: *Let the child own his problem.*

Too many parents immediately react to the child's message with some such feeling as, Oh, no! What kind of problem do we have with our youngster now? Parents are programmed to think of their child's school problem as *theirs.* If the child is in some kind of a predicament at school, this gives most parents a problem—fear, worry, disappointment, embarrassment, irritation, resentment, anger. When a parent reacts this way it is like saying, "Don't tell me about your problem, because I can't stand the thought that you're having one."

With that attitude, a parent simply cannot come across to a child as a potential counselor or helper. What gets communicated to the child is that he is at fault for shattering mom's or dad's peace of mind; he's bad; he shouldn't ever have a problem; he has hurt or disappointed his parent; he should never have mentioned it. And the parent has muffed a chance to be a counselor. What parent would be in the mood to listen empathically to a child's problem if the very news that a problem exists evokes feelings that are the opposite of empathy and understanding?

The *principle of separateness* rules all human relationships; to help another with his problem, the helper must remain separate from the helped. Translated into our rectangular window, this important principle means that the parent must keep the child's problem locked within the top area of the rectangle. The child must be accepted as a *separate person*, and *if he has a problem this must be felt as an acceptable event in their relationship.*

In the following incident reported by a parent enrolled in P.E.T., both separateness and acceptance are demonstrated by the father as he employs active listening to help his daughter, Charlene, deal with feelings generated by a school problem.

CHARLENE: (*Slams front door and throws books down on the coffee table*) Those teachers are screwed! If they think I'm going to do all this homework, they're crazy!

DAD: (*Biting his tongue*) Wow!

CHARLENE: They don't think anybody has anything to do but do their stupid homework! They don't care what happens as long as they get their precious papers turned in every morning.

DAD: You really feel shafted by them.

CHARLENE: That's the word all right, shafted! Do you know how long it would take me to do all of this? (*Points to the pile of books scattered on the table*) Years! They're supposed to take turns, you know. They're not supposed to all give homework on the same day. (*Flops down on the couch and stares morosely at the pile of books*)

DAD: It sure looks like an overwhelming job, huh?

CHARLENE: (*Sighs*) Yeah. I don't know where to start. (*Begins to pick up the books and papers*) Well, all I can do is what I *can*. If I can't finish, that's tough.

DAD: You'll do what you can do.

CHARLENE: (*Goes down the hall to her room*) Yeah. Call me for dinner, will you?

This father admitted to us that it was difficult for him to limit his response to active listening, because he knew his daughter was right and he felt that the teachers at her school were overzealous in handing out assignments. So his natural inclination was to agree with her or sympathize with her. When we asked what might have happened if he had agreed or sympathized, he laughingly said, "Most likely I'd have ended up doing part or all of that homework myself just because I felt sorry for her."

The more you can genuinely accept that the problems your child has with his various relationships at school *belong to him*, not you, the more helpful you can be. *Your child is not you*, so the more you can facilitate his handling of his own school problems, the stronger he will become, more able to take care of himself and more self-reliant.

This principle of separateness is not an easy one to accept for most parents, because children are so often looked upon as extensions of the parent, "a chip off the old block," "part of their flesh and blood." From some unknown source comes the expression, "The parent is joined at the hip with the child." Such symbiosis simply does not make a parent an effective counselor.

One P.E.T. class, never to be forgotten, got into a discussion about whether parents can justifiably assume ownership of children's problems because parents are "older and wiser." The discussion was brought to a dramatic conclusion when one of the parents, who up to that point had said hardly a word, replied to another father's strong statement about his "right to shape and mold my son at home and in school" by relating the following tragic story:

I haven't said much in this class, but I've learned a lot, and I think it's time I tell you all why I'm here.

The first night when we talked about ourselves and why we were taking the course, I said I wanted to learn how to get along with my fifteen-year-old son better than I have. Some of you know that I had another son. What most of you don't know is what happened to him. He was my pride and joy, everything a father could want. In fact, he was just about everybody's favorite: an "A" student all through school, valedictorian of his graduating class. He was active in the church and taught Sunday school classes. He was an Eagle Scout, president of the senior class, and a fine athlete. I saw to it that he got all the advantages I never had as a child, and, when he graduated, made sure he went to college.

In the middle of his sophomore year he killed himself. He left me a note. It said, "Dad, I don't know who I am. I think I am you."

"I never even knew there was anything wrong. He never said a word.

I'm here in this class to find out how to keep from molding my other son, to find out how to help him become his own person instead of whatever I want him to be. It's hard, but I'm learning.

This father is right—it *is* hard to keep from molding children. Often the effect on them is not known until it is too late.

WHAT TO DO ABOUT HOMEWORK HASSLES

One of the most frequent sources of conflict in families is homework. It brings on a whole range of problems, and any one of them can release a Pandora's box full of anger, resentment, frustration, and mutual hostility in families.

How *are* parents to handle the homework problem? Can they influence their youngsters to do their homework regularly? Should they try?

Homework is a very controversial issue among educators, too—some favor it, others oppose it. Many teachers consistently give homework assignments. Some put excessive demands on children, as in the case of Charlene, related earlier in this chapter. Conscientious students often feel compelled to work far into the night on homework assignments, which makes their working day, including their seven to eight hours at school, far longer than most adults would tolerate on their jobs. It is a cruel deception that children are protected from overwork by child-labor laws.

Some parents may agree with us that, at least below the college level, homework seldom serves any positive purpose unless (1) the student chooses to do it out of his own natural desire to learn, or (2) it is something that can be better done outside the classroom (field trips, visits to museums or art galleries, etc.). In fact, many teachers do not want to assign homework; they do so only because parents expect it or demand it, or because it is a school policy to which they must conform. Teachers recognize that the very students who do not need homework do it, and those who could benefit from additional drill or practice seldom open a book at home.

In the eyes of most students, homework is a dreaded chore hanging over their heads each night. If they do it, they miss out on other activities, some of which can be far more educational. If they don't, they feel guilty and go to school with a deep fear of being embarrassed in class, chastised by the teacher, penalized by an unannounced test, or given a failing mark for that day, as some teachers do.

Later we will suggest what parents might do to influence teachers or schools to give up homework assignments. But until schools drop this useless and harmful tradition, most parents will find their children having many problems brought on by homework. What can they do?

In our P.E.T. classes we encourage parents to think of homework as being in the No-Problem area; that is, it's best if homework is regarded as having no concrete negative effect on either the parents' lives or the child's life. Of course, if a child sends a message that his homework *is* causing him a problem, his behavior would be located in the top part of the rectangle, as a problem owned by the child.

When homework gives the child some sort of a problem, the parents' principal tool for helping will be active listening, as we illustrated in the case of Charlene, whose dad helped her discharge her strong anger toward her homework-happy teacher. Active listening, in addition to fostering a cathartic release of pent-up feelings, sends these parental messages to the child:

I hear you.

I understand what you are feeling.

I accept your having those feelings.

I'm willing to help you work through this problem and come to some solution of your own choosing.

If, unlike Charlene, the child is sending no messages—no cues or clues—that indicate he is experiencing a problem, we urge parents to assume that he is not having a problem. Then the parent-child relationship is in the No-Problem area and the parent need say nothing and do nothing.

To look at homework from a different perspective, here is a hypothetical dialogue between a wife and her husband. George, the husband, has just arrived home from a day's work, his briefcase bulging with work. Alice, the wife, greets him at the door and responds to him very much as many parents respond to a youngster coming home from school with an armful of books and notebooks.

GEORGE: Boy, what a day! My boss thinks all I ever have to do is work, work, work. Look at all this paperwork!

ALICE: Well, I'm sure it must be important or he wouldn't have asked you to do it.

GEORGE: Are you kidding? Do you realize that I spend half my day filling out dumb papers like these at my desk? You don't have to have my kind of training to do simple jobs like these. I'm going to have two martinis.

ALICE: No martinis until after the paperwork, George. You get right in there to your desk and get started without another word! Work before pleasure, you know.

GEORGE: You always take *his* side. You always think my boss is right. Well, he's not! Any stupid secretary could do this stuff.

ALICE: It's not nice to call names, George. I'm sure the secretaries at your office are very bright, so you shouldn't say they're stupid.

GEORGE: Okay, Okay! (*Throws briefcase on the desk, angrily*) Well, I'll get to it right after the news. (*Turns on TV*)

ALICE: (*Snaps off TV*) No you don't! Get started on those papers *right now*! I'll call you when dinner is ready, and after dinner I'll go over some of your work to see if you're doing it correctly.

Few wives would ever talk to their husbands the way Alice did, but many might very well say those things to one of their children. Why doesn't it seem ridiculous to talk to kids this way?

Often fathers are worse hasslers about homework than mothers. They use inane statements like "It's a tough world out there, kid"; "You gotta get prepared"; "You never know when you'll have to use what you're learning;" "It's forming good habits you'll need later on." If parents just used good common sense, they could easily see that most of the stuff called "homework" that kids bring home from school is almost never worth even a momentary spat, let alone the open warfare that breaks out in some families over it. As one very sensible mother said:

Randy usually has homework. Sometimes he really likes it, and he'll sit up until all hours of the night doing it. Other times he doesn't do it, because he says it's dumb or he has something else more important to do. I figured out a long time ago that Randy has got to decide these things himself, and I don't know of anything better than homework that he can use to practice learning about self-responsibility.

Parents are often in a dilemma when children run into something they don't understand in a homework assignment. Should the parent help?

Our answer is yes, provided the parent has the time and the energy. But there are different ways of helping, and each can be effective in different situations. Here are three:

1. *Active listening* may be appropriate and effective in helping a child to find the correct approach to a task:

CHILD: I don't know what to do for my oral presentation. Could you help me?

PARENT: You're really stumped about what to select.

CHILD: Yeah. I don't want to pick one that's too broad, because I'll have to work harder.

PARENT: You don't want a topic that would require you to do a whole lot of work, is that right?

CHILD: Yeah. I'd like to go kinda deep into a narrow topic and really get to know my subject.

PARENT: You really want to learn something from this assignment.

CHILD: What I'm most interested in is the Greek warriors' weapons, but I'm not sure my teacher would think that's legitimate enough.

PARENT: You'd like to pursue that but you're worried about your teacher's evaluation of that topic.

CHILD: But, darn it, why should I care as long as I'm really learning something?

PARENT: You're thinking maybe that's all the justification you need.

CHILD: I think I'll give a speech on weapons and take my chances that she'll think it's an okay topic.

PARENT: You've decided to do what you want to do and live a little dangerously, huh?

CHILD: Right.

2. *Door openers* may facilitate problem solving in certain situations. ("Well, how about talking about what you've tried so far in trying to solve this problem?")

3. *Being an effective consultant* may be the best way to help on some kinds of problems. ("Do you want to get another person's ideas on this? All right, from my experience I've found it damned important to first find the 'unknown factor' and put it on the left side of the equation, right off the bat. Start there first. So in this problem, what is it that's not known—what is it that the problem asks you to make known?")

"LOOK, MOM, I ONLY GOT TWO C's"

As big a problem as homework, and for some families bigger, is the problem of grading and report cards. At some time or another probably every school district in the United States has had a committee (occasionally with parents as members) to study grading and report cards. This seems to be the most researched area of public education. Not surprisingly, grades and report cards continue to be a major unresolved problem for everybody: the many teachers who universally detest the whole idea; the students who are victimized by the process; and the parents who want information but have to settle for a report card that tells them little, if anything.

We will not take up space here with a detailed explanation of *why* traditional grading (the A-B-C-D-F type) inhibits the learning process; nor why report cards, no matter how detailed, convey almost no useful information to parents about *learning*. We will simply affirm that these are the findings of the researchers and most of the "report-card committees."

Still, as with homework, most families are going to have to deal with grading and report cards of some sort. And, like homework, report cards are seldom worth making a fuss over and certainly not worth the risk of damaging your relationship with your child.

Even though report cards, as the name implies, are supposedly reports to parents about the progress of their children, the children usually attach undue importance to them and have strong feelings regarding them, even if the parents do not. When this happens, parents can be really helpful by active-listening to their youngsters' feelings, helping them work through their problems and find better ways to handle them in the future.

It is also very helpful for parents to talk to their children about grades and report cards at a time when there are no problems about them. During these "quality time" periods, parents can best convey what they know about grades and grading, college boards, entrance examinations, scholarships, graduation requirements, and any other information they may want to share. It is at these times that parents and their children can safely talk about academic performance, about feelings toward school achievement, and about the values they hold about education.

It is a wonder that grades and report cards don't cause far more problems for youngsters, considering all the deficiencies and inequities in the whole system of grading and reporting.

1. Grading systems are very subjective, open to the many biases of teachers—e.g., sex, color, nationality, physical attractiveness.

2. They cause children to compare themselves with others, often with devastating results on students who get high grades as well as on those who get low grades.

3. They cause children to work for grades rather than work because learning offers intrinsic rewards.

4. They use terms and symbols that are often difficult to understand and are thus open to misunderstanding and misinterpretations—e.g., "Satisfactory" or "Average" or "Good" or "Needs Improvement."

5. It is often not clear whether a student is being graded on the curve or against grade level. A very bright student, for example, may get a "B" or "C" in a class of superior students, but would get an "A" in what kids call a "dummy class."

If parents only knew how complicated, subjective, and confusing grading systems are, they might not make such a big issue of their children's grades.

In our P.E.T. course we encourage parents to try to keep their youngsters' grades above their "acceptance line" (in the area of Acceptance). When the child brings home his report card, accept it for what it is—the school's way of evaluating the child's performance. If you get no indication from the child that he has a problem about his grades, then the relationship is in the No-Problem area—you simply assume his grades are not causing him a problem, nor should they cause you a problem.

If you receive some cue or clue (a message) from the child indicating that he has a problem concerning his grades, then use active listening to help him identify his problem and find some solution to it.

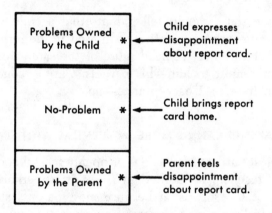

FIGURE 34

Unfortunately, many parents simply cannot leave their children's grades in the area of Acceptance. They become upset or frightened by a poor report card. They have strong feelings about their children's academic achievement and can't hide those feelings. So for many (if not most) parents, report cards cause *them* a problem. (See Fig. 34.)

What can these parents do to try to solve their problem? They can try all of the methods we offered in Chapters V through X:

1. Parents can send an I-message, telling the child honestly how they feel: "When I look at your report card, I feel very disappointed and worried about your performance at school." Note that the I-message has to be a self-disclosure message with no mention of the tangible effect on the parent because it is almost impossible to convince a child that *his* grades or *his* school performance in any way *tangibly or concretely* interferes with the parent's life.

2. Parents can be alert to the need to "shift gears" into active listening if their I-message provokes a feeling response from the child.

3. Parents can offer themselves as consultants to the child, hoping that the child might get to feel that his grades are as much a problem to him as they seem to be to his parents, and as a result be willing to seek consulting help from his parents. ("I don't know if this is also a problem to you, but if it is I think I might have some ideas. I would like to try to help you.")

Common sense should tell parents that a child who has received a negative evaluation of himself in the form of low grades certainly doesn't need more of the same from those who matter most to him—his parents. Caring, concern, an offer to help—yes. Unacceptance—no.

HOW PARENTS CAN BE MORE INFLUENTIAL WITH TEACHERS

Most parents are anxious or openly fearful about talking with teachers in more than the most superficial ways. This is not too surprising because most parents still have negative feelings about teachers from their own school days. Most parents are surprised when we tell them that many teachers are just as anxious and fearful of encounters with parents. Despite these mutual fears, parents, using active listening, I-messages, and Method III, can be very influential in meetings with teachers.

When meeting with a teacher it is very important to keep the relationship rectangle always in mind, constantly viewing the teacher through your window. In this way you will always know whether to be a sender or a listener in the communication process.

Following are two hypothetical examples of parent-teacher conferences. In the first, the parent will use active listening and I-messages. In the second, she will use the typical communication roadblocks. The teacher in both examples is untrained in T.E.T. skills.

TEACHER: Come in, Mrs. Gross. Won't you sit here? (*Points to chair near her desk*) I'm so glad you could come. (*Leans back in her chair and brushes a lock of hair off her forehead*) Whew! What a day!

PARENT: You seem really tired. (*Active listening*)

TEACHER: Well, they're really valuable, but these conferences really take a lot out of you. You're the fourth one today.

PARENT: You sort of pay a price for having conferences, huh? (*Active listening*)

TEACHER: Yes. But as I said, they're worth it. Even though I get tired, I go home feeling good. Well, enough about me. I guess you want to talk about Robbie.

PARENT: Well, yes.

TEACHER: He's doing just fine. A real hard worker.

PARENT: I know. But that's a problem, believe it or not. You see, when you assign him several pages of homework every night, he spends a lot of his time doing it and misses out on other things—things he likes to do that we think are important. I worry about him getting turned off to school by all the work. (*I-message*)

TEACHER: Robbie gets the same homework that everyone else gets. He just works slower than some of the others. Why, most of the children finish in an hour or less.

PARENT: You think the problem is Robbie's slowness. (*Active listening*)

TEACHER: Yes, and his perfectionism. He always does everything just right. Some of the others sort of give it a lick and a promise.

PARENT: There are big differences in the quality of work turned in. (*Active listening*)

TEACHER: You'd be amazed! (*Pause*) But I can see your point with

Robbie. He works hard at school and then he goes home and works hard some more, right?

PARENT: Uh-huh.

TEACHER: Of all the children I have this year, Robbie needs homework the least. I wish he'd be more like some of the others and goof off a little. (*Chuckles*) I don't really mean that. I really wish the others would work as hard as he does, then I wouldn't have to assign any homework at all . . . and I wouldn't have all those papers to check myself. I work harder than anyone.

PARENT: If I understand, you feel you have to assign homework even though most of the kids don't do it and it's a big job for you. (*Active listening*)

TEACHER: Yes. I've never really thought about it that way before. It sounds dumb, doesn't it? (*Pause*) Would you like for me not to give Robbie any homework?

PARENT: Yes, or at least cut it down to something he can do in his perfectionistic way in just a short time.

TEACHER: That seems reasonable to me. Except for some of the outside-reading assignments, I wouldn't think he really needs anything at all.

PARENT: That seems like a good idea. Then he can do some of the other things, like playing baseball and going to Scout meetings.

TEACHER: Okay. You've given me some ideas. I'm going to talk to Mrs. Farley next door about her differential homework program. Maybe I could use that for my class.

Now, let's see how the same conference might go when the parent uses the communication roadblocks instead of the communication skills:

TEACHER: Come in, Mrs. Gross. Won't you sit here? (*Points to chair near her desk*) I'm so glad you could come. (*Leans back in chair and brushes a lock of hair off her forehead*) Whew! What a day!

PARENT: Well, mine was pretty good until I had to come over here. The traffic was murder.

TEACHER: We hate to ask parents to come to the school like this, but we teachers feel that it's important that the parents and teachers pull together to make school the best we can for the children, and this is one way to do it.

PARENT: What ever happened to home visits?

TEACHER: They just take too much time. And besides, some people don't like teachers to come to their homes. I guess they're embarrassed or something.

PARENT: That's too bad.

TEACHER: Well, we're here to talk about Robbie. He's a fine boy. Hard worker.

PARENT: He does okay here?

TEACHER: Why, yes. He is at the top of the class.

PARENT: Well, from the amount of stuff you send home with him to do every night I figured he was probably flunking.

TEACHER: He gets the same as everybody else. I pride myself in treating the children all alike.

PARENT: Well, it's too much. I don't know about the other kids, but Robbie spends half the night doing all that stuff and it's spoiling his chances to play ball or go to Scouts.

TEACHER: That's a shame, but schoolwork is certainly more important than playing.

PARENT: We don't consider the Scouts exactly playing. Besides, Robbie needs a change of pace. Do you go home and work another two or three hours every day?

TEACHER: You bet I do! Who do you think checks all that homework?

PARENT: Did you ever think that if you didn't assign it you wouldn't have to work so much?

TEACHER: Are you trying to tell me how to do my job?

PARENT: No, of course not, but I wish you'd let up on Robbie's homework. If you don't, I'm just going to have to tell him to quit doing it.

TEACHER: If he doesn't turn it in, he won't get credit for it.

PARENT: You seem to care more about your homework assignments than you do about the welfare of the children.

TEACHER: Most of the parents back me up. They want their children to have homework. It gives them a chance to see what they're doing at school and they appreciate it. You're a very difficult person to deal with in that respect.

PARENT: Yeah. I guess I am. Who do I see to get Robbie transferred?

With these contrasting conferences we have tried to convey that parents will have a much greater chance of enlisting the help of teachers if they employ the skills of active listening and I-messages. Teachers are human—they have problems, and they have feelings, too.

In Chapter IV we recommended to teachers that students be included in parent-teacher conferences. As a parent you may want to insist on the inclusion of your child in these conferences. After all, the child (and whatever problem he may have at school) is the only reason for a parent and a teacher to have a relationship, and most of the decisions that will be made in these conferences will involve or affect him in some way. Therefore, he should be present.

HOW TO USE THE PARENT–TEACHER–PRINCIPAL TEAM

One of the most effective ways for parents to be influential in shaping a better educational program for their youngsters is to form a problem-solving team that includes the school principal as well as the teacher. The inclusion of the principal considerably increases the area of freedom for decisions. In most cases the principal will be an excellent source of educational information as well. Such a team must use the six-step problem-solving process (see p. 227) in order to avoid the typical pitfalls of getting into arguments about competing solutions or working with inaccurate definitions of the problem. It may be necessary for you to explain the problem-solving process to the teacher and the principal in some detail before starting to try to solve any problems.

Some of the problems that might appropriately be tackled by such a team are:

1. Your child's special learning problems—such as:

    hyperactivity

    dyslexia

    poor visual acuity

    poor auditory acuity

    short attention span

    distractability

2. Enriching the curriculum for your child

3. Modifying the classroom environment to fit your child's needs

4. Medical problems of your child

5. Psychological problems of your child

For example, if your child is diagnosed as "hyperactive," schools generally have two pat solutions to the problem: (1) they recommend medication (something that should only be prescribed by a qualified neurologist) or (2) they recommend special-class placement. These special classes have different names in different places, but they are characterized by lower teacher/pupil ratios, special materials, and often specially trained teachers. These standard solutions may be very good ones for your child, or they may not. A special principal-teacher-parent problem-solving team using the six-step process might develop many alternative ways to handle your child's special learning problem.

HOW TO EVALUATE YOUR CHILD'S SCHOOL

Over the past several years, schools have come under attack from all sides. Public education seemed to be getting the blame for all the ills of society.

As a result of the clamor, public schools *have* changed (sometimes *despite* the "help" of the critics). They have improved in many important ways. But most of the improvements have been in "hardware" (buildings, equipment, teaching machines, laboratories) and "software" (books, libraries, films, tapes, programs, curriculum designs). What has changed the least is what matters the most—the schools' human relations, the way people treat each other. Many students are still treated with a disrespect unequaled in any other institution of society. The latest building designs, carpeting, air conditioning, and other new equipment, and the most modern "relevant" curricula are of little value if Method I (power) is still the format for resolving conflicts and if students are still targets for a daily liturgy of destructive you-messages.

We propose that when you judge your child's school you look not only at its material benefits but at the attitudes of its adults toward the young people they serve. Here are some questions you can answer by observation and by discussion with teachers and administrators:

1. Do students participate in setting the rules and policies by which they are governed in the classroom? In the school?

2. Do adults spank or paddle students?

3. Do teachers hold student-centered class discussions?

4. Do students plan with their teachers what they are going to learn, at what rate, and how it will be evaluated?

5. Do students do a great deal of self-management or do teachers seem to be constantly "riding herd," directing, ordering, commanding?

6. Are students unruly, disrespectful, and inconsiderate as a result of too much teacher permissiveness?

7. Is it common to see faculty members and students having informal "rap sessions"?

8. Do teachers try to resolve their conflicts with students themselves, or do they send the students to "the office"—to a counselor, vice-principal, or principal?

9. Do counselors (if there are any) actually do counseling, or are they disciplinarians and programmers?

10. Is the general atmosphere relaxed and informal, or tense and rigid?

11. Do teachers confront students with I-messages, or do they rely on threats, put-downs, and other such you-messages?

12. When conflicts arise in classrooms, is Method III used to find creative no-lose solutions?

13. Do teachers provide opportunities for students to have individual time, time away from the hubbub of a large group?

14. Do teachers schedule optimum (one-to-one) time with students?

15. When you go to the school can you see signs that people care about people? Do students speak to you, welcome you? Do adults recognize you?

16. In informal (unstructured) situations, do the students seem to be able to organize themselves and treat each other with consideration, or are they fiercely competitive and argumentative?

The answers to these and many other questions that you may ask yourself about your child's school as you read this book will be clues to the quality of the human relationships in that school. We believe that before schools can educate well they must *first* be firmly committed to quality relationships between all the people in the school.

Parents can have more influence in bringing about better human relationships in the schools than they sometimes think. The chief reason why they have failed to achieve changes is that generally parents have yielded to using *their* power, and this has cost them their potential influence. School administrators and teachers are no different than other people. When faced with power, they, too, develop coping mechanisms. Not the least of these is resisting and fighting back.

Organizing parent groups for the purpose of "taking on" or battling with the schools is probably the least effective way to promote change. This authoritarian posture is hardly the appropriate model if parents are trying to achieve more democratic relationships in the schools. Administrators and teachers who see parents and parent groups as adversaries or power blocs are not going to be very open to problem solving.

Parents interested in helping to promote change within the schools can use already existing groups such as the P.T.A. to spread the word. "In unity there is strength" does not necessarily imply resorting to Method I. The P.T.A. represents a large number of parents, teachers, and administrators who are dedicated to improving the quality of education for the sake of the children. Introducing the skills of effective communication and Method III to such a "union" could greatly increase its effectiveness and make the job of improvement much easier.

There are several ways to introduce T.E.T. skills and techniques to such a group. Inviting one of the authorized instructors of the T.E.T. course to speak at a meeting or to hold a mini-workshop for interested parents and educators is one very effective method. Forming study groups using this book as a text is another. Having teachers who are trained in T.E.T. conduct demonstrations with students at a P.T.A. meeting is impressive. A panel of parents who have taken the P.E.T (Parent Effectiveness Training) course could be asked to discuss the effects that program has had on their own homes.

Some P.T.A. units, after being informed about the problem-solving process, have taken a new look at their organizations' goals and objectives and have started to use the six-step process to generate far more creative ways to meet those goals. In some cases, principals and teachers, using the P.T.A. as a vehicle, have formed groups to perform Step 1 of the process: identify and define the problems of the school. This can be a meaningful initial example of school-community planning and involvement.

One final suggestion. The key to change within any school is the principal. Share this book with your principal. There is a chance you will never get it back, but the payoff may be worth the risk.

BUILDING BETTER RELATIONSHIPS

LET US SAY it again: what goes on between parents, teachers and students will be determined more by the quality of those relationships than by any other factor. Our Effectiveness Training programs provide the skills and methods for improving the quality of those relationships. What is most needed is a new philosophy of human relationships—a credo to help people relate more effectively, more democratically.

Credo

For My Relationships

You and I are in a relationship that I value and want to keep. Yet each of us is a separate person with his own unique needs and the right to try to meet those needs. I will try to be genuinely accepting of your behavior when you are trying to meet your needs or when you are having problems meeting your needs.

When you share your problems, I will try to listen acceptingly and understandingly in a way that will facilitate your finding your own solutions rather than depending upon mine. When you have a problem because my behavior is interfering with your meeting your needs, I encourage you to tell me openly and honestly how you are feeling. At those times, I will listen and then try to modify my behavior, if I can.

However, when your behavior interferes with my meeting my own needs, thus causing me to feel unaccepting of you, I will share my problem with you and tell you as openly and honestly as I can exactly how I am feeling, trusting that you respect my needs enough to listen and then try to modify your behavior.

At those times when either of us cannot modify his behavior to meet the needs of the other and find that we have a conflict-of-needs in our relationship, let us commit ourselves to resolve each such conflict without ever resorting to the use of either my power or yours to win at the expense of the other losing. I respect your needs, but I also must respect my own. Consequently, let us strive always to search for solutions to our inevitable conflicts that will be acceptable to both of us. In this way, your needs will be met, but so will mine—no one will lose, both will win.

As a result, you can continue to develop as a person through meeting your needs, but so can I. Our relationship thus can always be a healthy one because it will be mutually satisfying. Each of us can become what he is capable of being, and we can continue to relate to each other with feelings of mutual respect and love, in friendship and in peace.

We need a new generation of teachers and parents who will accept the challenge contained in this credo. Then they will bring out the best in the young people they teach.

Acknowledgments

For providing me with the help I needed to design this T.E.T. course, I wish to thank a number of the early P.E.T. instructors whose regular jobs in the school gave them the experience to make valuable contributions as T.E.T. was being developed and subsequently improved. While I may have forgotten some of these early contributors, I will always remember Robert Hall, Lee Livingstone, Jack Danielson, Leona Thornton Rife, Al Carr, Ernie Jackson, Ron Leppke, and Barbara Peterson.

Particularly, I wish to acknowledge the substantial contributions of my first associate, Ralph Jones, who collaborated with me in developing the original Instructor Outlines or "lesson plans" for the T.E.T. course as well as helped with all subsequent revisions.

I am also indebted to a number of authors whose writings have reaffirmed my own convictions about what schools need in order to develop more humanizing relationships or whose creative ideas I adapted for use in the T.E.T. course: John Holt, William Glasser, Charles Silberman, Carl Rogers, Neil Postman and Charles Weingartner, Noel Burch, A.S. Neill, Nathaniel Cantor, George Dennison, Wilma Randolph, Harold Besell, Uvaldo Palomares, and (of course) John Dewey.

Additions and improvements to T.E.T. have been made continually as a result of the thousands of teachers who have participated as students in the T.E.T. course, adding their ideas and sharing their firsthand experience with using T.E.T. skills in their own classrooms. I am grateful for what they have taught me and all of our T.E.T. instructors, particularly for giving us more insight into the "institutional" pressures and restraints that make it so difficult for teachers to foster effective human relationships with their students.

I am also grateful for the T.E.T. instructors and school teachers who provided me with some of the rich illustrations and case materials for this book. Marlene Anderson and Kathy Piggott Newman generously contributed far "beyond the call of duty." Dr. Mike Lillibridge and Dr. P. Gary Klukken shared their creative ideas about the quality of teaching-learning time.

T.G.

Suggested Reading

Clark, D. H., and Kadis, A. *Humanistic Teaching*. Columbus, Ohio: Charles E. Merrill Books, 1972.

Valuable "how to" skills, learnings, and techniques developed by two psychologists applying their insights to the learning process.

Dennison, George. *The Lives of Children*. New York: Random House, 1969.

Story of a pioneering experiment in running a free school in New York's East Side. Filled with practical ideas for teachers who want to make their classrooms and schools more democratic and productive.

Friedenberg, Edgar Z. *The Vanishing Adolescent*. Boston: Beacon Press, 1964.

Adolescence and its pressures can be devastating. The author, a keen observer, sees these young people as victims of hostile social pressures which often goad them toward hostile behavior. Written with wit and understanding.

Ginnot, Haim. *Teacher and Child*. New York: The Macmillan Company, 1972.

Full of contrasting examples of destructive and therapeutic verbal interactions between teachers and students. Stresses need for teachers to learn how to listen with empathy and acceptance.

Glasser, William. *Schools Without Failure*. New York: Harper & Row, 1961.

Useful to show teachers how to conduct various kinds of classroom meetings to facilitate learning and solve conflicts. Stresses putting responsibility on child for behaving constructively.

Gordon, Thomas. *P.E.T.: Parent Effectiveness Training*. New York: Peter H. Wyden, 1970.

The companion book to T.E.T. Presents a complete theoretical system for better understanding of the parent-child relationship. Highly recommended for parents of children whose teachers wish to implement the skills taught in T.E.T.

Greenberg, Herbert. *Teaching with Feeling*. New York: The Macmillan Company, 1969.

A book written by an educational psychologist as a result of his encounters with teachers struggling to become not only teachers, but human beings as well. A rich resource. Full of understanding, empathy, and practicality.

Herndon, James. *How to Survive in Your Native Land*. New York: Simon and Schuster, 1971.

Strongly recommended for all teachers. Captures the subtle nuances of classrooms in middle class suburbia. Shows the picture of what junior high schools are really like and how they systematically destroy children's spirit.

Holt, John. *Freedom and Beyond*. New York: E. P. Dutton & Co., 1972.

A penetrating look at how schools are organized to deprive students of decision-making and how they can be changed to give students greater influence in their own education.

Holt, John. *How Children Fail*. New York: Pitman Publishing Corporation, 1964.

A teacher provides a penetrating analysis of what teachers and classes do to children to make them fail—even children who get good grades. Shows effects of evaluation. Shows how schools make children bored, afraid, and confused.

Holt, John. *How Children Learn*. New York: Pitman Publishing Corporation, 1967.

The sequel to Holt's *How Children Fail*. Presents ideas for tapping the native capacity of children to learn. Gives examples of how children can teach themselves. Excellent ideas for getting children to learn through talk.

Holt, John. *The Underachieving School*. New York: Pitman Publishing Corporation, 1961.

Points to specific deficiencies in schools, such as grading, testing, reading, instruction, poor teaching. An insightful analysis of the failure of our schools.

Holt, John. *What Do I Do Monday?* New York: E. P. Dutton & Co., 1970.

Rich in practical ideas for teachers to make their classrooms more interesting and relevant. Suggests ways teachers can begin to make changes desperately needed in our schools.

Klein, Thomas, et al. *Spinach Is Good for You: A Call for Change in the American School*. Bowling Green, Ohio: Bowling Green University Press, 1973.

The experiences of three high school teachers in a large metropolitan area as they attempt to put into practice their theories of humanistic education. Required reading for idealists (whether beginners or old hands) on how to make idealism work within the educational system.

Kohl, Herbert. *Open Classroom*. New York: New York Review, 1970.

A practicing teacher explains how classrooms can become student-centered, exciting learning environments without the teacher abdicating the role of teaching.

Kozol, Jonathan. *Free Schools*. New York: Bantam Books, 1973.

A teacher and organizer shares the wealth of information he has accumulated about how to start and operate a Free School. Although aimed primarily at low-income situations, it is equally applicable for parents and teachers of any social or economic stratum who are interested in alternative education.

Leonard, George. *Education and Ecstasy*. New York: Delacorte Press, 1968.

A renowned futurist examines schools and the educative processes as they might be, especially in the affective realm.

Neill, A. S. *Summerhill*. New York: Hart Publishing Co., 1961.

Report of a pioneering school in England in which an attempt has been made to incorporate in an educational institution the principles of democracy and the elements of a therapeutic community.

Neill, A. S. *Freedom—Not License*. New York: Hart Publishing Co., 1961.

A sequel to *Summerhill*. More of Neill's philosophy. Excellent for reinforcing some of the concepts in T.E.T. Recommended very strongly.

Postman, Neil, and Weingartner, C. *The School Book*. New York: Delacorte Press, 1973.

A valuable resource for parents and teachers who would like to have a better understanding of the language of education and who are interested in improving schools.

Postman, Neil, and Weingartner, C. *Teaching as a Subversive Activity*. New York: Delacorte Press, 1969.

A penetrating diagnosis of the sickness of our schools based as they are on fear, coercion, and rote learning. Suggests alternatives to bring more meaning into the classroom.

Rogers, Carl. *Freedom to Learn*. Columbus, Ohio: Charles E. Merrill Books, 1969.

A basic philosophic statement about learning as a process and how schools can choose to enhance the process. Drawn from the years of experience of a recognized giant in the field of psychology and human growth.

Silberman, Charles. *Crisis in the Classroom*. New York: Random House, 1970.

Required reading for all teachers. Not only documents how schools are harming children but offers some promising ideas for changing the schools. Rich in real-life examples. Shows empathy for the difficult job of teachers.

Index

Acceptable and unacceptable behaviors, 27–42
  changes in the self (teacher), 31–32
  crucial difference between, 27–29
  dividing line for, 30–31
  feelings toward different students, 32–33
  influence on, 33–34
  no-problem area (teaching-learning area), 41–42
  pretended acceptance, 34–38
  problem ownership, 38–40
    importance of, 39–40
Acceptance, language of, 55–60
Acknowledgment responses, 61, 88
Active listening, 66–79
  for classroom discussions, 90–102, 112–117
  for classroom success, 77–78
  counseling, 77–79
  decoding process, 67–69
  feedback, 88–89
  to handle resistance, 102–106
  to help dependent students, 106–112
  how to learn, 66–75
  need for, 63–64
  for parent-teacher conferences, 117–122
  for parent-teacher-student conferences, 122–123
  requirements of, 75–77
  uses of, 90–124
    results of, 123–124
Acton, Lord, 211
Adler, Alfred, 25
Advising, offering solutions or suggestions, 48, 82, 132
Allen, Dwight, 213
Anderson, Marlene, 96, 111, 236, 255
Apple polishing (student coping mechanism), 207
Assigned authority, 192–194

Authoritarian-permissive controversy, 17–18
Authority and power, 191–216
  effects of (on the winner), 211–212
  kinds of, 191–195
  limitations of, 195–201
  parental, 332
  rationalizations and justifications for, 212–216
  student coping mechanisms, 201–209

Better relationships, building, 355–356
Blaming others, tattling (student coping mechanism), 203–204
Bossing, bullying, pushing others around (student coping mechanism), 204–205

Caring, teacher-student relationship, 24
Changes in the self (teacher), how to understand, 31–32
Cheating, copying, plagiarizing (student coping mechanism), 204
Classroom discussions:
  effective content facilitators, 90–102
  student-centered, making the most of, 112–117
Classroom environment, modifying (to prevent problems), 156–178
  creative thinking and, 158–160
  to enlarge, 163–164
  to enrich the learning, 161
  to impoverish, 162
  planning ahead, 166–168
  potential of teaching-learning area, 175–178
  to rearrange, 164–165
  to restrict, 162–163

Classroom environment(*con't.*)
to simplify, 165–166
systematical thinking about, 160
to systematize, 166
teaching-learning area for, 178
thinking creatively about change,
158–160
typical classroom inadequacies,
157–158
upgrading quality of time and,
168–175
diffused time, 169–170
individual time, 170–172
optimum time, 172–175
Communication process:
active listening and, 66–75
language of unacceptance, 47–55
common misunderstandings, 52–
55
reason for ineffectiveness, 50–52
twelve roadblocks to, 47–50, 136
verbal, 80–89
facilitators, 87–89
roadblocks, 80–87
what it's about, 64–66
Conflicts, 179–306
classroom, 179–216
authority and power in, 191–
216
causes of, 181–182
defined, 181
teacher vacillation and, 190–191
typical resolving of, 182–184
win-lose approaches to, 184–191
no-lose resolving of, 217–282
approaches to, 220–221
benefits and rewards of, 241–
249
how it works, 221–226
other uses of, 250–282
prerequisites for, 226–227
problem-solving process, 277–
234
putting to work, 250–282
tape-recorded meeting, 236–241
working with, 234–236
value collisions, 283–306
See also Teacher-student relationships
Conforming, taking no risks, trying
nothing new (student coping
mechanism), 208

Content classroom facilitators, 90–
102
Coping mechanisms students use,
201–209
apple polishing, 207
blaming others, tattling, 203–204
bossing, bullying, pushing others
around, 204–205
cheating, copying, plagiarizing, 204
conforming, taking no risks, trying
nothing new, 208
feelings, 200
lying, sneaking, hiding feelings,
202–203
needing to win, hating to lose, 205
organizing, forming alliances, 205–
206
rebelling, resisting, defying, 201
retaliating, 202
submitting, complying, buckling
under, 206–207
withdrawing, dropping out, fantasizing, regressing, 208–209
Crisis In the Classroom (Silberman),
217–218

Daydreaming behavior, 46–47
Dependent students, helping, 106–
112
Different feelings, how to under-
stand, 32–33
Diffused time, problems of, 169–170
Discipline, 15–17
achieving, vocabulary for, 16–17
"Door openers," invitations to talk,
61–63, 88
Double standards, teacher phoniness
and, 36

Earned authority, 192–194
Environment, classroom, modifying
to prevent problems, 156–178
Erickson, Eric, 25

Facilitators, communication, 87–89
Farber, Jerry, 107
Firm, but fair, myth of, 215–216
Freedom and Beyond (Holt), 11
Freud, Sigmund, 25

Grading and report cards, 343–346
Guilt, 212

Holt, John, 11
Homework, 338–343
Hoop-jump-biscuit game, 11–13
  alternative to, 11–13
  rules of, 12

I-messages, 136–155
  anger of teachers and, 147–151
  effectiveness of, 139–142
  putting together, 142–145
  risk factor in sending, 151–153
  shifting gears after sending, 145–147
  value collisions and, 286–288
  versus you-messages, 136–139
  what they accomplish, 153–155
In loco parentis, 192
Indirect messages, why they fail, 135–136
Individual time, how to get it, 170–172
Ineffective confrontations, student problems and, 129–130
Interdependence, teacher-student relationship, 24
Interpreting, analyzing, diagnosing, 48, 85, 133

Judging, criticizing, disagreeing, blaming, 48, 83–84, 113

Klukken, Gary, 166

Lillibridge, Michael, 166
Listening, to facilitate learning, 4
Lying, sneaking, hiding feelings (student coping mechanism), 202–203

Moralizing, preaching giving "shoulds and oughts," 48, 81–82, 132
Mutual needs meeting, teacher-student relationship, 24
Myths about teachers and teaching, 21–24

Name-calling, stereotyping, ridiculing, 48, 84–85, 133
Needing to win, hating to lose (student coping mechanism), 205
Newman, Katherine Pigott, 234, 252, 259, 261

Niebuhr, Reinhold, 306
No-lose method (of resolving conflicts), 217–282
  approaches to, 220–221
  benefits and rewards of, 241–249
    fostering responsibility in students, 247–249
    motivation, 241–242
    mutual respect, 246
    no power or authority, 245
    no resentment, 241
    no selling, 245
    two heads better than one, 242–245
    uncovering real problems, 246–247
  between students, 258–265
  dealing with, 272–279
    competing solutions versus competing needs, 272–274
    non-agreement of solution, 277
    outside teacher's area of freedom, 274–277, 278–279
    when students don't stick to agreement, 274
    when youngsters build punishment into solution, 277–278
  how it works, 221–226
  prerequisites for, 226–227
  problem-solving process, 277–234
    assessing success of solution, 233–234
    defining the problem (conflict), 228–230
    determining to implement decision, 232–233
    evaluating solutions, 231
    generating possible solutions, 230–231
    making the decision, 231–232
  putting to work, 250–282
  rules and policies, 265–279
    benefits of, 270–271
    conducting the meeting, 269–270
    how class meetings work, 267–272
    overcoming the threat, 268
    preparations, 268–269
    setting, 265–267
    teacher's role, 270
    time factor, 271–272

No-lose method (*con't*)
tape-recorded meeting, 236–241
Teaching-Learning area, 251–258
uses of, 250–282
working with, 234–236
No-problem area (teaching-learning
area), 41–42, 53

Openness or transparency, teacher-
student relationship, 24
Optimum time, how to create, 172–
175
Ordering, commanding, directing, 48,
80–81, 131
Organizing, forming alliances (student coping mechanism),
205–206

Parent-teacher-student relationship,
323–354
authority and power, 332
child's learning, 326–329
evaluating the school, 351–354
grading and report cards, 343–346
home learning environment, 329–
330
homework controversy, 338–343
including principal in, 350–354
influence with teachers, 346–350
problems at school (child's), 334–
338
as teacher to the child, 324–326,
330–333
values and, 332–333
Passive listening (silence), 61, 87–
88
Postman, Neil, 21
Power-based authority, 194–195
Praising, agreeing, giving positive
evaluations, 49, 84, 133
Pretended acceptance, 34–38
Probing, questioning, interrogating,
134
Problems, teachers and, 125–155
classroom environment, how to
modify, 156–178
in conflicts, 179–306
in the classroom, 179–216
resolving (no-lose method),
217–282
value collisions, 283–306
indirect messages, 135–136

ineffective confrontations, 129–
130
I-messages and, 136–155
put-down messages, 133–135
solution messages, 131–133
student-owned problems, 43–79
constructive ways of helping,
60–64
teacher-owned problems, 126–129
Punishment, disciplining by means
of, 16
Put-down messages, 133–135
categories of, 133–134
why they fail, 133–135

Questioning, probing, interrogating,
cross-examining, 49, 86–87

Reassuring, sympathizing, consoling,
supporting, 49, 85–86, 134
Rebelling, resisting, defying (stu-
dent coping mechanism), 201
Resistance, how to handle, 102–106
Responsibility to transmit the cul-
ture, myth of, 214–215
Retaliating (student coping mech-
anism), 202
Roadblocks to communication, 47–
50, 80–87
Rogers, Carl, 25
Role playing, teacher, 21–24

Saturday Evening Post, The, 204
School Book, The (Postman and
Weingartner), 21
School system, teachers and, 307–
322
accepting importance of role, 310–
311
becoming an advocate for students, 321–322
becoming a consultant, 319–321
characteristics of problems for
teachers, 308–310
dealing with authority figures,
313–316
decision making, 309
group meeting effectiveness, 316–
319
imposition of uniform values, 309–
310

School System (con't)
increasing effectiveness within organization, 310–313
interaction through "rectangular window," 311–313
putting blame on others, 310
rigidity and resistance to change, 309
subordination, 308–309
Separateness, teacher-student relationship, 24
Shelley, Percy Bysshe, 197
Silberman, Charles, 217–218
Skinner, B. F., 25
Solution messages:
kinds of, 131–132
why they fail, 131–133
Student As Nigger, The (Farber), 107
Student-centered classroom discussions, 112–117
Student-owned problems, what teachers can do, 43–79, 126
active listening and, 63–64, 66–79
counseling, 77–79
how to learn, 66–75
need for, 63–64
requirements to be effective, 75–77
communication process for, 64–66
constructive ways of helping, 60–64
acknowledgment responses that work, 61
door openers, 61–63
passive listening (silence), 61
language of acceptance, 55–60
language of unacceptance, 47–55
common misunderstandings, 52–55
reason for ineffectiveness, 50–52
twelve roadblocks to communication, 47–50
and why teachers fail, 46–47
Submitting, complying, buckling under (student coping mechanism), 206–207

Teacher Effectiveness Training (T.E.T.) course, 6–8

Teacher-learner relationships, 1–18
as alternative to hoop-jump-biscuit technology, 11–13
authoritarian-permissive controversy, 17–18
communication skills and methods, 3–6
discipline problem, 15–17
philosophy of, 13–15
student growth and development, 8–11
T.E.T. course, 6–8
Teacher-owned problems, 126–129
"Teacher's Prayer" (Niebuhr), 306
Teacher-student relationship:
model for effectiveness, 19–42
acceptable and unacceptable behaviors, 27–42
characteristics for, 24–25
myths about, 21–24
rectangular viewing of, 25–27
problems, 125–155
classroom environment, 156–178
student-owned, 43–79
teacher-owned, 126–129
when students give teachers problems, 125–155
uses of active listening, 90–124
verbal communication, 80–89
when students have problems, 43–79
See also Conflicts
Teaching, lecturing, giving logical arguments, 48, 82–83
Teaching, using logic, giving facts, 132
Teaching-learning area (no-problem area), 41–42
potential of, 175–178

Unacceptance, language of, 47–55

Value collisions, 283–306
how to deal with, 293–306
as effective consultant, 293–298
model the behavior, 298–301
Niebuhr's prayer for, 306
self-modification, 301–306
how to identify, 285
I-messages and, 286–288

value collisions (*con't*)
   ineffectiveness of Methods I, II,
     and III, 289–293
Verbal communication, 80–89
   facilitators, 87–89
   roadblocks, 80–87
   See also Communication process

Warning, threatening, 48, 81, 131
Weingartner, C., 21

Wisdom of age and experience, myth
   of, 213
Withdrawing, distracting, being sarcastic, humoring, diverting,
   49, 87
Withdrawing, dropping out, fantasizing, regressing (student
   coping mechanism), 208–209

You-messages, *see* I-messages